THE MENTAL HEALTH OF THE SCHOOL CHILD; THE PSYCHO-EDUCATIONAL CLINIC IN RELATION TO CHILD WELFARE; CONTRIBUTIONS TO A NEW SCIENCE OF

John Edward Wallace Wallin

www.General-Books.net

Publication Data:

Title: The Mental Health of the School Child
Subtitle: The Psycho-Educational Clinic in Relation to Child Welfare; Contributions to a New Science of Orthophrenics and Orthosomatics
Author: John Edward Wallace Wallin
Reprinted: 2010, General Books, Memphis, Tennessee, USA
Publisher: Yale University Press
Publication date: 1914
Subjects: School hygiene
Psychophysiology
Children with disabilities
Exceptional children
Atypical children
Child guidance clinics
Psychology, Physiological
Education / Special Education / General
Psychology / Developmental / Child
Psychology / Physiological Psychology
Psychology / Mental Health
BISAC subject codes: EDU000000, EDU026000, PSY004000, PSY024000, PSY036000

1

THE MENTAL HEALTH OF THE SCHOOL CHILD; THE PSYCHO-EDUCATIONAL CLINIC IN...

PREFACE

The publication of these papers and addresses in a single volume was prompted, first of all, by the widespread interest which is rapidly manifesting itself in all sections of the country in the grave social and educational problems which spring from the presence in every populous community of large numbers of mentally abnormal children. It is now generally recognized that many of the most vexatious problems in our present-day social economy are somehow bound up with the mental and educational abnormalities of childhood. Educators, physicians, sociologists, penologists, criminologists, lawyers, clergymen, philanthropists and parents, therefore, welcome any attempt to gain deeper scientific insight into the nature, extent and causes of the mental, moral and educational arrest, deviation or deficiency of children. The papers included in this collection aim to show in slight measure the aid which the practical psychologists and expert educational consultants hope to render in the important work of diagnosing, identifying, studying and training feeble-minded, backward and mentally abnormal children in the schools.

During the last three or four years the writer has published a number of experimental memoirs, articles and addresses in American and European periodicals dealing, from different points of view, with a common theme: the scientific study and the care and improvement of the mental and physical misfits in the schools, or, in a word, the conservation of child life. These studies when brought to a focus form a fairly unitary, but by no means a sym metrical or systematic, whole. The more systematic treatment of the study and training of mentally unusual children is reserved for later volumes. A practical motive for bringing together the studies of this volume is the fact that the demand for reprints has exhausted the supply of several of the articles.

Most of the chapters of the book are reprinted, with the kind permission of the editors, from various periodicals. Several of the reprints, however, have been so completely revised that they constitute, in effect, new contributions, while the new chapters added contain important data which have recently been gathered at first-hand and which are nowhere else available.

A certain amount of repetition is ordinarily unavoidable in the publication of a series of scattered studies which deal with very closely related topics. While many articles have been considerably abbreviated and others somewhat expanded—sometimes to the detriment of the unity of the individual articles—in order to avoid needless iteration, certain repetitions have been designedly retained, because there exist today among both lay and professional workers serious and widespread misapprehensions regarding the aims, functions and administrative affiliations of the psychological or psycho-educational clinic, regarding the qualifications of Binet testers, amateur psychologists, professionally trained clinical psychologists, special teachers, nurses and physicians. Owing to these misconceptions we are today tolerating and fostering a type of work in applied psychology which often is scientifically barren and sometimes positively pernicious. Clinical psychology promises to make a very important contribution to the worlds sum total of knowledge, but it is in its infancy, and, therefore, its development needs to be guided

CHAPTER I

MEDICAL AND PSYCHOLOGICAL INSPECTION OF SCHOOL CHILDREN1

The question as to the need of the inspection of school children for the detection of contagious and communicable diseases (e. g., diphtheria, scarlet fever, measles, whooping-cough, chicken pox, smallpox, tuberculosis) may be said to be closed. All intelligent observers are agreed that the schools, unless properly medically supervised, may, and frequently do, become virulent foci for the dissemination of fatal community diseases. As a matter of fact, all enlightened urban communities in this country and in Europe have recognized this imperative need by providing some form of school inspection for the contagious child diseases. The modern school medical-inspection movement, indeed, began as a form of inspection for infectious diseases by officers of Boards of Health.

But there is another function of school medical inspection which is even more important for the proper development of the individual child, though this function is not so generally recognized; namely, the physical examination of school children for the detection of physical defects: defective vision, defective hearing, defective nasal breathing, adenoids, hypertrophied tonsils, cardiac diseases, defective teeth and palate, malnutrition, orthopedic defects, tubercular lymph nodes, lateral curvature of the spine, stoop i Reprinted, with extensive alterations, from The Western Journal of Education (now The American School Master), 1909, pp. 433-446.

. " . .

shoulder,-. nervous exhaustion and pulmonary disease. We ore/just awakening to the necessity of this type of pupilinspection because we are just beginning to realize the extent to which children are physically handicapped. The statistics of defective children, wherever gathered, are fairly appalling. Space permits reference to only a few American surveys.

Of more than 5,000 school children examined in Los Angeles, 61 per cent suffered from defective eyesight, 31 per cent from adenoids, 25 per cent from enlarged tonsils and 22 per cent from defective hearing. In Chicago in 1909, 123,900 children were examined (this was not an ultimate examination, only the major defects being noticed), and of these 36 per cent had defective teeth, 22 per cent enlarged tonsils, 13 per cent enlarged glands, 5.5 per cent nasal defects, 3.5 per cent adenoids and 2.3 per cent hearing defects. In another examination of 3,963 children in the same city 60 per cent were said to need the attention of a physician, the most prominent defects requiring treatment being hypertrophied tonsils, enlarged glands and adenoids. Seventy-two and three-tenths per cent of 230,243 children examined in New York City in 1911 were reported as requiring treatment. The percentages of defects found were as follows: Defective teeth, 59 per cent; hypertrophied tonsils, 15 per cent; defective nasal breathing, 11.9 per cent; defective vision, 10.6 per cent; malnutrition, 2.5 per cent; cardiac disease,.7 per cent; defective hearing,.6 per cent; orthopedic defects,.5 per cent; chorea,.4 per cent; pulmonary disease,.4 per cent; tubercular lymph nodes,.2 per cent. Of 1,442 children, largely of Irish, Jewish and Italian stock, examined in three schools in this city in 1908, 73 per cent suffered from defective teeth, 59 per cent from nasal breathing, 42 per cent from visual defects, 39 per cent from hypertrophied tonsils and 15 per cent from anemia. Based upon another medical census of 23,000 children in all grades, the following distribution was found at the ages of six and fifteen:

At 6 years At I5 years
Defective teeth 65 per cent 81 per cent
Enlarged tonsils 40 14
Enlarged glands 40 7
Adenoids 28 8
Defective breathing 28 9
Defective vision 17 26

About 80 per cent of these children were physically defective in some way. Gland, mouth and throat troubles, it will be observed, are typical childhood infirmities, while defective vision (as well as defective teeth) constitutes the bane of youth. In Worcester, 758 pupils examined in two elementary schools showed enlarged glands in 64.5 per cent of the cases, affected tonsils in 37 per cent, adenoids (suspected) in 21 per cent, eye defects in 15 per cent, anemia in 4.5 per cent, poor nutrition in 5.5 per cent, medium nutrition in 36 per cent and good nutrition in 57.5 per cent. Decayed teeth were found in 86.5 per cent of the pupils, the average number per child being 4.85, and the corresponding averages in the different grades (given in order from the first to the ninth grade), 7, 6.54, 6.08, 4.90, 4, 3.50, 4, 4 and 3.66 per pupil. There is a noticeable falling off in the five upper grades. The figures show a wide variation from grade to grade in some of the defects. Of over 50,000 pupils examined in the public schools of Cleveland, 62.5 per cent suffered from one or more physical defects; and of 1,284 pupils examined in about equal numbers in a congested section and in the east end (where the living conditions were more favorable), 18.5 per cent of the former suffered from various kinds of defects as against 28.4 per cent of the latter. Of 156 pupils examined in the seven grades of the school of observation connected with the Summer School of the University of Pennsylvania, 38.5 per cent had decayed teeth, 20.5 per cent suffered from eyestrain, 13.5 per cent from nasal obstruction, 5.1 per cent from defective hearing and enlarged tonsils, 4.5 per cent from poor nutrition and 2 per cent from nervous exhaustion and stoop shoulders. It may be assumed that these children came from the better social ranks. A survey of a special class of 41 Philadelphia retardates–these pupils assumedly came from the lower social strata–yielded 48.7 per cent of eye defects, 34 per cent of defective speech, 26.8 per cent nose and throat troubles, 19.5 per cent nervous temperaments, 17 per cent each of orthopedic defects, lack of motor control and hearing defects. Of the children examined in Jefferson City, Missouri, for eye, nose and throat troubles, 41 per cent were in need of glasses, while 7.7 per cent had defective hearing, usually in one ear. In the rural districts of St. Louis County, 30.6 per cent of the 2,000 cases examined had subnormal visual acuity in one or both eyes, 14 per cent had less than two-thirds normal vision and 3 per cent less than one-half normal vision (these figures do not include hyperopia or mild astigmatism), 7 per cent had defective hearing in either of the ears, somewhat less than 2 per cent could not hear a whisper with either ear and.9 per cent were seriously troubled with adenoids. From a study of twenty-five Massachusetts, New York and New Jersey cities Rapeer2 estimates that the percentages of serious defects requiring treatment Rafeeb. School Health Administration, New York, 1919, p. 226. among elementary pupils are as follows: dental defects, 66 per cent; visual defects, 7 per cent; enlarged tonsils, 6 per cent; adenoids and nasal obstruction, 5 per cent; malnutrition 2 per cent; anemia and enlarged glands, 1 per cent; spinal curvature,.8 per cent; strabismus,.7 per cent; hearing defects and weak lungs (not tuberculosis),.5 per cent and nervousness,.2 per cent. (See also Chapter XVI.)

School medical inspection statistics, which are now available from the examination of millions of pupils in all sections of the country, show clearly–in spite of the unreliability of many of the reports–that physical defects in children are not restricted to any clime, race, environment or social condition. The children in sunny Southern California no less than the children of the cold or humid North, East and West, the children of the country no less than the children of the city, the children of the rich no less than the children of the poor, labor under various forms of physical handicap which are usually subject to melioration or cure. It is impossible to estimate the percentage of physically defective pupils even with approximate accuracy, because the standards of the examiners differ very widely and because some defects increase with age while others decrease. Any reliable inspection surveys must be made in relation to age. My own estimates, based on the study of numerous statistical surveys, of the percentage of grade pupils seriously affected with various defects are as follows: defective teeth (one or more cavities, serious malocclusion), from 50 to 95 per cent; defective vision and adenoids and nasal obstruction, from 5 to 20 per cent; seriously enlarged or diseased tonsils, 5 to 15 per cent; curvature of the spine, 2 to 7 per cent; malnutrition, 1 to 6 per cent; weak or tubercular lungs and defective hearing, 1 to 2 per cent. It is estimated that 12,000,000 of the pupils in the public schools of the country are to some extent handicapped by one or more physical defects. The typical American school child in the grades everywhere suffers more or less from some form of physical defectiveness. Sometimes the defects are so numerous and serious that the childs body is but a tissue of malfunctioning, misshapen, diseased or disordered organs.

The defective condition of the physiques of our pupils must be a matter of very serious moment to all people who have the welfare of children at heart. The parent cannot fail to be concerned about conditions which cause discomfort, restlessness, pain or disease in his children. The school administrator and teacher must be vitally interested in any conditions which may cause irregular attendance or impair the pedagogical efficiency of the learner. Likewise the city and the state, because they have made large investments in school plants and school paraphernalia and have appropriated large sums for the support of teachers, have vital interests at stake which must be rigorously conserved. They have set children apart for a long term of years and have thereby denied them the opportunities of engaging in productive labor. This they have done in order to provide for the children such mental and bodily training as will eventually so increase their productive capacity as to insure them increased returns upon their investment of time and energy. In order to guarantee its own perpetuity the state demands an output from the schools that shall manifest a capacity for social and industrial efficiency, and any obstacle to the attainment of this end must be removed. The state demands, as of right, that it secure adequate returns upon the invest
ment of money and human sacrifice which it has made in the interest of the schools.

But are the schools under existing conditions able to meet this just demand imposed upon them by the state? Manifestly not, for numerous investigations have shown that there is a veritable army of handicapped pupils in the schools who are unable properly to profit by the instruction. The slow-progress pupils outnumber the accelerated pupils eight to ten times (the average for twenty-nine cities), while over one-third of all the elementary pupils are pedagogically retarded (see also Chapter II). A certain amount of this pedagogical retardation is undoubtedly due to physical defectiveness. This would seem to be so on a priori grounds, for the body and the mind are indissolubly knit together. They are merely two aspects of the same unitary life process. There can be no psychical activity without a correlated physical activity, no psychosis without a correlated neurosis. When the physical machine is crippled the mental mechanism cannot as a rule work harmoniously. Rarely, perhaps, does the mind reach its highest potential so long as the bodily organs function defectively. It is impossible by ordinary school processes to make defective sense organs to function properly. That physical defects often constitute a positive deterrent to normal mental action and thus produce pedagogical retardation has been shown by various observations and statistical and experimental studies. Those studies are discussed at length in Chapter XV (which see).

It is true that in some investigations no marked correlation between physical defects and retardation in school progress has been found. This may sometimes be due to the fact that the dull, physically defective child has been pushed along irrespective of his merits, or to the fact that the progress of the whole class has been adjusted to meet his needs; or the factor of age has complicated the question; or physical defects have been included which exert no influence upon neuronic and mental development. But it is certain that one of the causative factors of retardation and elimination (retardation usually results in elimination) is physical defectiveness.

Not only so: the physically defective child tends to become the juvenile criminal. For the physically defective, who tends to make the dullard, becomes dissatisfied with himself and discouraged with his school work and thus plays truant or permanently drops out of school. In one investigation over 95 per cent of truants were found to have physical defects. In many cases these eliminated physical defectives become the street vagrants or loafers; and the loafers are the embryo criminals. Ninety per cent of criminals began their careers as truants or loafers, according to A. J. Pillsbury. Undoubtedly there is frequently a direct relation between physical defectiveness and moral perversity and youthful criminality. Much precocious criminality is traceable to physiological maladjustment.

The physical examination of school children would thus seem to be one of the important present-day public duties. It is false economy to allow the progress of whole classes to be impeded by the presence of pupils whose physical defects make it impossible for them to keep step with the normal procession. The mere removal of a physical obstruction will sometimes revolutionize the life history of a child, while years of mental training, with all their attendant strain and depression may accomplish practically nothing for physically handicapped children. The first step in mental training should be the removal of those physical obstructions which stand in the way of the free, spontaneous activity of the mind. Nor is this work needed for the sake of the self-protection of the classroom; society must assume the work for the sake of its own self-protection. A child abnormal in body probably cannot remain normal in mind; he will tend, as has been said, to become morally perverse and criminal. Civilization is thus coming to face a new menace in the presence of rapidly multiplying multitudes of physically defective children in every community. Instead of penalizing and trying to reform the child after he has developed his degenerate tendencies and committed his offense, would it not be more sane for society to turn right face about and remove one of the causes of the young childs perverse tendencies before the latter have become ineradicably ingrained? This can only be done through the school medical clinic and dispensary. The day will come when the first thing the schools will do for the first-day entrant will be to give him a thorough physical examination. First the natural; afterward the spiritual.

That the American public is rapidly becoming awake to the necessity of providing for the inspection of physical defects in school children is apparent on every hand. Although school medical inspection started in this country only about nineteen years ago (Boston appointed fifty school physicians in the fall of 1894; Chicago followed in 1895, New York in 1897 and Philadelphia in 1898), and although thirteen years ago only eight cities had established medical departments in the schools (but without the school nurse), the development has been so rapid during the last decade that in 1911 443 cities (or 42 per cent) of 1,038 cities reporting were supporting depart ments of school medical inspection or school hygiene (but only 214 were providing physical examination by doctors)–this according to a report of the Russell Sage Foundation–while in 1912 nine states had mandatory laws and ten states had permissive laws in regard to school health work. Nevertheless, fully half of the cities of the country are either making no provisions whatsoever or very inadequate provisions for the routine physical examination of school children, while the rural districts are doing practically nothing (Minnesota, Michigan and Virginia employ specialists to visit the rural schools, in order to instruct teachers in school and child hygiene). Very few school systems conduct dental and medical dispensaries for the free treatment of certified indigent children, while only seventy-six cities (in 1911) supported staffs of school nurses and eighty-nine cities employed school dentists. We are still lagging behind Europe, where the school physical examination work had its inception (Sweden appointed school physicians for every secondary school in 1868, France organized departments of medical inspection in 1879, while Germany followed in 1889), and where it has been organized in some countries as a function of the national government, notably in France, Germany, England, Norway, Belgium, Switzerland and Sweden. In England and Wales the Education Act of 1907 makes school medical inspection compulsory and universal (even in the most remote rural districts). The work is conducted by 317 local educational authorities, who employ 943 school medical officers, and is under the administrative control of the Chief Medical Officer of the Board of Education for England and Wales. Every child is given a routine physical examination at the time of entering and leaving school (an intermediate examination at the age of eight will be required after April 1, 1915), which includes an examination of the special sense organs, the heart, lungs, lymphatic system, height, weight and personal and family history. Not only so, in 1913 the educational authorities had established ninety-five medical clinics and fifty-eight dental clinics for the free treatment of minor ailments and physical defects (exclusive of thirty-eight clinics which provide X-ray treatment for ringworm).

The campaign for the establishment of school medical and dental clinics in the United States must go on until the work has been made compulsory and universal. Not only so, dispensary dental and medical clinics should be established by schools for the free treatment of certified indi-gents, and nurses should be appointed for examination and follow-up work, for treating and instructing the affected pupils and for socio-hygienic service in the homes. For the work of diagnosis will be largely worthless unless the correction or mitigation of defects can be secured. Moreover, it is not sufficient merely to mitigate or correct the physical defects in the clinic; the success of the treatment will often depend on the subsequent physiological and mental habits of the child. The effects of the removal of adenoids and enlarged tonsils are often rendered nugatory because proper breathing exercises are not subsequently followed. Since the schools (through their teachers, nurses and medical inspectors) are in a position to follow up and properly supervise the child after treatment, it seems desirable to treat all the minor ailments and defects in a school dispensary. The time must come when physical reclamation work will be recognized as one of the regular, fundamental duties of the city and state school systems.

Incidentally it may be pointed out that the qualitative standards of many medical inspectors must be elevated if our highest hopes for child betterment from this service are to be realized.

But a further step must be taken in order to supplement and render effective in the highest measure the results of medical inspection and treatment and of pedagogical training. That is the psychological inspection of our large army of mentally exceptional school children. We do not know the complete status of the child when we have merely examined his bodily aspect by the available instruments of precision. The child possesses a mental aspect which needs to be just as thoroughly explored by instruments of precision. For the mental examination the instruments and the methods of medical inspection do not suffice; this work requires a technique of its own. Thus it is important to know how the childs motor functions vary, in respect to strength, steadiness, power to coordinate and speed of reaction; how his powers of memory, association, imitation, adaptation, observation, attention, judgment, reasoning, speech, ability to withstand fatigue, pressure and pain thresholds, perception of color (color blindness) and intellectual level vary, etc. Until such facts as these are known, we can have nothing but the most general knowledge of the childs mental constitution. Only by tests of this nature will it be possible to reveal striking departures in fundamental mental make-up; only thus will it be possible to determine whether the mental variations in a given child are of the nature of aberrations or abnormalities. And only when this knowledge has been obtained will it be possible to make the training of a mentally defective or unusual child scientifically accurate, because the training of exceptional children must be adapted to the exigencies of each case; it must be made to fit the special needs of every special child. In the absence of thorough knowledge of the childs mental peculiarities instruction must remain a hit-and-miss process. So far as the teacher is concerned, medical inspection and treatment yield knowledge of minor importance for her guidance. Medical treatment is, of course, primarily of value to the individual pupil. It is a means of freeing him from his physical impediments, so that heredity may come to her own. And it is, indeed, a God-send to the schools in the case of the child whose abnormal physical functions impede educational progress. Nevertheless, the psychological examination yields knowledge more directly valuable for the teachers guidance, because her work is chiefly with the childs psychical functions. In the absence of any exact knowledge of the peculiarities of the pupils mind her work must blunder along with a mixture of happy hits and unfortunate misses. It is not sufficient that the teacher adapt method to subject-matter; she must also adapt method to the mind which is to assimilate the subject-matter–the latter being the more important in the case of the atypical child.

That the public is rapidly becoming awake to the necessity of segregating the atypical or special child is becoming increasingly evident. This need has been long recognized by the state so far as the idiots, imbeciles and low-grade morons are concerned. More recently this need has been recognized by about 350 cities which have established as an integral part of the school system so-called ungraded and special classes for the retarded, the seriously backward–for pupils whose mental caliber is superior to the feeble-minded but considerably inferior to the normal child–and for the feeble-minded. It is absolutely necessary that we segregate the subnormals in the public schools for at least two reasons: first, they constitute an intolerable drag upon the regular classrooms, impeding their progress and consuming more than their just share of the teachers time; and, second, by grouping subnormals together in small classes they may be given individual attention by the teacher, and, what is more important, be provided with a type of school work which fits their needs and which will maximally equip them for the socio-indus-trial responsibilities which they are able to assume.

Unfortunately the method of classifying and segregating subnormal children is in most cities in many respects pitiably inadequate. These children have almost invariably been segregated simply upon the classroom teachers, principals, superintendents or medical inspectors recommendation, because they have been unable to furnish the required classroom output. They have not been subjected to a prior thorough scientific psycho-educational examination, except at the hands of amateur psycho-clinicists. The special teacher usually gets the laggards without adequate diagnosis, or with mistaken diagnosis. Without having any precise or adequate knowledge of their mental and educational abnormalities, she is expected to give them skilled differential pedagogical treatment. As a matter of fact, many special class teachers are simply shooting in the dark, and many administrators seem to feel that provided the teacher keeps eternally at the laggards she is doing all that can be reasonably demanded of her.

In the light of the above facts, does it not seem the part of public wisdom and economy to establish in every school system a psycho-educational clinic for the educational and the psychological examination of all types of educationally misfit children? Should there not be connected with every school system of any considerable size an expert clinical psychologist to supervise the examination and training of educationally exceptional children?

So far as relates to the medical inspection of all school children, departments have been organized in the schools of nil the large cities of the country. But it must be conceded that so far as organized psychological inspection is concerned we have made only a beginning, even in the large city systems. True, a number of schools have done pioneer work of great intrinsic value in this line of endeavor, notably the Chicago public schools, which for years have conducted as an integral part of the school system a department of Child Study and Pedagogic Investigation. Many other city school systems are beginning to establish psychological clinics (see Chapter XVIII), but the work is usually conducted by medical inspectors or teachers who are profoundly ignorant of the detailed psychology and pedagogy of mental and educational abnormalities. This is, I feel, but a temporary stage in the work; eventually the schools will demand the services of competent experts for this work. The fact that many institutions for the feeble-minded have established psychological clinics and are demonstrating their value for the proper educational classification and treatment of their inmates, and the fact that many universities have established psychological chnics not only for the examination of cases but for the training of competent examiners, augur well for the rapid development of the public school clinic. (The Russell Sage Foundation has rendered some aid to the cause by the compilation of retardation and elimination statistics, but it has done only a modicum of what, with its vast resources, it could be reasonably expected to do in the direction of establishing the normal mental norms which are so much needed for the more exact psychological diagnosis of mentally unusual children.) The school public will soon come to realize that their duty toward the educationally exceptional child has not been discharged until, in addition to providing him with the advantages of medical inspection and treatment, they also supply the adequate machinery for determining his psychological and educational abnormalities.

The first line of psycho-clinical work undertaken by the schools should be the expert examination of the so-called laggards or dullards (more properly the feeble-minded and seriously backward). The laggard is the one who creates the grave administrative problems of the schools; he it is who binds a millstone about the neck of the educational organism, who impedes the progress of the regular classes, who causes expensive repetition or early elimination; who has bottled up within his self the concentrated mischief of the school community; who gives little or no returns for the excessive demands which he makes upon the teachers time and energy. The normal child, thanks to his hereditary endowment, is fairly well able to fight out his own salvation. In him nature will assert herself even in the face of untoward environing circumstances. I would not, of course, have this type of child neglected; he ought to be offered every facility to work at his maximal potential; the normal and bright pupils are the children of greatest promise to the state. But as long as retarded children are permitted to encumber the progress of the regular grades we cannot do our duty by the gifted pupils. Our first duty, then, is the removal of the laggards from the regular grades: this is the Macedonian cry. Any plan of psycho-educational inspection must first aim to reach the retarded children.

As a matter of fixed school policy every child who has spent not more than two years in the same grade (i. e., who is retarded not more than one year) should be given a physical examination by a medical expert for the detection and treatment of defects of the eyes, ears, nose, throat, teeth, glandular system, lungs, heart, nutrition, nervous disorders, etc.; and a psychological examination by a competent consulting psychologist for the detection of intellectual retardation and anomalies of sensation, movement, memory, imagination, association, attention, imitation, color perception, speech, number sense, fatigue and for the determination of indices of stature, weight, vitality and dynamometry, etc. The determination may very well, in each case, be restricted to the most essential tests. These examinations, together with the previous academic record and family history of the child, would determine whether he should remain in one of the regular classes or whether he should be assigned to one of the special classes for backward or feeble-minded children. It would also determine details of pedagogic treatment. A retarded child found mentally defective through this winnowing process should be compelled, by school enactment, to enter the special class where he can be educated with a small number of his likes. The first attention which some of these children should receive should be medical: any physical handicaps which impede the efficient activity of the mind should be removed before the child is compelled to undergo the educative processes of the schoolroom. Whether such treatment could by due process of law be made compulsory would be a matter for judicial decision. The child is compelled under the law to attend school; is it not his right, under a parity of reasoning, to demand that the state put him in such condition that he can assimilate those con tents demanded of him by a compulsory attendance law? Certain it is that mere recommendation is not sufficient: there is a large gap between advising a parent to provide proper medical treatment for his child, and actually getting the child treated in accordance with the recommendation. Until the public is sufficiently educated on the question, some form of pressure must be applied. Following this, however, each child should be subjected to such pedagogical and mental treatment or training as the prior psychological and medical examinations have indicated as specially pertinent to his case. When a child is transferred to a special school a brief transcript of the psychological examination, together with the examiners recommendation, should accompany him. With this record in her possession the classroom teacher will be able to proceed with eyes open to a systematic and rational development of those functions which have become atrophied or remained dormant.

In order that there be no misapprehension it should be stated that a large percentage of subnormal children are purely educational and not medical cases. Their mental improvement depends almost entirely upon proper pedagogical training and little, if at all, upon medication or surgical interference.

Under the above scheme of segregation of the feebleminded and backward from the average and bright pupils, the psychological clinic (together with the special classes) would naturally become an educational clearing house. Some pupils sent to the special classes would eventually be returned to the regular classes; others, on the contrary, would be sent to the feeble-minded institutions. Some of those who proved to be retarded because of physical defects would eventually catch up with their fellows after having received proper medical treatment and special mental training, and could thus be returned to the regular classrooms. Likewise, many pupils merely standing in need of specific, corrective pedagogic treatment would be considerably improved, and often could be restored to their regular grades. On the other hand, those who failed to make any appreciable progress would thereby indicate that their trouble was more fundamental, a condition of general neural and mental arrest. Such incurably weak pupils should, after due training, be relegated to institutions for the feeble-minded or institutions of a similar nature. Their defects are an irremediable condition and not a disease or a specific defect amenable to curative treatment. Even moronic defectives can be trained to become self-supporting under direction only, and should be permanently isolated in custodial institutions where the conditions render it possible for them to support themselves, instead of being turned adrift upon society, to become the victims of its vicious members and designing rapscallions, or to become fresh recruits to its armies of vagabonds, miscreants, social delinquents and criminals.

This rational method of selecting, treating and educating the mentally defective or subnormal pupils must appeal, not only to the generous instincts aroused in any normal human soul by the contemplation of the sad story of these unfortunates, but also to our sense of business economy and instinct of self-preservation. Society must do this work for its own protection. Preventive medicine, preventive philanthropy, preventive didactics, mental hygiene, are better and cheaper in the end than alms-houses, jails, prisons and an army of penal officers. The plan here advocated would yield results out of all proportion to the money expended.

, The psychological inspection in the city schools, to which I have referred, might be made a function of the department of psychology of training schools for teachers supported by municipalities, until the work has been thoroughly organized and developed in a separate division of the school systems. The director of the psychological laboratory (but only provided he possesses adequate clinical training and experience) might serve as the director of the psychological clinic. Three-fourths of his time might properly be devoted to the work of routine inspection, and one-fourth to the work of regular classroom instruction in the school of education. This plan would render it possible to inaugurate the work with a comparatively small outlay of money, as the laboratory apparatus could be used for a twofold purpose: instruction in the normal school and pupil inspection. This plan would tend to vitalize the instruction in psychology by bringing the instructor into first-hand contact with important concrete situations. It would give a new significance and content to child study, and afford enriched opportunities for the students in the observation courses. What applied science signifies in contrast with pure science, individual psychology would come to mean in contrast with general psychology. Individual psychology would assume a clinical significance, and become of service for mental diagnosis and educational guidance.

Psychology is destined to have not only a pedagogic but a clinical value for education. Eventually we shall have an independent science of clinical psychology or clinical education, instruction in which will be afforded in all of the large progressive normal schools and colleges

Schools of education under private or state control could make similar arrangements with public school systems.

of education. And we shall also have psychological or psycho-educational clinics in the large school systems, manned by psychological and educational experts, for the purpose of classifying the educational misfits.

CHAPTER II

THE NEW CLINICAL PSYCHOLOGY AND THE PSYCHO-CLINICIST1

Scientific psychology is essentially a modern creation. It is only about a half century since the scientific methods of induction and experimentation were systematically applied to the study of mental phenomena. Yet we possess, after this brief half century of labor, not only a fairly complete body of reliable theoretical psychology, but the promising beginnings of a number of applied psychologies. The methods and results of the new psychology have been applied, with gratifying results, during the last decade or two to the study of problems in history, literature, art, anthropology, sociology, economics, business, hygiene, medicine, insanity, feeblemindedness, criminology, law, education and paidology. Its services thus far have been most valuable, perhaps, to education and medicine, and the outlook in these fields justifies the expectation that we shall soon have to christen various new independent sciences, namely, the sciences of experimental pedagogy, experimental psycho-pathology (with psycho-therapy) and clinical psychology (or better still, perhaps, psycho-educational pathology).

In the present chapter we shall discuss one of the most promising of the recent applications of psychology, namely, the new psycho-clinical movement, which has won recognition, within a decade, in a number of universities, normal and medical schools, hospitals for the insane, institutions for the feeble-minded and epileptic, reformatories and correctional institutions, immigration stations, juven... and public schools. The discussion will pertain more particularly to the educa... cts of the movement–the psycho-clinical and psycho-educational examina... ool children.

1 Reprinted, with extensive alterations, from The Journal of Educati... ology, 1911, pp. 121-132, and 191-910.

1. The psychological clinic in the higher institutions of learning: th... ies, colleges, normal schools and medical schools. Dr. Lightner Witmer, to whom we owe the name clinical psychology,2 is the pioneer psycho-clinician in connection with the university laboratories of psychology. His interest in the phenomena of mental retardation began in 1889, when his attention was drawn to a boy who suffered from retardation through speech defect; but it was not until March, 1896, that he opened the Psychological Clinic of the University of Pennsylvania and received his first case, a chronic bad speller (34, 35). Since that time Witmers work has continued uninterruptedly and has grown apace, so that three hours daily are now (since 1909) devoted to the examination of children. These children come from homes, institutions, public and private schools and juvenile courts of Philadelphia and the surrounding territory. Witmers work embraces a physical, psychological and sociological examination, in which a number of experts cooperate–a psychologist, neurologist, dentist, oculist, nose and throat specialist and social worker. The social worker makes a first-hand examination of the childs home conditions, renders aid in the mitigation of bad environmental influences, and by means of follow-up work sees that the treatment prescribed for the child is carried out. The clinic does not limit itself to the problem of diagnosis; an orthogenic home school, or hospital school, was established in July, 1907, for the medical and pedagogical treatment of pay and free cases. This is a combined home, hospital and training school, where the child is provided with proper food, baths, outdoor exercise, sleep, medical attention, discipline, motor training and intellectual drill in the rudiments of the school fundamentals. This school also serves as a school of observation and a clinic for further diagnosis. Records of the childs hereditary, family and personal history (accidents, diseases, educational record, present mental and physical status) are preserved for reference. Courses in clinical psychology are offered to teachers during the regular and summer sessions, while classes for mentally exceptional children are conducted during the summer for purposes of training and observation. Witmer also edits The Psychological Clinic, now in its eighth volume, which is devoted to the study of the psychology, hygiene and education of children who are mentally and morally deviating.

2 Clinical psychology is not synonymous with medical psychology or psychopathology or psychiatry (see Chapters III, V and X). Clinical means literally bedside, and was applied originally to the first-hand (bedside) method of studying the individual patient. In psychology it designates the method of determining the mental status or peculiarities of an individual by a many-sided process of firsthand observation, testing and experiment. The clinical method may be used in the study of normal as well as of abnormal mentality. I suggest the use of the words psycho-clinical, psycho-educational and medico-clinical to designate, respectively, psychological, educational and medical examinations by the clinical method.

e last few years the psychological clinics have multiplied very rapidly. In order to obtain more accurate knowledge concerning the psycho-clinical work attempted, and the courses offered in the psychology and pedagogy of mentally exceptional children in the colleges, universities, medical and normal schools in the United States, a questionnaire was sent out in January and again in September and October, 1913, to the professors of psychology or education in all the universities and in all the larger colleges, to the principals of all the state and city normal schools and to the deans of all the medical schools of the country. My thanks are due to the many respondents whose replies made this study possible. The following were the questions asked: 1. Do you conduct a psychological clinic for the actual examination of all mentally exceptional cases referred to you? (Date of organization, name and preparation3 of clinician, and equipment.) 2. What per cent of the clinicians time is given to the actual clinical examination of cases? What per cent of his time is given to teaching? To teaching branches other than clinical psychology and the study, care and education of exceptional children?

8. Do you conduct a training clinic for training students in the methods of psycho-clinical and anthropometric examination and diagnosis?

4. What didactic courses (lectures or recitations) are offered in clinical psychology and the psychology and pedagogy of exceptional children?

5. Do you conduct training classes for exceptional children? If so, are they open to students for observation and cadet teaching?

6. What plans are being made for the organization or extension of this type of work?

Replies were received from sixty-six colleges and universities, thirty-three state and city normal schools and twenty-five medical schools. The replies are topically summarized under the above captions in the following pages. When the questions are left blank it is to be inferred that the answers are negative. The dates given refer to the time when the clinical work or courses were first organized. Hours means the number of hours per week.

3 The academic data are given in the subsequent pages only for specialists who are actually conducting psychological clinics.

Several institutions which were known to offer the type of work contemplated in the questionnaire failed to make reply, although two or three inquiries were addressed to them. In some of these cases data have been gathered from the catalogues and included in this tabulation.

The replies are tabulated separately for the universities and colleges, the normal schools and the medical schools, in accordance with the following grouping:

Group I comprises institutions which have established bona fide psychological or psycho-educational clinics; that is, laboratories whose regular, primary and essential function is the psychological or educational examination of individual cases, for purposes of diagnosis and advice.

Group II comprises institutions which either have given in the immediate past or which do at the present time give a slight amount of attention to the psychological testing of children with a view to arriving at individual mental diagnosis. These institutions can scarcely be said to conduct psychological clinics, although more or less psycho-clinical work may be attempted in the laboratories of psychology, education or psycho-or neuro-pathology (in the case of medical schools).

Group III comprises institutions which do absolutely no clinical work in psychology or education (or at most a very negligible amount of it), but which either give some attention to the study of mentally exceptional children or which are ready to develop certain lines of this work.

Universities And Colleges

Group I

University of Pennsylvania

(From the catalogue, 1912-1913) 1. Psychological Clinic organized in March, 1896, in the department of psychology. Director, Lightner Witmer, Professor of Psychology (Ph. D. in psychology), assisted by a staff of psychologists, physicians and social workers.

8. Yes.

4. (1) Growth and Retardation (Witmer).

(2) Tests and Measurements, 8 hours one or two terms. (8) Social Research in Clinical Psychology, 4 hours one term.

(4) The Exceptional Child, 1 hour one term.

(5) The Training and Treatment of Exceptional Children, 1 hour one term.

(6) Clinical Psychology, 1 hour one or two terms.

(7) Mental Defects, 1 2 hours one term.

(8) Orthogenics, iva hours one term.

5. Yes.

Didactic and clinical courses and an observation class are conducted during the summer term.

University of Washington 1. Clinic in operation in the department of psychology since the fall of 1909; conducted since 1911 by the Bailey and Babette Gatzert Foundation for Child Welfare. A fund of 80,000 was given to the University in December, 1910, for the maintenance of a Bureau of Child Welfare in the School of Education, whose purpose is to provide expert diagnosis of mentally and physically exceptional children, to cooperate with local authorities throughout the state in the establishment of psychological laboratories and special classes, to furnish teachers and experts for the work, and to collect and publish data. Director, Stevenson Smith, Assistant Professor of Orthogenics (Ph. D. in psychology; additional work in the Psychological Clinic of the University of Pennsylvania and in the Vanderbilt Clinic, New York City); one assistant, two graduate student assistants and four medical assistants. The Director holds the appointment of psychologist to the Public Schools and Juvenile Court, and does a certain amount of field work throughout the state. Rooms are provided in the university psychological laboratory.

2. Seven-eighths of Directors time given to clinical examination and instruction of children; rest of time given to teaching. No teaching of subjects other than those pertaining to the clinical work.

8. Instruction given to graduate and undergraduate students in psychological, anthropological and medical methods of diagnosis, in courses given in 4 below.

4. (1) Psychology and Education of Exceptional Children, in School of Education, 4 hours during one semester (Smith).

(2) Laboratory Course in Experimental Child Study and Clinical Psychology, in department of psychology, 8 hours (4 credits) for one semester.

(8) A Graduate Course in the Education of Exceptional Children (practical work in the Psychological Clinic and special classes in the public schools), in the School of Education, 4 credits (Smith).

(4) A Practical Graduate Course in Clinical Methods/ in the Department of Psychology, 4 credits.

All of the above given since September, 1911.

6. Classes are conducted at the university for feeble minded, backward and speech-defective cases. Open to student observation. Partly in charge of graduate teachers.

6. Plan to increase didactic courses at the university.

The courses are also offered during the summer term.

University of Minnesota 1. Free Clinic in Mental Development, organized in the year 1909-1910, in the department of psychology. Director, J. B. Miner, Professor of Psychology (Ph. D. in psychology), assisted by Herbert Woodrow, Instructor in Psychology (Ph. D. in psychology); by Fred Kuhlmann, Director of Psychological Research, Minnesota School for Feeble-Minded and Colony for Epileptics (Ph. D. in psychology and education); and by J. P. Sedgwick, M. D. Full laboratory equipment in special room at University. Examinations are also made in reserved room in City and County Court House and in public school buildings.

2. One or two days a week, including work in Juvenile Court; work, which is divided among several men, is equivalent to three-fourths of the time of one man.

8. Students attend psychological clinic; they have their attention directed to the simpler matters in medical diagnosis; and are privileged to visit pediatric clinics and the State School for the Feeble-Minded at Faribault.

4. Mental Retardation, since February, 1910, 8 hours for one semester (Woodrow); given to a separate division during the fall of 1912 by Kuhlmann. Also includes psycho-clinical examinations, and lectures on the application of facts to delinquents, by Miner, and medical examination by Sedgwick. Optional to students with one years work in psychology.

5. Graduate students sometimes work with individual children. A class was at one time conducted for the correction of stuttering.

Courses are offered by various specialists in the summer school.

Johns Hopkins University and Phipps Psychiatric Clinic 1. Psychological clinic established in February, 1911. Director, E. B. Huey,4 Lecturer on Mental Development in the Johns Hopkins University, and Assistant in Psychiatry in the Phipps Clinic of Johns Hopkins Hospital (Ph. D. in psychology and education; special work in institutions for the feebleminded and in clinics here and abroad); under the general direction of Dr. Adolf Meyer. Several rooms available in the new Phipps Clinic, but no apparatus secured as yet.

2. Six hours per week. About one-half of the Directors time is given to examination and treatment.

8. No training clinic, but students in medicine and psychology assist in the testing.

4. (1) Feeble-minded and Backward Children, January, 1911, 1 hour for one term (Huey).

(2) Clinical Psychology, in the Medical School, consisting of lectures and tests, 1 hour for one term (Huey). No courses in other than clinical work.

5. Experimental class for defective children was to be established in the Baltimore schools, enrollment limited to 15, none under the mental age of six, under Hueys direction.

University of Kansas 1. Clinic established in 1911, in department of education. Director, A. W. Trettien, Assistant Professor of Education (Ph. D. in psychology and education; additional work in hospitals in Worcester). Two rooms available; use of equipment in Medical School. Visits to homes. Have tested inmates in Boys Industrial School.

2. Two hours. 8. No.

4. (1) Educational Pathology, since 1910, 2 hours for

Dr. Huey died December SO, 1913. No data as to what extent of the work in this clinic will now be devoted to psycho-educational as distinguished from psycho-pathological examinations.

18 weeks, with clinical work (Trettien and Prof. R. A. Schwegler).

(2) School Hygiene/ 8 hours for 18 weeks, covers certain aspects of the work (Trettien).

(8) Mental Measurements, 2 hours (Schwegler).

5. No, but have placed children under instruction and observation.

6. Plan to enlarge the work, under the direction of the School of Education and School of Medicine.

Leland Stanford, Jr., University.

1. Clinic established in the year 1911-1912, in the School of Education. Director, Louis M. Terman, Associate Professor of Education (Ph. D. in psychology and education). Work done in the laboratory of the department of education and in neighboring schools. About 400 worth of materials for mental and physical testing.

2. One to 5 hours per week. About one-half of the Directors time.

8. No, but major students in education are afforded practice in giving Binet and other tests.

4. (1) Clinical Child Psychology/ since 1911-1912, 2 hoars throughout the year (Terman).

(2) Seminary and Research Course in the Psychology and Pedagogy of Backward Children (Prof. Percy E. Davidson).

5. A class was conducted from 1910 to 1912; now conducted by the town of Palo Alto, with the aid of the university clinic; enrollment, 15.

. University of Missouri 1. Clinic organized in the year 1911-1912, in the School of Education, by W. H. Pyle (Ph. D. in psychology).

2. Irregular; in fall about two afternoons per week for two or three months. The chief duties consist in teaching educational psychology.

8. Yes, in connection with the clinic and a course on The Scientific Testing of Method.

4. The Abnormal Child/ since fall of 1911, 1 hour (Pyle).

5. No, but plan to conduct classes eventually.

6. Plan to train teachers of subnormal children, and to develop this work in the state.

University of Pittsburgh 1. Dispensary Psycho-Educational Clinic, established in March, 1912, in the School of Education. Director, J. E. W. Wallin, Director of Psychological Clinic and Professor of Clinical Psychology and Mellen Research Fellow on the Psychology of Smoke (Ph. D. in psychology, philosophy and education; special work in institutions for epileptics, feebleminded and insane, and in medical clinics and schools). Rooms in temporary quarters in the School of Education. An initial supply of about 850 worth of equipment for psychological and anthropometric testing. Student assistant for record work on part time. Clinical examinations conducted in cities in Western Pennsylvania and various other states.

2. Varies from 10 to 20 hours per week. Somewhat less than two-thirds of Directors time devoted to clinical work; the rest to teaching. One course temporarily offered in another department.

8. Clinic Practicum, since June, 1912, optional. Open to a restricted number of students who desire a practical command of the technique of mental and anthropometric examination methods. Designed particularly, though not exclusively, for capable students who seek expert preparation for research or clinical work.

4. (1) Clinical Psychology and the Clinical Study of Mentally Exceptional Children, lectures with demonstration clinics, since April, 1912, 2 hours for one term. Elective, but required in the department (Wallin).

(2) The Care and Education of Feeble-minded and Back ward Children, lectures, with clinics and visits to institutions, since April, 1912, 2 hours for two terms. Elective, but required in the department (Wallin).

(8) Psycho-educational Pathology and Educational Therapeutics, a detailed treatment of corrective pedagogics, since September, 1912, 2 hours throughout the year. Elective, but required in the department (Wallin).

(4) Social Investigation, field work, since September, 1918, 2 to 4 hours throughout the year, elective but advised (Wallin).

(5) Manu-mental and Industrial Work for the Backward, Feeble-minded and Insane, since April, 1918, 2 hours throughout the year (Prof. H. R. Kniffin and Mr. Leon Winslow).

5. No; expect to utilize the special classes in the public schools for observation and cadet teaching. Have selected pupils for many public school classes.

6. Plan to expand the scope of the work in various directions.

The didactic and clinical courses are repeated during the summer term, and classes of feeble-minded and backward children are conducted for training, observation and practical teaching.

Yale University 1. Juvenile Psycho-clinic, established in April, 1912, in the department of education; examinations conducted in dispensary of Medical School. Director, Arnold Gesell, Assistant Professor of Education (Ph. D. in psychology and education; additional work in the Medical School).

2. Half of Directors time given to teaching subjects other than clinical psychology.

8. Offer a Clinical and Research Course for Advanced Students, 1 hour; includes visits to institutions and schools.

4. (1) Backward and Defective Children in the Public Schools," since October, 1912, 2 hours throughout the year. Elective graduate course (Gesell).

(2) Norms of Development, scheduled 1 hour for second half of second term. 5. No.

Harvard University 1. Clinic conducted in the out-patient department of the Psychopathic Hospital, Boston, since September, 1912. No technically trained clinical psychologist, but consultation and examination work is divided between E. E. Southard, M. D., Director; R. M. Yerkes, Ph. D., psychologist; W. F. Dearborn, Ph. D., psycho-educationalist; Herman Adler, M. D., chief of staff; V. V. Anderson, M. D., and F. D. Bosworth, Jr., M. D., examiners.

2. Clinics conducted by different examiners every afternoon except Sunday. No data as to what extent the examinations are psycho-educational.

8. Clinical training afforded in Psychopathic Hospital.

4. (1) Psychology of the Abnormal, since 1912, summer session, 89 lectures, with clinics (William Healy, M. D.).

(2) Mental Heredity and Eugenics, in department of psychology (Yerkes).

(8) Educational Psychology, in department of education (Dearborn).

(4) Aspects of Mental and Physical Development, in department of education (Dearborn).

(5) Psychopathology, in department of psychology, with clinics, since 1918-1914 (Adler).

5. No.

6. Plan to perfect clinical and educational organization in the out-patient department of the Psychopathic Hospital.

Certain courses are offered during the summer term.

University of Cincinnati 1. Clinic established September, 1912, in department of psychology. Director, B. B. Breese, Professor of Psychology (Ph. D. in psychology), assisted by Mr. S. Isaacs. Use of six rooms in the Psychological Laboratory of the University.

2. Three hours per week, or one-seventh of Directors time.

8. Yes.

4. Mental Measurements/ since September, 1912, 8 hours for 86 weeks (Breese and Isaacs).

Psychology of Mentally Defective Children (seminar), 2 hours.

5. No; cooperate with special classes in public schools.

Tulane University 1. Clinic established in October, 1912, in School of Education of H. Sophie Newcomb Memorial College for Women. Director, John Madison Fletcher, Assistant Professor of Experimental and Clinical Psychology (Ph. D. in psychology and education); supported jointly by Tulane University and the New Orleans Board of Education.5 Board of Education contributes 1,500 annually. Clinic rooms in Psychological Laboratory of School of Education. Assistants comprise a supervisor of social investigation, a recorder and secretary, student assistants and an advisory medical staff.

2. Three-fourths of Directors time given to clinical exami- 5 The joint arrangement was terminated during the summer of 1913, owing to the resignation of Dr. David Spence Hill from the acting directorship of the School of Education. Dr. Hill is now director of the recently created Department of Educational Research in the New Orleans public schools. The department at present has a budget of 3,500 and during the present year is undertaking the following program of work: a vocational survey, the individual study of exceptional children and statistical studies of retardation. A brief lecture course is also offered to the students at the city normal school. A psychological laboratory is being equipped in the directors rooms in the city hall.

Hm. Notes on the Problems of Extreme Individual Differences in Children of the Public Schools. Department of Educational Research, New Orleans Public Schools, 1913.

nation and teaching in the department; rest of time given to teaching experimental psychology. 8. No.

4. (1) The Psychology of the Abnormal Mind/ 8 hours for one term (Fletcher).

(2) Clinical Psychology, advanced course (Fletcher). (8) The Psychology of Retardation and Mental Deficiency (Fletcher).

5. No, but classes have been organized in the public schools.

University of North Dakota 1. Clinic started in September, 1918, in the department of psychology. Director, John W. Todd (Ph. D. in psychology, educational psychology and philosophy). Modest equipment. Aim to examine both normal and deviating children.

2. Varies; the laboratory is regularly open from 2 to 4 p. m., Mondays, Wednesdays and Thursdays.

8. No.

4. None.

5. No.

State University of Iowa 1. Clinic established in department of psychology, September, 1918. Director, R. H. Sylvester (Ph. D. in psychology; special preparation in clinical psychology). Aim to examine children anywhere in the state.

2. Indefinite.

8. Plan to conduct a training clinic.

4. (1) The Backward Child, 2 hours throughout the year (Sylvester).

(2) Orthogenics, 2 hours one semester (Sylvester).

(8) Tests and Measurements, 2 hours for one semester (Sylvester and Mabel Clare Williams).

5. No, but expect to treat speech defectives.

Courses are offered during the summer term.

University of Oklahoma 1. Clinic work conducted in conjunction with city schools and the state asylum for the insane, since the fall of 1918, in the School of Education, by W. W. Phelan, Director of the School of Education and Professor of Psychology and Education (Ph. D. in psychology).

8. No.

4. Seminar course, 2 hours, since September, 1918 (Phelan).

5. No.

6. Plan to organize the-work in the School of Education.

Group II

Clark University 1. No psycho-clinic at present, but more or less clinical work, supplemented by a course of lectures, has been carried on by various men during the last four years in the department of psychology.

Cornell University 1. No, but occasional cases are referred to Educational Laboratory for examination, by G. M. Whipple, Ph. D., Assistant Professor of the Science and Art of Education. The laboratory has been examining by Binet scale and other tests various children in the George Junior Republic, with a view of determining advisability of requiring in future a prior psychological examination of all candidates for admission.

8. No, except as noted in 4.

4. (1) Education of Exceptional Children, since 1908, 2 hours for one semester. Elective (Whipple).

(2) Conduct of Mental Tests, since 1908, for graduate and advanced students, 3 hours for one semester. Also given in summer session since 1912, 2 hours daily, with examination of cases (Whipple).

School of Pedagogy, New York University 1. A psychological clinic is conducted for demonstrating cases in connection with the lecture course given by Henry H. Goddard, Director of Research, New Jersey Training School (Ph. D. in psychology and education).

8. Yes, in the summer session.

4. Education of Defectives, since October, 1906, 8 hours on alternate Saturdays during the academic year. Also given during summer term (Goddard).

5. Six special classes conducted during summer session 1912, 15 pupils in each class.

Numerous courses are offered during the summer term by various instructors.

Girard College 1. Boys in the school and candidates for admission have been examined since September, 1910, by Ralph L. Johnson, A. M. (University of Pennsylvania and New Jersey Training School). Have a laboratory with two rooms.

2. Half of examiners time given to examination and half to teaching morons.

8. No.

4. No didactic courses given.

5. Conduct classes for morons.

Group III

Alfred University 4. Brief discussions on mental defectives in courses in child study and educational psychology (Bessie L. Gambrell).

Barnard College 4. Occasional reference to topics in courses in experimental psychology (L. H. Hollingworth).

Bryn Mawr College 1. No.

8. No, but students visit the psychological clinic of the University of Pennsylvania and schools for deficient children.

4. The Psychology of Defective and Unusual Children, a graduate seminar throughout the year, first given in 1918-1914. Five months (J. H. Leuba).

College of the City of Nen York

(From the catalogue, 1913) 4. Education of Backward and Defective Children, lectures, demonstrations of tests, visits to classes (S. B. Heckman).

Columbia University, Teachers College

(From the catalogue, 1913) 4. The Psychology and Education of Exceptional Children" (Naomi Norsworthy and E. A. Thorndike).

Normal Diagnosis and Anthropometry, with demonstrations (W. H. Mccastline). Didactic courses are offered daring the summer session.

Dartmouth College 1. A few of the students of the department of psychology tested the pupils in the public schools during the fall of 1912 by means of the Binet scale (W. B. Bingham).

Depauw University 4. Abnormal Psychology, including some clinical work, formerly given.

Mount Holyoke College 5. No, but use is made of Whipples Manual in course in Experimental Psychology (Samuel P. Hayes).

4. Reference reading on exceptional children in course in Educational Psychology.

Northwestern University 4. Abnormal Psychology, since 1909-1910, 8 hours for one semester, elective (R. H. Gault). A certain amount of time devoted to mental tests in course in Educational Psychology- 6. It is possible that psycho-clinical work will be undertaken within a year or two by the public schools or the University.

Ohio State University 4. The Defective Child, lectures, recitations and demonstrations, one semester, 8 credit hours (T. H. Haines).

Ohio University, Athens 4. Incidental reference to these topics in courses in psychology (Oscar Chrisman), and Educational Psychology (Willis L. Gard). Expect to give a systematic course in the near future.

Pennsylvania State College 4. Occasional lectures given to students on exceptional children (A. Holmes).

Princeton University 4. Topics are referred to incidentally in course in Genetic Psychology, since February, 1910 (Howard C. Warren).

Rutgers College 4. About 10 hours in all given to these subjects in courses in Elementary, Advanced and Educational Psychology and School Administration (W. T. Marvin and Alexander Inglis).

6. Plans for future development not yet matured.

University of California 1. No.

4. During the summer session of 1918, the following courses were offered:

Clinical Psychology and the Teaching of Exceptional Children, with demonstration clinic (F. G. Bruner, Ph. D., Clinical Psychologist to the Board of Education, Chicago).

Clinical Examination and Training of Subnormal Children (Mrs. Vinnie C. Hicks).

5. Training class for Subnormal Children/ open for observation (Mrs. Vinnie C. Hicks, Miss Nellie Goodhue and Miss Frances H. Ney).

6. Plan to establish a psychological clinic, in affiliation with departments of education, psychology and medicine.

University of Chicago, School of Education 4. Psychopathic, Retarded and Mentally Deficient Children/ 4 hours for twelve weeks, given only in 1910-1911.

University of Idaho 4.   Referred to incidentally in courses in Educational and Experimental Psychology (P. H. Soulen).

University of Illinois 1.   No clinic, but apparatus is available for starting work. 4. Three hours during one semester devoted to these topics in course in Educational Psychology (W. C. Bagley).

University of Indiana
(From the catalogue of the summer session, 1913) 4.   Orthogenics/ recitations and laboratory work, open to advance students 5 credit hours (E. E. Jones and Mr. John E. Evans).

5. School of Orthogenics/ for diagnosis, laboratory study, observation and training of a limited number of defectives.

University of Michigan 1. No.

8. No.

4. Education of Backward and Defective Children, since July, 1911, 2 hours for one semester (C. S. Berry).

6. No, but a class for backward children in an affiliated public school is open to students for observation.

Dr. Berry has recently been appointed consulting psychologist to the public schools of Detroit and to the Michigan Home for Feeble-Minded and Epileptics, at Lapeer. Courses for the training of teachers will be offered at the latter institution during the summer of 1914.

University of Montana 4.   Mental Pathology, 2 hours for one semester; visits to institutions (Bolton).

Exceptional Children, lectures and laboratory work, summer term, 1918.

6. Will establish a clinic at the University. Director, Thaddeus L. Bolton, Professor of Psychology and Education (Ph. D. in psychology).

Courses are offered during the summer term.

University of Nevada 4.   Lectures on exceptional children in course in Child and Adult Psychology, during six weeks, in Department of Psychology (George Ordahl).

University of North Carolina 1.   Have tested suspected cases in several city school systems and have induced Boards to provide training for special class teachers (H. W. Chase).

4. Treated incidentally during regular and summer terms in course in Educational Psychology (Chase).

University of Oregon 4.   Three or four lectures on the subject are given in course in Mental Hygiene and Abnormal Psychology (Edmund S. Conklin).

University of Southern California 4.   Education of Exceptional Children, given since 1911-1912, 2 hours for one semester; visits to institutions (Howard L. Lunt).

University of Tennessee 4.   Was emphasized in a course in Child Study and Adolescence given in summer session 1918 (Bird T. Baldwin).   Two brief didactic courses will be offered during summer of 1914.

University of Texas 4.   These topics treated only incidentally in course in Educational Psychology (J. C. Bell).

Will establish a clinic in School of Education.

University of Utah 6.   Legislature has been asked to establish a clinic in the Department of Psychology and provide for didactic courses. Thus far only a few cases have been examined (Joseph Peterson).

University of Wisconsin 6. Plans already considered to establish a Psychological Clinic in the Department of Education.

William and Mary College 4. These subjects are treated briefly in the course in Child Study (H. E. Bennett).

State And City Normal Schools

Group I

Colorado, The State Teacher College, Greeley 1. Psychological clinic, established in 1908 in the department of psychology. Director, J. D. Heilman (Ph. D., special training in clinical psychology).   Physical and mental examinations are provided. Children in the Denver schools have been examined once every two weeks. One room with fair laboratory equipment.

2. About 5 hours. One-third of clinicians time given to teaching clinical subjects and two-thirds to teaching other subj ects.

8. Psycho-clinical Practice, elective, 2 hours, fall term (Heilman).

4. Clinical Psychology, since March, 1910, elective, 8 hours throughout the term; also given to Denver teachers and principals (Heilman).

Lectures on retardation and exceptional children, summer term, 1918, by various psychological specialists.

5. Yes. Special classes for the feeble-minded, backward and dull, and for children with speech, reading, spelling and number defects; from 1 to 4 pupils per class, although the classes for the dull are larger.

Group II

California, Lot Angelet State Normal School 1. Since 1912 have examined a few children from the training school and juvenile court, and a few delinquent girls and feeble-minded children. Examiners: Grace M. Fernald (Ph. D. in psychology; special work in the Psychological Institute of the Juvenile Court, Chicago), and C. W. Waddle (Ph. D. in psychology and education). Limited equipment. Two rooms provided for in plans for new building.

2. One or two hours per week, not programed.

8. No; a week or two in the course in Child Study is given to familiarize students with the signs, and the means of discovering, physical defects, with demonstrations. A few students are taught to give psychological tests.

4. Frequent reference to these topics in the courses in Child Study and Advanced Psychology.

5. Some work with exceptional children done in training school. One or two special rooms provided for in the new training school.

6. Plan to enlarge work if the legislature authorizes extension of course to four years.

Michigan, Central State Normal School, Mount Pleasant 1. Clinic conducted by Department of Psychology and Education for testing children in the training school. Examiner, E. C. Rowe (Ph. D. in psychology and education). Have the usual supply of apparatus.

2. Four hours per week.

8. No, but testing of pupils in training school is observed by students of the Normal Department.

4. Clinical Psychology/ since January, 1911, 4 hours for 12 weeks (Rowe).

5. No.

Group III

Alabama, State Normal College, Florence 6. It is possible that at some future date some of this work may be programed.

Connecticut, State Normal Training School, Willimantic.

5. Pupil teachers do individual work with exceptional children.

Illinoit

Chicago Normal College 1. No, this work is done by the department of child study of the public schools.

2. No work regularly programed.

8. Students and instructors (John T. Mcmanis and Mabel R. Fernald) make a simple anthropometric and psychological examination of normal and exceptional children in the courses in education. One large room equipped with apparatus for psychological tests.

5. No, we conduct classes for the deaf only in one of the practice schools.

Expect to train teachers for backward children.

State Normal University, Normal 8. No, but students assist in physical measurements. Physical and mental data are entered on a card which accompanies the child through the training school.

Matsachusetts

State Normal School, North Adams 5. A class for defectives is being established.

State Normal School, Worcetter 4. Two special lectures and incidental reference to feebleminded children, and an annual excursion to the School for the Feeble-Minded at Waltham, since February, 1910 (J. Mace Andreas).

Michigan

Northern State Normal School, Marquette 1. A few pupils in the training school have been tested since 1910 (G. C. Fracker).

2. Nominal.

8. No, but students are afforded some training in giving the Binet tests.

4. A few lectures are given on exceptional children, and on methods of diagnosis and treatment, in courses in Psychology and Principles of Education (Fracker and G. L. Brown). The diagnosis and treatment of physical defects are considered in the course in Hygiene and Sanitation.

Western State Normal, Kalamazoo 1. No programed work, but Binet-Simon tests are used and teachers are in touch with the problems.

Minnesota

State Normal School, Duluth 4. Treated incidentally in courses in Psychology and Pedagogy.

State Normal School, Winona 1. No, but a few cases have been examined since 1898 (J. P. Gaylord).

5. Some special provision has been made for retarded (especially) and bright pupils. Open to observation by student teachers.

6. If course is lengthened will develop work with unusual children.

New York City, Brooklyn Training School for Teachers 8. Teachers in training give anthropometric and psychological tests to pupils in the ungraded room.

4. Psychology of Mental Defectives, since November, 1912, 5 hours for six weeks; now 60 hours (W. J. Taylor). Required of those teachers already conducting ungraded classes who may be designated by the supervisor of ungraded classes.

5. One ungraded class, with one teacher and sixteen pupils (high grade imbeciles and morons).

Oregon, Normal School, Monmouth 4. About five weeks is devoted to these topics in course in Educational Psychology (E. S. Evenden).

5. A flexible scheme of grading in the training school allows better adjustment of work to the needs of backward and bright pupils.

6. Contingent on growth of school, it is planned to offer a separate course in this work.

Pennsylvania

Bloomtburg State Normal School, Bloomsburg 4. Treated incidentally in courses in General Psychology and Child Study.

East Stroudsburg State Normal School, East Stroudsburg 4. Incidental attention is given in course in Educational Psychology to tests of intelligence, and methods of studying and training exceptional children (D. W. Larue).

Indiana State Normal School, Indiana 4. Brief presentation of subject of defective eyes and ears to senior class in Methods, since fall of 1911 (Frank Drew).

Millersville State Normal School 4. Incidental lectures in pedagogical courses on the Psychology of Abnormal and Subnormal Children.

Philadelphia Normal School for Girl 4. The mental and physical differences of children are studied in the course in Child Study. Students are given some training in giving tests, since 1910 (Grace Hamill).

Washington, State Normal School, Bellingham 4. No, but Binet and desanctis tests are used in a course in Child Study (Frank Deerwester).

5. Special attention is given to dull, bright and peculiar children in the training school.

Wett Virginia, Training School of Marshall College,

Huntington 6. Plan to develop some phases of this work in future.

Wisconsin, State Normal School, Milwaukee 6. Psychological Laboratory is gradually being equipped and some clinical work may be done next year (W. T. Stephens).

Medical Schools

Group I Columbia University, College of Physicians and Surgeons 1. Clinic in psychology and psychotherapy, conducted in the Vanderbilt Clinic (out-patient department of the college), since 1908, especially for the examination of the exceptional and psychopathic child (idiotic, imbecile and psychotic children are not received). Director, J. V. Haberman (M. D., Columbia and Berlin), and several assistants.

2. From 9.20 to 12.00 a. m. three days a week.

8. Yes, in connection with clinic and didactic course.

4. Psychopathology and Therapy, which includes mental examination methods and pedagogical treatment, since 1909, optional in fourth year, 2 hours during one-quarter year (Haberman).

6. Hope in near future to affiliate with (a) Childrens Courts, for the purpose of examining the psychopathic cases; and (b) the public schools, for the purpose of examining and treating children afflicted with abnormalities of disposition, the psychopathic constitutions of Ziehen (rather than the mentally defective and backward), who if not given timely treatment tend to recruit our classes of hystericals, instables, delinquents, criminals and the insane. A very interesting program which, however, will not touch the psycho-educational problem of many educational deviates.

Harvard Medical School See Harvard University, p. 84.

Johnt Hopkins Medical School

See Johns Hopkins University and Phipps Psychiatric Institute, p. 80.

Nero York Pott-Graduate Medical School and Hospital 1. Clinic, since May, 1911; has served as clearing house for the New York Department of Public Charities since January, 1918. It is reported to be a part of the city system of caring for the feeble-minded children at Randalls Island. Director, Max Schlapp, M. D., assisted by seven neurologists and three psychologists. Twelve clinic rooms and a completely equipped laboratory.

2. Every day from 9.00 a. m. to 1.00 p. m.

8. Graduates in medicine are permitted to witness the examinations.

4. Amentia, Dementia and Exceptional Ckildren, daily (Schlapp).

5. No, we attempt supervision of the classes in tke city residential institution for the feeble-minded.

University of Chicago, Rush Medical College 1. Clinic started in the fall of 1912, as part of neurological department. Two rooms, with psychological and neurological apparatus. Clinician in charge, Josephine E. Young (M. D., supplementary work in psychology in the University of Chicago and Columbia University). No clinical psychologist as such. No data as to what percentage of the work is strictly psycho-educational.

2. Two periods per week. 8. None as yet.

4. None. Later will give a course to medical students in psychological methods of examination, eugenics and the pathology of the feeble-minded.

5. Conduct a class Saturday mornings for all grades, one teacher.

6. As soon as the money is available, expect to organize a well-equipped school, with a specially trained teacher in charge, assisted by cadets from the University of Chicago. Will also engage a field worker who will see that patients report at the referred medical clinics and that they receive proper care and attention at home. Aim to work in the school classes with border-line cases difficult to diagnose, and with small groups of low-grade children. The latter will come two or three times a week with their mothers, who will be instructed by the teachers how to care for the pupils at home. Ultimately hope to have a small institution where research can be prosecuted.

Yale University Medical School 1. Psychological clinic conducted by the Department of Education in the New Haven Dispensary, since April, 1912 (Arnold Gesell, Ph. D.).

3. No.

4. None.

Students entering the medical school without elementary psychology are required to take such a course in the university. A course on the physiology of the special senses is given in the psychological laboratory to second-year students (R. P. Angier, Ph. D.).

Group II

Georgetown Medical College 1. No purely psychological clinic, but the Child Study Laboratory in the dispensary division of the University Hospital affords opportunities for giving the Binet-Simon tests and an anthropometric and physical examination to children who are referred because they do not get along well at home or in school. By D. Percy Hickling, M. D., J. J. Madigan, M. D., and Miss Margaret Stewart (public teacher in ungraded schools). Surgical and medical treatment is afforded in the dispensary; parent or guardian is told how to apply hygienic treatment.

8. Cases examined in the child-study laboratory are explained in clinics given to the fourth-year class.

4. Psychiatry, including facts of psychology, 60 hours each year, to third-and fourth-year classes (Wm. A. White, M. D., and Hickling).

5. No, but cases are recommended to ungraded classes, or sometimes mothers are instructed in home treatment and training.

Two years of required work for entrance involves a certain amount of instruction in psychology.

University of Michigan, State Psychopathic Hospital 1. This hospital is available for mentally abnormal and insane children.

Psychology required for entrance in the Medical School.

Group III

Boston University School of Medicine 4. Incidental reference in courses in Nervous and Mental Hygiene. Psycho-analysis and Psychotherapy/ since 1918-1914 (A. S. Boomhower-Guilbord, M. D.).

5. No.

Cornell University Medical College 1. No psychological clinic, but abnormal children from the schools are frequently referred to out-patient clinic for examination and advice (C. L. Dana, M. D., and August Hoch, M. D.)-

Hahnemann Medical College, Chicago 1. No, not apart from other clinical work. 4. None.

6. Are planning to organize didactic and clinical courses in a department of psychology for the study and care of exceptional children and all kinds of mental deviates.

New York Homoeopathic Medical College and Flower Hospital 1. No. 8. No.

4. Treated only incidentally in courses in Neurology and Psychiatry.

Tufts College Medical School 4. Mental Diseases, lectures with eight or ten clinics at the Boston State Hospital, and two clinics on defective children at the Massachusetts School for Feeble-Minded Children, from January 1 to May 15 (Edward B. Lane, M. D., assisted by Walter E. Fernald, M. D.).

Psychopathology and Psychotherapeutics (Morton Prince, M. D., J. J. Thomas, M. D., and A. W. Fairbanks, M. D.).

University of Buffalo, Medical Department 6. Now conduct a psychiatric clinic, and plan to open a psychological clinic with laboratory equipment in the dispensary for the examination of exceptional children.

University of Wisconsin, Medical School 1. No.

4. A course in Psychology is given to medical students which includes reference to methods of psychological diagnosis (Joseph Jastrow). Also a course in Abnormal Psychology.

Washington University, Medical School 6. Plans are gradually crystallizing for the development of a psychological clinic.

Results And Conclusions It is difficult to state unequivocally from the returns just how many genuine psychological clinics there are in the higher educational institutions of the country. The difficulty is due to the fact that the psychologists, educationists and physicians do not as yet have a clear idea—a definite standard—as to what constitutes a psychological clinic. The physician tends to confuse the neurological clinic, and especially to identify the psychiatric or psycho-pathological clinic, with the psychological clinic. He inclines to the view that no special preparation is needed to conduct a psychological clinic for the examination of mentally exceptional school children, beyond taking the ordinary courses in neurology and psychopathology, learning how to administer a few stock tests in psychology and spending a few days visiting psychological clinics. Ninety-nine out of every hundred physicians have no tech nical knowledge of those branches of psychology and pedagogy which bear on the teaching of educationally exceptional children. As a result we are today confronted with an anomalous situation throughout the country; medical inspectors and physicians, very few of whom have any special training in neurology and psychopathology and nearly all of whom lack technical training in education, are attempting to differentiate educationally exceptional children in the schools and to direct their educational training. It ought to be evident to anyone who has worked in the neurological, psychopathological and psychological clinics, or who has taken serious pains to inform himself, that the methods of examination employed in these three clinics frequently differ very widely, while the standpoint and aims of the examinations often have little in common. Owing to these confusions medical schools are inclined to report that they have psychological clinics when the clinics are really neurological or psychopathological clinics.

Again, the psychologist or educationist is inclined to regard a psychological or educational laboratory—any room containing psychological and educational apparatus and test materials, and a psychologist or educationist—as a psychological clinic, although it ought to be evident that a psychological laboratory and an experimental psychologist no more constitute a psychological clinic than do an anatomical laboratory and an anatomist constitute a medical clinic. The psychologist also seems to feel that he, too, is qualified to mentally examine children without special training in mental examination methods, and in case-taking and in clinical procedure. He seems to think that the ordinary courses in psychology and education prepare him for this work (most of the respondents did not answer the question regarding the character and extent of the special, technical training possessed by the director of the clinic, whether the latter was a psychologist or a physician). In consequence of these opinions certain universities report that they have a psychological clinic although the examiner has no special training for the work. In other institutions the practice obtains of parceling out the clinical examination work among the members of the departmental staff, none of whom may have definitely prepared for the work. The fact is that we have recently developed a new type of clinical work without the full recognition that it cannot successfully be done by either the physician or the psychologist without a definite technical preparation. The time must come when the work of educational diagnosis and guidance for mentally and educationally exceptional children will not be entrusted to physicians who have no definite preparation in psychology and educa-tion, or to psychologists or educators who are wholly lacking in clinical training and experience. We are met with a further difficulty in attempting to evaluate the existing clinics: some of the clinics are devoting a bare hour or two per week to clinical work, while the remaining time of the clinicist is given to teaching, usually branches quite remote from clinical psychology and the education of juvenile mental deviates. With these clini-cists the clinical work is entirely incidental, albeit the laboratory may have been established as a bona fide clinic. It is evident that a clinic in which the actual work of psycho-educational examination is regarded as a mere byplay to teaching, to be indulged in an hour or two a week, cannot afford even sufficient practice to keep the clinicist instrumentally efficient. It is, therefore, only by a liberal construction that such an exercise can be called a clinic. Fortunately some of the laboratories in higher institutions of learning are devoting themselves very largely if not exclusively to clinical work. In the University of Washington seven-eighths of the directors time is devoted to the actual examination of cases; the clinic is supplied with a considerable staff of assistants, and all the teaching courses of the director are limited to the study and education of exceptional children. At the University of Pittsburgh about two-thirds of the directors time has thus far been given to the work of clinical examination and to the supervision of the examination and investigation of children, but two courses foreign to the department have temporarily been carried. The ideal university clinics, from the standpoint of the amount of time actually given to clinical examinations, are those of the University of Pennsylvania, the University of Washington, the University of Minnesota (save for the division of the work among several experimental psychol-ogists rather than its assignment to a duly qualified specialist), and the University of Pittsburgh.

Recognizing that the definition and standards of any science must be more or less fluid during its early stages of development, it has seemed advisable to place a rather liberal construction on what constitutes a psychological clinic and this has been done in the grouping attempted in the above classification. Accepting this grouping as approximately correct we have today in the higher institutions of learning nineteen psychological clinics in Group I and seven in Group II, or a total of twenty-six (exclusive of Girard College).

Sixteen of the clinics are in universities. Thirteen of these are in Group I, namely those of the University of Pennsylvania, Washington, Minnesota, Kansas, Leland Stanford, Missouri, Pittsburgh, Yale, Cincinnati, Tulane, North Dakota, Iowa and Oklahoma. Three are in Group II: Clark, Cornell and New York University. Seven are in medical schools. Of these five are in Group I: the Vanderbilt Clinic of the College of Physicians and Surgeons of Columbia University, the Psychopathic Hospital connected with the Harvard Medical School, the Phipps Psychiatric Institute of the Johns Hopkins Hospital and Medical School, New York Post-Graduate Medical School, Rush Medical College of the University of Chicago; and two are in Group II: Georgetown Medical School and the State Psychopathic Hospital of the University of Michigan. Three are in normal schools: one in Group I, Colorado State Teachers College; and two in Group II: Los Angeles State Normal School and Mount Pleasant, Michigan, State Normal School. It is thus evident that over 61 per cent of the psychological clinics in the higher educational institutions are in the universities.

Fourteen of the clinics are in private institutions and twelve in state institutions. All the clinics in the normal schools, one clinic in the medical schools, and exactly one-half of the clinics in the universities (including the city institution in Cincinnati), are in state institutions.

Sixteen of the clinics are in populous centers (nine university, six medical and one normal), as against ten in small cities (seven university, two normal and one medical). The urban centers, no doubt, offer a very much better field than the rural districts for the successful organization of psychological clinics.

Thirteen of the clinics are in departments of education (including the clinics in the three normal schools), seven are in departments of medicine (including the Johns Hopkins and Harvard Clinics) and six in departments of psychology. The clinics at the University of Washington and Yale are supported by the department of education, although the laboratory of the former is in the department of psychology and of the latter in the dispensary of the medical school.

It is significant that one-half of the clinics are in departments or schools of education. Three years ago I expressed the opinion that the university clinic dealing with mentally exceptional children (specifically the feebleminded, backward, retarded, speech-defective, blind, deaf, precocious, word-blind, word-deaf, children with specific deficiencies in reading, spelling, number work, writing) should preferably be located in the school or department of education. I am more strongly convinced than ever of the wisdom of that judgment. There seems to me to be no very convincing reason for locating the clinic in the college department of psychology. As well might we place the medical clinics in the college department of biology. Psychology is a science rather than an art, while the psycho-clinical examination of children is primarily an art (which, to be sure, presupposes a groundwork of scientific knowledge), just as teaching and medicine are primarily arts. Moreover, the aim of a clinic in the department of psychology cannot be other than the aim of a psycho-educational clinic, namely correct educational classification and advice regarding the corrective pedagogical training of the child.

Similarly there is no very convincing reason why the psycho-educational clinic dealing with the types of mentally unusual cases mentioned above (which are primarily educational cases and not medical) should be located in the medical school, unless it were placed in charge of a psycho-educational expert thoroughly trained to prescribe pedagogically for the school cases examined. To be sure, there are certain positive reasons that can be advanced for locating the psychological clinic in the central clinic or hospital of the medical school: parents customarily bring children who appear to be not right to medical clinics; it facilitates the transfer of cases coming to the psychological clinic which require medical care to the appropriate medical specialists, and, vice versa, cases coining to the medical clinics which require special educational care can be readily transferred to the psychological clinic; it will foster greater harmony and cooperation between examining physicians and examining psycho-educationists, and this will remove some of the misguided opposition and unjustified prejudice against the psychological examiner which now obtains in various quarters.

On the other hand, if the clinics are located in the medical school they will frequently, perhaps generally, be manned by physicians who are neither psychologists, educationists nor experts in the differential methods of educating pedagogical deviates. On the whole, the best plan for the organization of a psycho-educational clinic in a university is to place it under the direction of a well-trained psychological and educational examiner, and to affiliate it with, or place it under, the joint administrative control of, the schools of education and medicine, or of the schools of education and medicine and the department of psychology.

In so saying, however, I wish to voice the opinion that every first-class medical school ought to establish a psychological clinic in conjunction with its clinics in neurology, psychiatry and psychopathology, primarily for the more detailed psychological study of neurasthenic, psychotic, psychopathic and psycho-neurotic cases, and only secondarily for the study of the types of cases which appeal primarily to the educational clinic. The director of the medical school psychological clinic (preferably a neurologist or psychopathologist with extensive training in normal, abnormal and clinical psychology) should offer didactic, clinical and experimental courses (covering mental tests and psychological diagnosis) to all students specializing in psychiatry, psychopathology, psychas-thenics, neurology and psychotherapy.

Not only have the medical schools of the country neglected adequately to provide for these and-allied courses for students specializing in psychopathology (our returns indicate that about a dozen medical schools are attempting a certain amount of this instruction and training; possibly a couple of dozen schools in this country are offering measurably satisfactory courses);" but until recently any student who did not have the bachelors degree could graduate in any medical school in the country without having taken a single systematic course in psychology–a fact which physicians themselves have lamented (Jones, Munro, Taylor, 17, 22, 27, 4). Most physicians are given not five minutes training in psychology in the five years of their student life. There is no teacher of clinical psychology in any medical school in the country (Jones). The average physician probably has less technical knowledge of the science of psychology

See, however, the recent report of the committee of physicians and psychologists appointed by the American Psychological Association (7): It is apparent that students and graduates in medicine who incline toward practice in diseases of the mind and nervous system have few or no opportunities in the medical schools in this country to acquire a broader acquaintance with the subjects of neurology and psychiatry, than the clinical courses which are offered. At present the teaching of psychiatry appears to be in an earlier stage than surgery was in the two-or three-year course in medicine twenty years ago.

than the average city grade teacher–all normal school graduates have been required to take at least one systematic course in psychology. And yet the physician is expected to minister not only to the bodily but also to the mental well-being of his patient. Happily the situation in the medical schools is gradually changing for the better. Franz finds in his recent census that ten medical schools have already introduced, or plan to introduce next year, psychology into the curriculum or require it for entrance, and one advises students to take a course in psychology in the preparatory premedical years. Moreover, of the sixty-eight medical deans or professors who answered the question, 75 per cent favored giving the medical students special instruction in psychology, while only 10 per cent gave negative and 15 per cent qualified affirmative or negative replies (7).

There is, therefore, no need to hold a brief for the introduction of a required course in psychology for all the students in the premedical or medical curriculum. But it is well to reemphasize that the medical schools should make distinctly better provisions for teaching the specialties in psychology for students preparing to specialize on mental cases. In justification of this contention it is only necessary to say that it is becoming generally recognized that the malfunctioning of mental processes may play a dynamic role in the production of certain nervous and mental disorders, and that mental factors play an impor-tant role in therapy (psychotherapy). The influence"-/ of suggestion, mental strife, latent complexes, suppressed wishes, morbid fears, obsessions, etc., in the causation of certain forms of abnormal behavior has been established by the researches of Freud and Jung and many of their followers, by the clinical observations and results of

Dubois (5) and of other medical practitioners, and by the net results, however distorted, exaggerated and unreliable most of the reports are, of healing cults of a pseudo-scientific character (24).

Among the disorders which are now believed by many to be largely psychogenic in origin are the neuroses proper (neurasthenia and anxiety neuroses, both related to disordered sexuality, according to the Freudians), the psycho-neuroses (classical or Freudian conversion hysteria, anxiety hysteria and compulsion neuroses, all related, so says Freud, to suppressed yearnings or wishes of a sexual nature), the lighter forms of hypochondria and melancholia, and various disequilibrations bordering on insanity. Since the pathology seems to be partly or wholly psychogenic, the treatment of these disorders must be partly or wholly ideogenic. It must consist in the modification of the patients abnormal stream of thought, his faulty associative mechanisms, his morbid emotional complexes and attitudes and his perverted instinctive reactions, by the methods of suggestion, reeducation or psycho-analysis. The efficacy ascribed to drugs, physical agencies, healing thoughts, or absent treatment in the treatment of the true psycho-neuroses probably comes from the force of suggestion: the innate impulsiveness or tendency of ideas to express themselves in appropriate physiological adjustments or glandular activities (the law of dynamogenesis). Whatever the expla-nation, there is nothing occult in scientific psychotherapy: it is a legitimate division of psychology and medicine. The successful operator must be, first and foremost, a skilled clinical or medical psychologist. He must be able to inspire confidence by his manner and by a correct diagnosis and prognosis, to awaken hope by emphasizing the favorable symptoms throughout the course of the treatment, to remove conflicting thoughts and suggest appropriate thoughts, to bring to the surface and to dissipate psychic complexes which cause mental strife, etc. Mental hygiene and therapy should not be left to dilettante and fakirs, as has been done: in psychotherapy the public has been left largely to its own devices, to become the victims of Christian Scientists and dabblers in the occult, or misguided clergymen. Various forms of mental affliction which have baffled medical skill have been left to untrained empirics and irregular practitioners, because medical curricula have made little provision for training physicians in the scientific mental therapy of psychic disorders. In consequence, we have for years been reaping a rich harvest of pseudo-psychotherapies.

If now–to repeat–suggestion and psycho-analysis are the basal principles in the psychic treatment of the above varieties of mental disorders, and suggestive and psychoanalytic therapeutics are a legitimate branch of psychology and medicine, the conclusion follows that every complete medical school should make provision for instruction and training in the science and art of psychological medicine. One of the divisions in the department of psychological medicine should be a laboratory of clinical psychology, in which the student may receive training in the psycho-clinical and psycho-laboratory methods of examining patients. Training should be afforded in the methods used for testing specific mental deviations, for ascertaining the extent of the involution changes resulting from various dementias, and for measuring the degree of subnormality and supernormality. Practice should be given in the hypnotic, psychoanalytic and association-reaction methods of mental diagnosis and treatment, possibly with some attention to the psychomotor or galvanometric tests. Lectures should be given on the psychological and therapeutical aspects of suggestion, psycho-analysis, hypnotism or any of the methods which enable us to lay bare dormant, unrecognized, suppressed mental complexes or conflicts, disorders and blockages in the associative mechanism, tendencies toward repetition or perseveration of test words, sensory and motor automatisms, dissociation phenomena, obsessions, fixed ideas, phobias and confusions, and which will enable us to construct a differential psychology of various psychic disorders. When the medical schools have given proper attention to these matters, psychological criteria will attain a diagnostic value they do not yet possess.

In attempting to determine how many institutions are conducting training clinics for preparing students to psychologically and educationally examine mentally exceptional children, we are again obliged, because of the vague standards of what a psychological training clinic is, to attempt an evaluation of the existing clinics. Some institutions offer merely didactic, demonstration or experimental courses in mental tests and regard these as training clinics; some institutions have the students test and experiment upon each other and regard these exercises as training clinics; and others open their dispensary clinics (often neurological or psychopathological rather than psychological or psycho-educational) to students for observation, and regard these as training clinics. It is clear that a genuine psychological (or psycho-educational) training clinic must afford students training in studying actual cases of mental deviation by the methods of psychological observation, testing and experimentation; it must afford training in the larger aspects of case-taking and clinical procedure; it must have access to a large variety and an ample supply of clinical material; and it must provide instruction, supervision and guidance at the hands of an expert psycho-clinical (and psycho-educational) diagnostician. It is evident that a student who has been trained in a clinic frequented by a limited number of feeble-minded or backward children may be entirely ignorant of the great variety of perplexing cases of mentally and educationally exceptional children which are certain to come to the psychological clinic in the large urban centers. And it is entirely clear to my mind that no student can be graduated from a university psycho-educational clinic as a thoroughly competent examiner unless he has made firsthand studies during an extended period of time (from two to four years, certainly not less than two) of a great variety of educationally unusual children—feeble-minded, border cases, backward, dull, normal, precocious, epileptic, aphasic, speech-defective, etc.

The best provisions for training students in the art of psychological diagnosis are probably offered in the following institutions: University of Pennsylvania, University of Washington and University of Pittsburgh. New York University offers good opportunities during the summer session—but the period is entirely too limited to make it possible to train experts. Among the other institutions reporting which afford students more or less opportunity for making observations, for conducting clinical examinations, or for making psychological tests and experiments are the following: the universities of Minnesota, Missouri, Yale, Leland Stanford, Cincinnati and Cornell; the College of Physicians and Surgeons of Columbia, the Psychopathic Hospital of Harvard, the Phipps Clinic of Johns Hopkins, the New York Post-Graduate Medical School and Hospital and the Georgetown Medical College; the State Teachers College of Colorado, the Brooklyn Training School, the Marquette, and Mount Pleasant, Michigan, State Normal Schools, the Los Angeles State Normal School, the Chicago Normal College and the Philadelphia Normal School for Girls.

Classes for the purpose of training subnormal children and for affording opportunities for observation are conducted in the following universities: University of Pennsylvania, University of Washington, University of Indiana, New York University (summer session), University of Pittsburgh (summer session) and the University of California (summer session); in the following normal schools: Brooklyn Training School, Los Angeles Normal School, the State Teachers College of Colorado and the North Adams, Mass., State Normal School, while special attention is given to exceptional children in the Winona, Minnesota, State Normal, Monmouth, Oregon, State Normal and the Willimantic, Conn., State Normal; and in Rush Medical School (one morning only for all grades, which is an almost negligible amount). Clinics in especially the following institutions are assisting public school systems in the diagnosis and selection of cases, or in the supervision of the classes, or in utilizing the classes for purposes of observation: the University of Pennsylvania, the University of Pittsburgh, Leland Stanford, the University of Cincinnati, the University of Michigan, the University of Minnesota, the University of Iowa, the University of Washington, Yale, the Phipps Psychiatric Clinic and the New York Post-Graduate Medical School and Hospital.

On the whole, very few of the clinics in any kind of higher institution of learning have at their disposal satis factory special classes in which mentally exceptional children can be properly trained, in which they can be studied under laboratory conditions and observed in a superior educational environment, and in which students in training may be afforded superior opportunities for observation and cadet teaching. Possibly this state of affairs does not invite serious criticism, for it is scarcely the function of departments of psychology in the universities or of medical schools to conduct elementary classes for mentally unusual children. The duty of providing training for these children clearly rests with the public schools, and (although perhaps not to the same extent) with the observation and practice departments of colleges of education and normal schools. It is very desirable that classes for the educationally exceptional types of children be established in the practice schools of the latter institutions, in order that the diagnosis and training of these children may receive proper scientific study, in order that opportunities for follow-up work may be afforded, and in order that proper facilities may be afforded for training special teachers and expert examiners. But, after all, the colleges of education and the normal schools cannot care for 5 per cent of all the children who require special educational treatment, and it is clearly the duty of the public schools to make adequate provisions for training all the children of all the people.

2. The psychological laboratory and clinic in the hospitals for the insane. The psychological clinic is rapidly finding a place in the public and private institutions for the mentally diseased and the mentally defective classes. In the hospitals for the mentally alienated much of the recent work of value in psychiatry has been done by psychologists or by alienists trained in the methods and imbued with the spirit of the new psychology. The pioneers in the new psychiatry are Wernicke, who, to be sure, recognizes the paramount importance of physical etiology in the consideration of mental diseases, but finds it inadequate for classification, and who makes the disorders of the content of consciousness primary (from him we derive the concepts of psychosensory, intrapsychic and psychomotor disorders; allopsychoses, somatopsychoses and autopsychoses; afunctional, parafunctional and hyper-functional disorders); Ziehen, whose classification is thoroughly psychological (based upon the Herbartian and association psychology); Kraepelin, who employs the methods of psychological experimentation and the longitudinal method of analysis of the stream of consciousness (sequential course) for making a composite picture of the distinctive traits of various disease types; and Freud, who has elaborated a unique method, the method of psychoanalysis, for purposes of diagnosis (disclosing submerged morbid mental complexes) and treatment, and who maintains that the etiological factors in various neuroses are of purely psychic origin. In this country the psycho-biological conception of various mental disorders has been ably championed by Adolf Meyer, M. D., the director of the recently opened Phipps Psychiatric Clinic at the Johns Hopkins Hospital, who has made notable contributions to the psychology of dementia præcox. Among other psy-chopathologists who are giving considerable study to the psychological aspects of mental disturbances may be mentioned Drs. T. A. Williams, A. A. Brill, Morton Prince, I. H. Coriat, Wm. A. White, Smith E. Jelliffe, Boris Sidis and August Hoch (the director of the Wards Island Psychiatric Institute). Dr. Ernest Jones of the University of Toronto is an enthusiastic exponent of Freudian methods.

Psychological laboratories, manned by trained psychologists, have been established in the following institutions: Mclean Hospital, Waverly, Mass., since 1904, with F.

Lyman Wells, Ph. D., as director; the Government Hospital for the Insane, Washington, D. C., since January 1, 1907, with Shepherd Ivory Franz, Ph. D., as psychologist and scientific director; Friends Asylum for the Insane, Frankford, Pa. (work temporarily suspended), and the New York Psychiatric Institute at Wards Island (now apparently without a psychologist). Both Franz and Wells have published a considerable number of valuable experimental papers ranging over a wide field in the psychology of mental disease. The Massachusetts General Hospital maintains a psychologist (L. E. Emerson, Ph. D.), and more or less psychological research is being conducted at the Kings Park Hospital, in New York State, by A. J. Rosanoff, M. D., and very probably in numerous other hospitals for the insane and in psychopathic sanitaria.

Many clinical examinations and investigations of the alienated and psychopathic are necessarily partly psychological in nature, so that it is probable that psychological research and psycho-clinical examinations are conducted to some extent in the majority of state and private institutions throughout the country.

3. The psycho-clinical laboratory in institutions for the feeble-minded and epileptic. The initial impulse toward the organization of laboratories of psychological research in these institutions came from Dr. A. C. Rogers, who, in 1898, engaged a psychologist (who later also qualified as physician), Dr. A. R. T. Wylie, to devote about half of his time to the psychological study of the patients in the Minnesota School for Feeble-Minded and Colony for Epileptics at Faribault. The fruits of Wylies work, which continued for about three years, appear in a number of studies of the emotions, instincts, senses, memory, reaction time, and height and weight of the feeble-minded.

The main impulse, however, toward the development of the work came from Superintendent E. R. Johnston of the New Jersey Training School for Feeble-Minded Boys and Girls at Vineland who, in 1906, appointed H. H. Goddard, Ph. D., as director of research. The work in Goddards laboratory has progressed uninterruptedly during the last seven years, and has covered a wide range of interests in psychology and heredity. The laboratory at present commands the services of seventeen men and women including student assistants and heredity field workers. The following divisions have been organized: psychology (with Mr. E. A. Doll as assistant psychologist), physiology (directed by A. W. Peters, M. D.,) and psychopatholgy (directed by W. J. Hickson, M. D.).

The Vineland institution has also developed into a seminary of instruction. During the summer it offers training courses to teachers of retarded and subnormal children, and to school medical inspectors. Beginning with the summer of 1914 only teachers who have already specialized in the study of the subnormal will be admitted to the teachers courses. (Other institutions for the feebleminded which recently have conducted, or are conducting, training classes for teachers are The Herbart Hall Institute for Atypical Children, Plainfield, N. J.; Rome State Custodial Asylum, Rome, N. Y., and Michigan Home for Feeble-Minded and Epileptic, Lapeer, Mich.)

The result of the Vineland work is appearing in a number of studies of the psychology and heredity of feeble mindedness, including percentile growth curves of height, weight, vital capacity, hand dynamometry, endurance; mental classifications; heredity charts and studies; record forms; translations of graded tests for developmental diagnosis, etc. (10, 11, 12). The psychological laboratory has a fair equipment of apparatus and a well-chosen library of technical books and periodicals, domestic and foreign. This laboratory may be regarded as the first genuine laboratory of clinical psychology to be established at an institution for the feeble-minded, and has exerted a very wide influence in its special field.

Within the last few years departments of psychological research have been organized in a number of institutions for these defectives. In the fall of 1909 a laboratory–the second of the sort in the country–was established in the Lincoln State School and Colony of Illinois, under the directorship of Dr. E. B. Huey (14). This laboratory is now in charge of Dr. Clara H. Town. In the fall of 1910 the Faribault laboratory was reestablished with Dr. Fred Kuhlmann as director, and two new laboratories were established, one at the Iowa Institution for Feeble-Minded Children at Glenwood (this laboratory has been temporarily discontinued, but will probably be reopened in the near future), and one in the New Jersey State Village for Epileptics at Skillman. The latter laboratory, which was organized by the writer, is the pioneer psycho-clinical laboratory in colonies for epileptics. The work in this laboratory has been temporarily discontinued. In 1914 the Michigan Home for Feeble-Minded and Epileptics appointed a consulting psychologist (see p. 42).

Among the private schools for feeble-minded and backward children which are making some provisions for the psychological examination of their pupils may be men tioned the Bancroft Training School, Haddonfield, N. J. (E. A. Farrington, M. D., president) and Herbart Hall, Plainfield, N. J. (M. P. E. Groszmann, Pd. D., educational director).

The latter institution is now fostered by the National Association for the Study and Education of Exceptional Children. During the summer and fall of 1913 its director traveled extensively throughout the far West and Northwest, delivering addresses and organizing state associations in affiliation with the national organization.

Institutional positions in psychological research offer certain advantages. The incumbent is relieved of teaching duties and has ready access to an abundance of clinical material. He may also count on the sympathetic cooperation of the governing and administrative officers of the institution, for the view is now gaining acceptance that the functions of public hospital, custodial, training, correctional and penal institutions should not be limited to the care, treatment, occupational supervision and restraint of the inmates, but should include the scientific investigation of their present mental and physical status, and the conditions and causes which underlie various kinds of defective-ness and delinquency. Public institutions should be laboratories of research as well as places for treatment, refuge, confinement and profitable employment. In order to be made attractive centers of scientific research, however, the prerogatives and regulations affecting the research positions (in respect to the matter of stipend, rank, hours of service, vacations, publishing rights, personal prerogatives, freedom from unnecessary restrictions, and from the absurd regulations of tyrannically inclined superintendents, etc.) should be made to conform with the rules which govern similar positions in the universities and research institutions. Only thus will the best scientific talent find the field sufficiently attractive to forsake the scientific, cultural, library and laboratory advantages which the universities furnish in such rich measure. At the present time the universities have practically a monopoly on the scientific producers of the country. According to Cattells statistical study of American men of science, 75 per cent of the 1,000 scientists of the first rank are located in the colleges and universities (3). There is an inviting virgin soil for scientific investigators in institutions for defectives. Provided that proper inducements are offered, these institutions bid fair to become large productive centers of scientific work in the near future.

So far as psychological work is concerned, it is pertinent to point out that the function of the psychologist is to study mind in all its manifestations and under all its conditions. The psychologist should, therefore, have the freedom of the institution; he should have ready access to the patients in the cottages or schoolhouse or in the field, no less than in the laboratory. There may be a certain artificiality and formality about psycho-laboratory work, a certain unnaturalness in the attitude or the reactions of the subject toward the tests. This will sometimes render the results one-sided or partial, and, therefore, makes it desirable to do supplementary work under other conditions.

4,. Clinical psychology in the juvenile court. The application of the methods of clinical psychology to the study of the juvenile and adult offender is making rapid strides. The department of child study and pedagogic investigation of the Chicago public schools has for years done incidental work in this direction in connection with the schools for truants and delinquents. The first labora tory to be directly connected with a juvenile court is the Juvenile Psychopathic Institute, organized in Chicago in April, 1909, by Dr. William Healy, who secured a fund of 30,000 with which to defray the expenses of conducting clinical examinations of juvenile court delinquents for a period of five years. It was considered that five years was sufficiently long to demonstrate the value of the work. Dr. Healy, with the aid of psychological and sociological assistants, is engaged in the study of the underlying factors, physiological, psychological, social and hereditary, of juvenile criminality, and is working particularly with the juvenile recidivist. According to press reports this Institute is now supported by Cook County.

The city of Seattle established a division of diagnosis as an integral part of its juvenile court in 1911, with Dr. Lilburn Merrill as director, and Dr. Stephenson Smith as consulting psychologist. In September, 1913, Dr. V. V. Anderson was appointed assistant probation officer of the municipal criminal court in Boston, for the purpose of making psychological and medical examinations of criminal offenders. Various charitable agencies in many cities are now attempting to supply the facilities for the psychological, medical and sociological examination of juvenile court cases (e. g., according to report, New York, Newark, Baltimore, Minneapolis, Washington, Cleveland); but the psychological examinations are often made by amateurs or by physicians with little or no technical training in psychological diagnosis, or by psychiatrists with a distinct psychiatric rather than psychological and educational bias.

Let me, in passing, express the conviction, however, that the problem of the juvenile delinquent is less the problem of the juvenile court than the problem of the public schools. Instead of haling, a la wholesale, incipient or active child delinquents into court, only to parole the large majority of them–a procedure little calculated to impress the youthful offender with the gravity of his possible perversity, or with the respect due the legal statutes of the community, or with the dignity and importance of court procedure, and which in all events imposes a heavy tax on the community for the support of elaborate court machinery–all possible effort should be made to keep the young delinquents out of court altogether. This can most successfully be done by so organizing our schools that they will minister educationally to the peculiar needs of mentally and morally exceptional children. It is the public schools rather than the juvenile courts that should maintain in their educational divisions laboratories for the study and diagnosis of subnormal and delinquent children. Just as soon as the child manifests evidences of subnormality, or tendencies toward incorrigibility and truancy—according to A. J. Pillsbury, 90 per cent of criminals began their criminalistic careers as truants in the schools–he should be examined in the psycho-educational clinic of the schools, which should also afford a medical, hereditary and sociological examination. As a result of the examination the child should be provided with appropriate physical treatment, if such is indicated; he should be correctly classified psychologically and educationally, and he should be placed in the type of class which can provide the educational training which he requires. With a proper adjustment of the course of study to meet the needs of the individual delinquent the problem of juvenile delinquency largely solves itself. If you give abnormal children the kind of school work that they can do and that they like to do, and place them in a school environment that they enjoy, you will supply the most efficient and humane system of correctives for juvenile truancy and delinquency.

Very suggestive in this connection is the experience of Los Angeles (Psychological Clinic, 1913, p. 84). In the public schools of this city special classes for persistent truants (boys) were started in 1905, dedicated to the proposition that no pupil shall fail or be suspended or expelled. In these classes the boys were provided with adaptable men teachers and with curricula more closely related to the life interests of boys. The boys were given the type of school work which appealed to their interests, and was adapted to their varying capacities. In 1912 there were nine of these classes. Among the notable results of this experiment are the following: (1) No boy was ever suspended or expelled from the special classes: the habit of suspending and expelling boys from the public schools practically ceased.

(2) The average attendance in these classes for a period of seven years was 99 per cent: the fit school environment practically solved the non-attendance and truancy problems.

(3) The truancy work of the juvenile court was practically abolished: before the classes were organized all / persistent truants were arrested and haled before the court. In 1905-1906 there were fifty-six of these cases; in 1906-1907, thirty; after that, never more than three a year, and one year none at all. Now the schools handle the truants, and more economically and efficiently.

I repeat: the problem of the juvenile delinquent is primarily a problem for the schools–first, a problem of scientific diagnosis and, second, a problem of supplying a fit school environment. Juvenile courts should be courts of last appeal–for the persistently refractory cases and for cases which cannot be brought under the compulsory education laws.

5. The psychological laboratory in penal institutions and correctional homes. Psychological tests (usually only the Binet and other simple tests by amateur psychologists) are now being given as a matter of daily routine to the boys and girls in

a considerable number of reformatories and correctional institutions throughout the country.

Examinations have been made since 1908 of the inmates (whose average age is 20.5 years) in the Massachusetts Reformatory for Boys at Concord, in order to determine their mental and moral status. These examinations have been made by Guy G. Fernald, M. D. Physical tests are also employed for the purpose of selecting and segregating mental defectives.

The most notable research institute in a correctional institution is the Laboratory of Social Hygiene in the New York State Reformatory for Women at Bedford Hills, occupying a ten-room building, equipped at a cost of 250,000 for the study of the causative factors and the best methods of training female (social) delinquents. The work in this laboratory began in July, 1911, under a 1,500 grant from the New York Foundation, but is now fostered by the New York Bureau of Social Hygiene. The director of psychological research and field work is Jean Weidensall, Ph. D. The staff will include a psychopatholo-gist, sociologist and educationist.

The Indiana Reformatory, Jeffersonville, organized a department of research August 12, 1912, with Prof. Rufus B. von Klein Smid as director, F. C. Paschal and W. Beanblossom as assistants in psychology, R. W. Merrifield as assistant in social research and J. M. Walker, M. D., as consulting physician and assistant in medical research. The cost of the psychological equipment to date amounts to about 500. The department administers the problem of the discipline of the inmates, and controls the disposition of their time (i. e., it determines the character of the work suitable to each case, the character of the schooling to be given different boys and the transfer of cases to other state institutions in which they more properly belong).

Among the institutions which have more recently established departments of psychological investigation are the following: Girls Industrial Home, Sleighton Farm, Darlington, Pa. (Miss Helen F. Hill in charge since 1913), and the State Home for Girls at Trenton, N. J. (Margaret Otis, Ph. D., resident psychologist). Psychological examinations are also conducted in the Massachusetts Reformatory for Women at South Framingham. In April, 1912, the New York Probation and Protective Association appointed Frederick Ellis, Ph. D., to conduct psychological studies of the socially delinquent girls who are in the care of the association.

Mention may also be made at this point of the fact that several states (thus New Jersey and Minnesota) have within the last two or three years made definite legislative appropriation for the study of the heredity and psychology of their mentally and morally abnormal dependents and delinquents.

The time is near at hand when our criminals and delinquents, juvenile or adult, whether in juvenile courts, jails, prisons, reformatories, houses of rescue or detention homes, will be given individual study from the points of view of anthropology, medicine, sociology and of clinical and criminal psychology. Not only so, the time must come when the truthfulness of testimony and the veracity of witnesses will be tested by methods other than the crude method of cross-examination (23). The laboratory method of determining capacity for correctness of description and report will prove an aid to the jurist. Psychology is destined to contribute something toward making criminology and jurisprudence more scientific. When the methods of science have been applied to the study of the delinquent and criminal, we shall be in a position to adapt the penalty, qualitatively as well as quantitatively, to the nature of the offender rather than to the nature of the offense. Frequently the roots of criminality lie embedded in a criminal neuropathic heredity, or in certain irresistible habits which have been engendered by vicious or criminal influences in the social environment, in a diseased or physically malformed organism which thereby has become functionally maladapted to its physical and psychical environment, or in mental deficiency. The role of the different causal factors must be rightly estimated for every individual offender before we can deal scientifically with the problems of crime and criminology. Our methods of criminal procedure have too long been on a par with that type of cure which treats effects but ignores causes. The Binet-Simon and other psychological tests will aid the alienist and jurist in determining the mental status and responsibility of persons in commitment. The arrest, deviation or degeneration revealed by such tests will often be found to affect precisely those higher psychical powers without whose integrity of function the individual cannot attain that standard of conformity to law demanded by his social environment. It will frequently be found that the arrest or atrophy of various mental processes may be so serious as to produce permanent mental and moral maladjustment to the community ethical requirements. Offenses by such individuals may be without conscious criminal intent. There is no immorality of intent in their criminal actions, though there is immorality of act. Such individuals are, subjectively considered, unmoral, like the infant who cannot appreciate the distinction between right and wrong. Their immorality and criminality are resolvable into mental deficiency. None the less, these persons are a menace to society, and require permanent restraint as a protective, rather than a punitive, measure.

6. The psycho-educational clinic in relation to vocational guidance. There are six essential functions of a vocational bureau.

First, the maintenance of a free placement agency. This is the function apparently exalted above all others by the existing bureaus.

Second, the making of a local vocational or industrial survey. This survey should include a tabulation of all the establishments of the community which afford employment to youthful wage-earners; an appraisal of the moral, hygienic, sanitary and labor conditions surrounding each plant or type of industry; a determination of the initial and prospective ultimate financial returns yielded by different occupations; a determination of the chances for promotion together with the probable rate of advancement, and the prompt listing of positions as they become available.

Third, the ascertainment of the physical health index and the salient anthropological indices of the applicants. It is unscientific and pernicious to place pupils in lines of employment for which they are unfitted by virtue of specific constitutional or acquired diatheses, diseases or defects, such as tubercular predisposition, gouty or rheumatic diatheses, neuropathic heredity, nasopharyngeal disorders, certain auditory, visual or olfactory defects, or palsies or deformities of certain bodily members. How many of the existing so-called guidance bureaus pay any consideration to the vital factor of bodily efficiency? Many of the directors of these bureaus have no technical knowledge of the physiological factors concerned, and apparently many do not seek to obtain this knowledge.

Fourth, the ascertainment of the individual vocational preferences, proclivities or inclinations of the applicants. Vocational guidance which directs children into lines of employment for which they have no taste and in which they lack all interest is not only a misnomer, but it is culpable, inexcusable, blundering empiricism. Most children, provided they possess the requisite psychomotor capacity, will succeed in any line of work in which they manifest a keen healthy interest. They will just as surely fail, or achieve an indifferent success, if they are placed in uninteresting, disagreeable occupations. Success in life work usually turns on hitching the right job to the right interest. How many existing bureaus make any effort to ascertain the real inclinations of the applicants beyond asking a few perfunctory questions? How many make any effort to secure the independent judgment of the observant teacher or parent or the psychological specialist?

Fifth, the determination of the general functional level of capacity or achievement–the mental or moto-industrial age–of the applicants. It is worse than folly to guide children into vocations to whose efficiency demands they cannot adjust themselves because of all-round lack of mental or motor capacity. Many of the adolescent breakdowns and adult neuroses and psychoneuroses are due to the inability of the persons to meet the exacting requirements of the vocations in which they happen to find them selves. To place a child with a nine-year mentality in a position which requires a fourteen-year mentality is to condemn him to repeated failure, perennial job-hunting and ultimate dependency, delinquency or mental and nervous collapse. Many children seeking the aid of the bureaus will rank in capacity with the pupils who are now in up-to-date schools placed in the special classes for morons, border-line and backward cases. We know that most of these children will not be able to support themselves in trades which require any considerable degree of technical skill or endurance. Without attempting to review all the available data as to the industrial inefficiency of the graduates of the special classes of the public schools, I may state that the Royal Commission on the Care and Control of the Feeble-minded concluded that 47 per cent of the pupils from the special classes of the London schools will never be able to earn their own living, 28 per cent probably will do so under proper direction, while only 22 per cent may be regarded as possible wage-earners. The After Care Committee of Birmingham followed up the careers of 650 graduates from the special classes of the city school during nine years and found that only 18 per cent were doing remunerative work (at an average weekly wage of 6s. Id.); a later statement (School Hygiene, February, 1913, p. 7) indicates that 42 per cent of those reported were employed. Because the children were unable to retain their jobs, particularly as they grew older, the committee abandoned the free employment bureau which it conducted for four years. In Liverpool only 28 per cent were employed, in Leeds 45 per cent were found in good promising or fair employment, while the combined statistics in 1908 from nine English cities showed that only 22 per cent were at work and 6.8 per cent were in irregular work. Of fifty cases selected at random from the ungraded classes in the New York City schools only 4 per cent held permanent positions, 10 per cent had worked steadily for a few weeks at an average of 3.50 per week, and the majority were utterly incapable. Of ten graduates of the subnormal classes in the Chicago schools who were investigated three were wholly unfit for responsible positions, and the average weekly wage of the others was only 5.73. In Germany the record is better–70 to 80 per cent of the auxiliary pupils can earn their living, according to Bottger–but that is largely because the pupils are placed in the type of work that they can do, and are given supervision by guardians and by masters-of-trade, under whom many of them labor.

Recently it was my fortune–or misfortune–to witness a director of a public school bureau of vocational guidance guide a boy of fourteen into a line of work in which he must certainly fail. It would have been quite evident to a psycho-clinical specialist from a cursory examination that the boy was a microcephalic moron! Was it not essential for purposes of scientific guidance that this director should have known that he was negotiating with a feeble-minded boy who presumptively cannot stand the strain of skilled factory employment under the conditions of modern competitive industrialsm? What justification is there for calling this a guidance bureau when it makes no attempt to call in the consulting psychologist to determine the general level of functioning of at least the obviously abnormal cases? It is very clear to me that employers will not continue to go to school vocational bureaus for applicants whose powers and capacities the bureaus have made no scientific attempt to evaluate.

The present nation-wide interest in the establishment of bureaus of vocational guidance is commendable. But let us not forget that many if not most of the existing bureaus are unconscious of any obligation to the community except that of making vocational surveys and listing and finding jobs for work-certificate pupils. They are merely free employment agencies. They fall far short of their highest function, namely, expert scientific gwd-ance. It would seem to be more rational and profitable to establish the bureaus as a division of the department of psycho-educational diagnosis, than as independent departments in the public schools, so that at least the more obvious cases may be given a psychological examination (not to mention the anthropometric and medical) to determine their general mental status. This should be done before any attempt is made to direct them into a vocation. To repeat: vocational guidance should include more than making industrial surveys: it should include the making of human surveys, that is, surveys of the mental (and physical) status of the applicants themselves. Only thus shall we be able to find the right man for the right job and the right job for the right man.

Sixth, the determination of the specific motor, mental or industrial gifts or deficiencies of each applicant. Successful workers in specific trades, handicrafts and occupations must possess a certain minimal amount of the specific traits or talents, or combinations of traits, demanded by the occupations in question. Those who possess in maximal degree the required traits constitute the preferred or talented class of workers. It is evident, for example, that successful typewritists must possess a high degree of psychomotor rapidity and accuracy; successful motor men require, for certain of their duties, a high degree of rapidity, accuracy and range of observation, of celerity of response and of presence of mind. It is possible experi mentally to determine what mental capacities are required by successful telephone operators, ticket sellers, paper wrappers, railroad engineers, or any operative engaged in any line of skilled work whatsoever, and it is also possible to determine to some extent by psychological tests whether a given applicant for a job possesses the qualifications required by that job (25). However, we are better able with our existing diagnostic refinements to determine an individuals all-round grade of mental development than his specific vocational longs or shorts.

Mention should be made in this connection of the study made of children who go into industry by the Schmidlapp Bureau and a number of private contributors, in Cincinnati. The investigation includes a study of the effects of industrial work upon the physical and mental development of fourteen-year-old work-certificate children (comparative physical and mental measurements are made of fourteen-year-old children who remain in school), a study of the children who fail in industry (including a comparison of their performances in psychological tests), the establishment of age-norms for various psychological tests, and a study of the childrens earnings, pay increases and amount of unemployment. The scientific work is directed by Helen T. Woolley, Ph. D. So far as I have been able to gather information no examinations have been made with a view to determining the general functional level or specific capacities of the applicants for clinical purposes, hence the bureau cannot be classed as a psychological clinic, as some writers have done.

7. The psychological clinic in the immigrant station. At the fifteenth International Congress on Hygiene and Demography held in Washington in September, 1912, I took occasion to comment substantially as follows, at one of the sessions of the subsection on mental hygiene:

Recently an attempt was made to induce Congress to enact a law excluding immigrants on the basis of tests of information or literacy. The bill passed by Congress deserved to be vetoed, because, in my opinion, it failed utterly to meet the situation. What we need on the side of diagnosis for detecting mentally defective foreigners is primarily not tests of information, erudition, literacy or mere acquisition, but tests designed to determine the strength of the power of acquiring information, psychological tests of the inherent strength of various fundamental mental traits. Illiteracy and mental deficiency (feeble-mindedness) are not synonymous terms. Many illiterates come to our shores who are perfectly normal in mental potentials, who are capable of making the best citizens, intellectually, morally, socially and industrially, and who should, therefore, not be deported. Their illiteracy is due to lack of educational opportunities or proper mental training. The problem is to distinguish this type of illiteracy from the type that is due to mental sub-normality. Really it is not a problem of literacy or illiteracy as such, but a problem of capacity and incapacity. It is therefore evident that what we want are not chiefly tests of literacy, but tests of mental capacity. If so, the task of diagnosing mentally defective or feeble-minded foreigners is distinctly a psychological problem, and requires the services of an expert consulting psychologist who has had extensive first-hand experience with feebleminded cases. The average medical immigration inspector is just as fully "at sea" when he tries to identify the subnormal immigrant as the average medical school inspector is "at sea" when he tries to diagnose the various types of educationally unusual children in the schools and prescribe appropriate orthogenic pedagogical treatment for each case. Neither the immigration nor the school medical inspectors have been specifically or professionally trained for these lines of highly technical and difficult work. Neither type of inspector would be able adequately to qualify for this branch of service in less than two or three full years of technical training–this is especially true of the school medical inspector. Moreover, it may be said that the stock psychiatric methods of examination have little value except for the psychotic cases. The specialist on the feeble-mindedness of immigrants must receive a course of training which is just as specific and technical as that received by the specialist on the eyes, on dental surgery, on metallurgical engineering, or on kindergarten teaching.

The position thus taken has been regarded as farfetched, but I believe it is essentially sound. Strong confirmatory evidence that this is so is afforded by an experiment carried out during the course of one week at the immigrant station at Ellis Island by the psychological assistants from the training school for feeble-minded children at Vineland, N. J., the results of which have since appeared in print (Training School, 1913, p. 109). The experiment indicated that the government physicians on duty were able to recognize only about 10 per cent of a given number of the mental defectives passing through the port. Moreover, more than half of those whom they selected were incorrectly chosen, while seven-eighths of those selected by the Vineland workers were properly identified, as determined by later tests.

Without raising the question as to the absolute reliability of the above data, there is no doubt that our immigrant stations, because of their defective and inadequate examining machinery,7 are annually permitting many hundreds of morons and imbeciles to land upon our shores. These immigrants will eventually become public charges and, unless restrained, will produce a prolific progeny of social and industrial incompetents. As long as the government allows this situation to continue, little headway can be made in the effort to reduce the defective, delinquent and dependent classes. The way to check this national evil is to establish psychological clinics in the immigrant stations, and put them in charge of thoroughly trained experts–either physicians or psychologists–who must do more than give a few psychiatric, literacy, or haphazard commonsense psychological tests. They must attempt a fairly comprehensive and systematic survey of the stage of mental development of the suspect.

8. The psycho-educational clinic and bureau of research in the public schools. Unquestionably one of the most fruitful fields for the application of clinical psychology is education. Nowhere are the practical benefits to be derived more patent. American public schools have shown commendable enterprise in securing increased physical comforts, the erection of costly material plants, the equipment of expensive laboratories for instruction, the organization of new courses to meet the enlarged demands of the altered social and industrial conditions of the twentieth century, but it must be confessed, to our shame, that they have lagged considerably behind the institutions

T Two questionnaires were addressed to the chief surgeon of one of the immigrant stations, with the expectation that definite, unambiguous information would be obtained regarding the character of the psychological examinations made of subnormal immigrants, but without avail. A psychological clinic, however, is evidently conducted at the Ellis Island station.

for the abnormal and defective in respect to the establishment of laboratories for discovery and research. So far as promoting or conducting departments for the scientific study of the problems which concern the normal health and development of the childs body and mind, the conditions under which such development can be most economically secured, the questions of the most expeditious learning and the most economic teaching methods, of fatigue, of the length of the school day and of the school year, of the scientific examination, and classification, segregation and treatment of the retarded, accelerated and delinquent, they have until recently done practically nothing. The one outstanding exception is the public schools of Chicago, in which a department of child study and pedagogic investigation was established in 1899 (20). This department, which now commands the services of D. P. Macmillan, Ph. D. (director), F. G. Bruner, Ph. D., and Miss Clara Schmitt, has, since its organization, made various studies or educationally normal and misfit children–the blind, deaf, truant, retarded, feeble-minded, etc.–has regularly examined candidates for admission to the city normal school and has issued a series of valuable annual reports embodying its findings.

During the last few years there has come a radical and gratifying change of attitude on the part of educational experts toward the exceptional child–the subnormal (idiot, imbecile, moron, border-line, backward and dull), the supernormal (bright, gifted, talented, precocious), the cripple, epileptic, speech-defective, blind, deaf and mute. It is now recognized by the intelligent public everywhere that the mentally deviating child sets a special problem. On a conservative estimate from 2 to 4 per cent of the retarded children in the schools are idiots, imbeciles, morons, border-cases, epileptics and pronounced neurotics and psycho-neurotics. From 15 to 30 per cent grade all the way from the border-line or seriously backward cases to the merely dull or slow-progress pupils. Fully one-third (in many systems one-half) of the public school children are pedagogically retarded when measured by the age-grade standard (approximately 6,000,000 pupils in the United States). About 2 per cent suffer from some form of speech defect. There is no more vital problem in educational administration, constructive philanthropy or race conservation than the organization of intelligent preventive, reconstructive, educational and reeducational work for the large army of mentally deviating children which encumber our schools. To neglect properly to care for these children would be to invite national disaster. The only effective method of dealing with defective children is to segregate them into special groups and to provide special treatment, care, training or restraint. Not only will this policy tend to remove dead weights and irritating impediments from the regular classes, so that the typical, hopeful, progressive children may receive their just dues, but in the long run it will prove the only way in which the mentally handicapped child can be saved to society from a life of idleness, pauperism or crime. He can be saved only by being sufficiently prepared to discharge the industrial and social responsibilities of citizenship or, in cases where special training proves unavailing because of grave permanent arrest or defectiveness, by being isolated from society in custodial institutions. Let us not forget that the first step in the successful solution of this vital school problem is the early selection of th-e abnormal children in the schools by the qualified psycho-educational examiner.

Owing to the combined influences of the laboratories of the Chicago schools, the University of Pennsylvania and Vineland, psychological tests are now being carried out in many public school systems throughout the country. In order to obtain accurate data in regard to the character of the work done in psychological diagnosis, as well as the educational provisions made for mentally unusual children in the public schools, a questionnaire was addressed October 29, 1913, to the superintendents of public schools in the United States. The returns will be given in Chapter XVIII.

At this point reference may appropriately be made to the state law enacted in California in 1908, authorizing the establishment of departments of health and development supervision in the public schools under the control of boards of education or of school trustees. The program of work contemplates the annual physical examination of pupils and a follow-up service, in order to correct physical abnormalities and to provide the conditions essential for the maintenance of continuous health and normal growth; the adjustment of school activities to meet the developmental needs of the individual in respect to health and growth; the scientific, systematic study of mental retardation and deviation; proper sanitary supervision; the physical examination of candidates for teaching positions and of teachers in service to determine their vital fitness and the amount of work which may reasonably be required of them without imperiling efficiency, and the appointment of expert educator-examiners to conduct and supervise the work. These examiners must qualify as experts in child hygiene and physiology. Above all, they should, in my judgment, be trained in the methods of clinical psychology and educational diagnosis. The pro jected California work thus rests upon a far broader basis than the system of medical inspection now in vogue, and will make it possible to grade children in health as well as in studies. The law is not mandatory.

Under this law quite a number of school systems in California have established departments of health and development supervision (although the work done is probably largely restricted to the ordinary medical inspection routine). But it is interesting to note that two of the most progressive school systems of the state have established psychological clinics independently of the department of health and development supervision, namely Los Angeles (with Mr. George L. Leslie, who was responsible for the health and development law, as director) and Oakland (Mrs. Vinnie C. Hicks, director). While theoretically it would seem desirable to locate the psychological clinic in the department of health and development supervision, practically it may be better to conduct the psycho-educational examinations in a separate department of the schools, in order that the work may not be identified with the usual routine of medical inspection, in order that it may not be unduly hampered by the red tape which attaches to large departmental organizations, and in order that this important work may not be assigned a wholly minor role in a department whose primary interests may be quite foreign to the pedagogico-corrective treatment of mentally unusual children.

The Possibilities Of A Bueeau Of School Research In view of the fact that the intelligent educational public is gradually becoming reconciled to the proposition that the changed industrial and social conditions of modern life necessitate the organization of various new school agencies—departments of medical and dental inspection, of school hygiene, of experimental pedagogj, of social survey work, of psycho-educational laboratories for the examination of exceptional children—I wish to pause a moment to outline briefly the work which a bureau of school research might profitably undertake for the good of the schools.

At the outset it should be said that the results of the various agencies which are being organized in the schools for purposes of educational investigation and diagnosis are liable to run to sand unless they are properly unified, correlated and brought to a focus. There is need, therefore, of a central, unifying bureau or department of school research, in charge of a director of school research, where the data collected by the various examining agencies may be gathered, preserved, compiled, compared, correlated, interpreted and turned to practical use.

The director of such a bureau should be an expert in child, educational and clinical psychology, who has done productive work of recognized merit in these fields. He should be thoroughly familiar with the methods employed by these sciences and by experimental pedagogy, and should have some knowledge of medical inspection work (a minimum of knowledge in regard to physical diagnosis and the signs and symptoms of physical defectiveness and nervous instability). He should be a technical educationist, with practical teaching experience, preferably in public and teacher-training schools, and must possess the ability to plan and direct the work along broad, progressive lines. His should be distinctly a position of leadership in the educational work of the schools, ranking as a directorship or assistant superintendency, and nothing but a thoroughly trained, broad-gauge, technical, psycho-edu cational consultant should be able to qualify. (Parenthetically let me say that since the above was first written, bureaus of statistics, reference or research have been established in the public schools of New Orleans, Rochester, Baltimore and New York City. Cleveland also maintains a statistician. While these bureaus have other functions than those given below, the program of work in some of them includes statistical and clinical studies of retardation and the giving of efficiency tests.)

The materials to be collected and correlated by our bureau should be derived from the following sources: 1. Records and charts of physical (medical and dental) examinations and treatment—nasopharyngeal and dental charts, showing the locations of nose and throat obstructions and defective dentures; vaccination records and charts, showing the dates of inoculation and the number of vaccine scars; abnormalities of the respiratory, circulatory, nutritive, muscular, osseous and nervous systems; sensory defects (visual, auditory); records of operations and of medical and dental treatment, with the carefully determined results of such treatment, etc. The data should be recorded annually, if possible, on duplicate cards, which should accompany the child from grade to grade. The originals should be filed in the bureau of records.

It would lead the discussion too far afield to consider what should be the detailed functions and relations of the department of physical or medico-dental examination. The matters in dispute revolve around the questions whether the work should be entirely confined to examination, or whether it should include free treatment, at least for the minor ailments (22); whether the system should be under the control of boards of health or of school boards; whether inspection should be supplemented by follow-up educational care, treatment and supervisory work by a corps of school nurses, both in and out of school; whether it should embrace the sanitary inspection and supervision of the school plant; whether it should include instruction and supervision in individual and school hygiene; whether it should include provision for, and supervision of, school lunches, gratuitously available to indigent anemics, for school baths, gymnasia, etc.

These questions cannot be answered in the abstract; in the near future they will loom large in the educational discussion of the day. They constitute one phase of the large eugenics or euthenics movement which has recently been forced into the focus of public attention by the threatened dangers of national degeneracy and racial decay of highly civilized races–dangers which, e. g., are evidenced in a lessened rate of fertility under the conditions of civilized life (which is mans conscious attempt to domesticate himself); continued high infant mortality in spite of hygienic progress; the enormous presence of physical defectiveness (cf. Chapters I and XVI), and the alleged prolific increase of degenerate or neuropathic offspring (feeble-minded, epileptic, criminal and insane). These problems cannot, in the face of present knowledge, be solved in any rule-of-thumb fashion; they must be solved according to the exigencies of the case and according to the results of experience. The ancient Spartans found it essential to their national safety to exercise practically unlimited supervision over the physical, hygienic, social and educational regimen of the child, and they therefore removed him entirely from the family home. During these latter days we have been rapidly approximating the Spartan ideal, because recent conditions have been at work which have forced a return toward it. The first law of individual as well as of national life is the law of self-preservation; against this primal law preconceived notions and paternalistic or communistic phobias avail naught. The patrons of the schools demand, as of right, that the schools shall foster those agencies and practices without which they cannot realize proper dividends upon their investments, and without which the forces in the modern environment which are destructive of the public weal cannot be successfully combated. Ultimately all those measures must surely be introduced into the schools which are essentially for national self-preservation; the fundamental imperative of national self-preservation will take precedence over all other considerations, and theoretical scruples will be powerless.

There is another important question affecting medical school inspection which we can here merely raise: Who should be eligible for appointment as medical or physical school inspectors? Many of the present incumbents possess neither technical training nor interest in the work. This is one reason why so much of the inspection work is perfunctory and thoroughly unscientific. A class of experts for this work scarcely yet exists, because at the present time there is probably not a university or medical school in the country that provides special, technical training in medical school inspection. Recently short courses of this character have been given by Dr. W. S. Cornell in the New Jersey Training School at Vineland. Until we secure a class of expert school health examiners–specialists in the neuro-physical and developmental defects and maladies of childhood, in school hygiene and sanitation, and in the theory and practice of dento-medical school inspection–appointees should be selected from the expert pediatricians or from the general medical practitioners who show a vital interest in the distinctive problems of medical school inspection. The dental work should be directed by a doctor of dentistry.

2. Sociological, personal and family data. We cannot satisfactorily diagnose a sub-normal or defective pupil by merely examining his present bodily conditions. There are other influences, hereditary, developmental and environmental, which have contributed to make him what he is. These we must understand. We must know something

of the social organism of which he is a constituent member–something of his home, his community, his street life. The out-of-school activities and the economic, sanitary, hygienic, moral and intellectual conditions of the home and neighborhood often make or mar the individual. Properly to diagnose his condition we must know something about his food and drink, about the adequacy of his raiment and sleep, about the purity of the air he breathes, about the wholesomeness of the games and amusements which he enjoys and the resorts which he frequents, and about the care and treatment which he receives in the home. We should obtain a record of his developmental history, of his past habits, diseases, disorders and eccentricities. Particularly important are records of early dangerous tendencies, tantrums, fits, outbreaks or disorders or diseases which are prodromal of oncoming adolescent or adult instabilities, neurasthenias and psy-chasthenias. And properly to estimate his hereditary dower–his inborn capital or native handicap–we must know something of the stock from which he springs, his direct and collateral antecedents.

The two fundamental factors which make or mar the life of every child are heredity and environment. But it is impossible to determine offhand, and frequently even after considerable study, which of these two factors is more largely responsible for a childs degeneracy or delinquency. The view that acquired degeneracy exceeds the inherited became rather prevalent some time ago, perhaps as a reaction against the Italian or Lombroso school of crimi-nologists who manifest an exaggerated tendency to refer all mental abnormalities to biological causes, and who maintain that there is a very preva-lent degenerate (specifically criminal) type which is born and not made. But recent heredity studies of feeble-mindedness, epilepsy and insanity show the preponderant influence of neurotic ancestral strains. Be this as it may, it is unquestionable that a vast amount of abnormal conduct is acquired from, or accentuated by, a bad environment; from physically and morally unclean slums, from squalid or unhealthy homes, from vicious resorts, social vices, unhygienic school practices and habits, etc. The first treatment which a child reared in the underworld needs is to be rescued: he must either be removed from his evil surroundings or his environment must be reformed. This accomplished, he must be supplied with proper training, food, sleep, exercise and clothing. Instances of children who have been transformed in body and mind by these measures have been frequently recorded; modern hospital or orthogenic schools are demonstrating what can be done through the work of scientific, educational and social reclamation.

Obviously it would be folly to aim to include in the above survey all the pupils of the school. At best we must be satisfied to include only the problematic or defective cases. Much valuable information can be gathered, of course, by teachers, principals and school nurses; but a field worker, trained in social survey work, should be added to the staff for this particular type of service.

3. Pedagogical records from the schools. The bureau we are advocating should also keep on file the pupils school reports and records, particularly the records of the problem pupils–feeble-minded, backward, neurotic, truant, etc. These records, to be made out by classroom teachers and principals, should contain facts in regard to the childs age and grade (pedagogical retardation), the number of months he has been in school, the grades repeated, the amount and type of work that he has been able and that

he has not been able to do, his attitudes, dispositions, demeanor, behavior, dominant interests and aversions, vocational bias, regularity of attendance, etc. Such records will attain a unique value when studied in the light of the data from other sources.

4. The results of controlled educational experiments. A department of experimental pedagogy should be one division of a complete bureau of school research. This department should study, under principles of scientific control, the important school problems in pedagogy: methods of teaching and learning various branches, rest and work periods, fatigue, recreation, the relation of temperature to working efficiency, the content and articulation of courses, etc. It should standardize efficiency tests and apply pedagogical measuring scales in the various branches of study. Some of the problems would be solved experimentally in the laboratory; others could best be solved by controlled school tests, and others would be studied in special experimental schools. The laboratory connected with the Chicago schools has devoted a slight amount of attention to problems of this character. The results of the pedagogical experiments should be correlated with the other data in the bureau.

5. Psycho-clinical records from the department of clinical psychology. One of the most important divisions of the bureau should be a laboratory of clinical psychology for the individual study of pupils, particularly subnormal, supernormal and delinquent children. The central aim of this department–we shall discuss it somewhat in detail presently—should be the scientific investigation of abnormalities of psycho-educational development.

Conceived in this large way, the bureau of school research would become a large scientific, educational clearing house, a vital agency for the scientific correlation of pedagogical facts and a potent instrument for the dissemination of reliable educational data. It is only when we view the child from all angles–from the bodily, the psychical, the pedagogical, the sociological, the developmental and the hereditary–that we are in a position thoroughly to understand him, and that we are able to deal effectively with the problems of mental exceptionality.

Perhaps we can best illustrate the point we wish to make by reference to the questions of retardation and acceleration, which are far more complex than would be supposed at first blush. When we are dealing with the development of a child we are dealing not with a single equation, but with a number of variable equations. Instead of one constant age, we may speak of a child as having six ages: a chronological, a physiological, an anatomical, a socio-industrial, a pedagogical and a psychological. So far as the chronological age is concerned, there can be no question of retardation; a child born precisely fifteen years ago is chronologically exactly fifteen years old. But physiologically, anatomically, pedagogically, socio-industrially and psychologically his development may spread over a number of ages. Physiologically, our fifteen-year-old child may be, say, only thirteen years old. Measured by the maturity of bodily functions, e. g., by the degree of pubertal or pubescent development (or size, which it is claimed,-roughly corresponds, 6), he has the body of a normal child of thirteen. He is physiologically two years retarded. Anatomically–i. e., measured by structural changes, particularly by the degree of ossification of the cartilage, Rotchs X-ray method–he may be fourteen years old, or only a year retarded. Measured by the gocio-industrial or motor standard–i. e., by his rate of acquiring the fundamental social functions and various motor or industrial operations–he may be sixteen years old, or a year accelerated.   Similarly, our fifteen-year-old child may be retarded pedagogically three years;., assuming that he started school on time and has arrived at his present grade three years later than his classmates in the first grade, he has a pedagogical development of twelve years. He is pedagogically retarded, whatever the cause–mental defect, physical handicap, frequent absence, transfer, lack of application, etc.   Finally, the psychical age of our fifteen-year-old may be, say, only eleven; he has the mental development of a child of that age.   It might be assumed that the pedagogical and mental ages would coincide.   At times they will, but by no means always.   The childs pedagogical retardation may be due merely to late entrance, irregular attendance, frequent transfers, lack of interest in the particular tasks set by the school, or because some temporary handicap may have especially crippled those mental functions (e. g., memory and attention) which play an important role in the learning processes of the school, in which case the pedagogical retardation may be greater than the mental.   On the other hand, his pedagogical retardation may be less than his mental, for he may have been promoted undeservedly (32); or his abilities may have been overestimated, owing to a heightened development of some special mental function (e. g., memory); or he may have been pushed forward because of the pressure brought to bear on the classroom teacher to eliminate failures or to minimize the number of non-promotions.   Accordingly, the childs actual mental development needs to be determined independently by serial graded age-tests, which are sufficiently comprehensive to include tests of the fundamental mental functions, capacities and powers.   Until recently we had no such tests–no measures of mental age that were regarded as scientifically valid.   Now, thanks to the laborious and ingenious investigations of Binet and his co-worker, Simon, we have a set of graded tests which render it possible somewhat approximately to ascertain, in terms of age, the intellectual status of a child below the teens or the degree in which his intellectual development varies from the average or typical child of his chronological age.   While these tests are neither exhaustively comprehensive, amazingly accurate nor infallible–as recent experimental studies show (1, 12, 15, 19, 21, 28, 31) and as I shall point out in later pages, they give us a consistent, practical, impersonal, objective, scientific method of determining psychological retardation, which is of considerable service to the expert psycho-diagnostician.   Standardized, graded intelligence tests should be given in all the large school systems under the direction of a qualified expert.

The School, Psycho-educational Laboratory

Where the establishment of a bureau of school research upon the comprehensive plan sketched above is not feasible, the most urgent need should be provided for, namely, the establishment of a clinical laboratory for the examination and grading of retarded children.

I do not intend to imply that only the retarded child should receive the advantages of scientific diagnosis.   No type of child has, perhaps, been so thoroughly neglected as the supernormal child, the child on the plus side of the curve of efficiency.   This is probably due largely to the fact that accelerated children are not nearly so numerous as retarded children, as shown by the available surveys, and to the fact that they do not encumber the machinery of the schools as do the retarded pupils.   The supernormal or precocious child is the incipient genius; and it is chiefly through the constructive achievements of its geniuses that civilization advances. Both of the extreme types of the special child merit special study and treatment: the subnormal child, in order that he may be relieved, so far as possible, of his physical and mental handicaps, so that he may become as little of a burden to society as possible; and the supernormal child, in order that he may be surrounded with those conditions which, on the positive side, make for the freest and largest development of his potentialities, and which, on the negative side, will not serve to distort, abort or repress his natural powers. Since it is probable that most of the new laboratories which will be established will be dedicated to the study of the subnormal child, it is to be hoped that a laboratory will be established with the express and exclusive aim of studying the supernormal child, and that, eventually, all the large public schools will organize definite plans for conserving and furthering the interests of its incipient geniuses. Nevertheless, the enormous prevalence of retarded as compared with accelerated pupils makes the identification and segregation of feebleminded and backward children the problem of paramount importance.

In New York City there are eight slow-progress pupils for every rapid-progress pupil; in a Massachusetts city the relation was found to be 21 to 1; in a Pennsylvania city, 14 to 1 (13); among 8,942 graded pupils in Bureau County, Illinois, 57.5 per cent were behind the normal, while only 8 per cent were ahead, and among 2,090 rural pupils, 53.5 per cent were retarded, and only 12 per cent ahead; of the 137 pupils whose records were traced through the grades in Princeton, Ill., 69.3 per cent were behind time, and only 4.6 per cent accelerated (8, 9); in a Baltimore class, where the progress and retardation was likewise traced for 43 pupils from the first to the eighth grade, 77 per cent arrived late, while only one arrived ahead of time (16); in three Chicago schools the per cent retarded was 68.1, the per cent accelerated 8.1; in Cincinnati (report of 1907: 26) the proportion was 58.4 per cent to 9.6 per cent; in Mauch Chunk township, Pa., 34.5 per cent to 16.6 per cent (for 842 pupils studied; most of the accelerated started early: 30); in five cities studied the retarded were from 10 to 150 times as numerous, and in 29 other cities from 8 to 10 times as numerous (Ayres). It has been said that three out of every four must do one room twice, and statistics show that from 33 to 50 per cent of the pupils in the schools are over age for their grade.

In the light of these statistics–and I have given a mere hint of the available data– it becomes imperative to undertake a thorough study of the extent, causes, results and treatment of retardation–the great threatening colossus of the modern school. It is particularly important to make psycho-educational examinations to determine the degree of the mental deficit of the retardate, to determine whether the retardation is a case of inherent deficiency or subnormal mental development, or whether it is the result of adventitious factors, such as late entrance, transfer, irregularity of attendance, illness, physical defectiveness, language deficiency, home abuse, poor teaching, lack of individual tuition, maladapted courses, indifference, etc. Until the schools make greater efforts to discover the cause of the lack of progress of the individual retardate, the orthogenic treatment cannot be made scientifically accurate or practically effective.

It is the worst sort of possible economy to attempt to train subnormal children without a prior scientific educational diagnosis.

The Specific Functions Of The Schools Psycho- Educational Laboeatoey 1. The clinical examination of exceptional children. Every child retarded pedagogically over one year should be given a special preliminary medical examination, and then referred to the laboratory for a psycho-educational examination. The tests should, where possible, include graded serial tests for determining mental age, form-board tests, sensory-motor tests, which have a diagnostic value (auditory and visual acuity, motor skill, coordination, hand dynamometry, endurance, body sway); selected standardized tests of fundamental intellectual traits (memory, spontaneous and controlled association, accuracy and quickness of perception and observation, recognition, linguistic construction, learning capacity); speech tests, certain physical and anthropometric growth measures (sitting and standing height, weight, thoracic perimeter, spirometry, head circumference, together with vital, ponderal and statural indices, and perhaps tests of anatomical age), and certain reflex action tests. In selected cases the psycho-analytic (Freud) and reaction-association (Jung) tests may be relevant for purposes of diagnosis of more fundamental or obscure mental abnormalities. Anthropometric percentile curves and indices should be plotted for each child, showing his status relative to the normal child of the same chronological, and perhaps also anatomical and psychological age. To plot such curves we stand in need of reliable norms for typical, average or normal children. Since we do not now have fully satisfactory norms, one of the functions of the laboratory at the present time should be: 2. The establishment of thoroughly reliable anthropo-metric norms for normal children. To be sure, we already have anthropometric norms for certain functions, e. g., those worked out by the Department of Child Study and Pedagogic Investigation of the Chicago schools. These norms are perhaps reliable so far as they go, and have sufficient validity to enable us to proceed at once, without awaiting confirmatory or more elaborate measurements, to measure and grade, with considerable confidence, any given child, whether subnormal, normal or supernormal. Yet the fact remains that it is still desirable to repeat Smedleys percentile measurements (or measurements designed to give anthropometric indices, whichever type of measurement ultimately will prove the more valuable) on height, weight, vital capacity, manuometry, endurance and other functions on a much larger scale and under more satisfactory conditions.8 For Smedleys norms are not entirely satisfactory in four respects: In the first place, they are based upon the examination of too few persons. To secure thoroughly reliable normal norms we should examine at least 1,000 persons of each

The task involved in gathering reliable mental and physical norms, for both children and adults, is herculean, and would require the combined efforts of many workers. The work should be organized sex for each year, and each one-half year during early childhood. Smedleys numbers for given ages ranged from 44 (ages nineteen and twenty, boys) to 448. I do not believe that in a country like the United States where so many nationalities commingle we can be satisfied with one hundred for each age.

In the second place, we have no evidence that the norms are normal norms; i. e., that they are based upon the examination of typical or normal children. In fact, the probability almost amounts to a certainty that a considerable number of the pupils examined were more or less subnormal or abnormal. It is, therefore, possible that the percentile curves or indices for any case of retardation plotted on the basis of these results will misrepresent the development of the pupil in comparison with normal children. Measurements seem to show that anthropological indices are atypical for mentally abnormal persons.

Of course, the concept of a normal norm–a typical, normal individual–is quite fluid or elastic. How shall we determine who is normal in advance of making the tests? This is extremely difficult to say. Unless we are satisfied to use random, unselected groups and assume a symmetrical curve of distribution, we must adopt some criteria. So far as I know there are only two criteria which are at all available for selecting normal school children: namely, school grade (pedagogical status) and degree of physical defectiveness.

by a public or endowed private bureau of research, so that it may be done with sufficient thoroughness, so that uniform or standardized methods may be used, and so that the results may be worked up in the most serviceable form. Properly to study any given individual–normal, criminal, insane, demented, amented–we must have individual and typical percentile curve or indicet of phyrical development, and ttandardt of mental attainment for various ages.

I know of no form of public service which merits more fully the liberal support of philanthropic persons who have the interests of child reclamation or eugenics at heart. It is a work that should be munificently endowed. One of the essential functions of the Russell Sage Foundation, and the Government Bureau of Child Welfare, might well be the establishment of mental and physical norms of development. Meanwhile, our psycho-clinical school laboratories should contribute their mite toward obtaining these norms for persons of school age.

On the basis of the first standard, the pupils of a given age who satisfactorily carry the work of the school grade to which they chronologically belong (or of an earlier grade in case of late entrance), may be considered mentally normal.

The other method of selection is based upon the physical and medical examination of the child. That child may be regarded as physically normal who does not possess serious physical defects, or in whom the ravages of infant and childhood diseases have not resulted in pronounced physical impairment. In other words, those children would be physically normal who suffer only from the ordinary amount of physical defectiveness. Even under the best conditions of modern life, the child with assumed normal motor and sensory equipment will show some traces of physical defectiveness (21, 22). It is, therefore, chiefly important to exclude all the extreme departures from physical normality.

Both of these methods of selection are practical, and the norms obtained by them ought more genuinely to represent normal norms than the norms obtained by testing unselected cases. The validity of the latter must always rest on the assumption that there are just as many supernormal or accelerated as subnormal or retarded individuals. This I regard as improbable. Norms secured according to the above suggestions would not only give us valuable measures of the mental and physical powers and capacities of people of the present generation–racial and national indices–but indices by means of which to determine the character and extent of the changes in human functions which are gradually taking place through hereditary propulsion and environmental influences.

In the third place, Smedleys range of ages, from four to twenty-one (or twenty-one years and over), is too limited. It embraces merely the periods of childhood and adolescence. We need norms for infancy and the adult or the ebb period of life as far as the age of forty or fifty, at least. Such norms would perhaps have no immediate practical value for the public schools, juvenile courts or correctional and rescue homes for the young, but to the student interested in the scientific study of the problems of human evolution or in the study of the degenerative, involution, senescent changes peculiar to the process of aging, or in the study of the various physical and mental deviations peculiar to various classes of defectives (feebleminded, epileptic, insane, criminal, paralytic, etc.), they would possess unusual value. At the present time we have little knowledge that is scientifically accurate regarding the growth (developmental or retrogressive) changes peculiar to middle and old age, because the norms are practically nonexistent.

In the fourth place, Smedleys percentiles are given for whole ages only–4, 5, 6, 7, 8, 9, etc. A child who is six years and one day old is grouped with one who is six years and 364 days old. Consequently, children who are practically one year apart in age may be grouped together. This tends to introduce a considerable error, owing to the kaleidoscopic developmental changes which occur during the growth period. During this period the results which are valid for the youngest child of a given age may grossly misrepresent the oldest child of that age. Accordingly, a better plan would be to group children by half-ages, thus: 4, 41/2, 5 5 5 etc. Thus, the six-year group would include children from five years ten months (beginning of tenth month) to six years three months (end of third month), while the six and one-half-year group would include children from six years four months (beginning of fourth month) to six years nine months (end of ninth month). (I am now establishing certain norms according to this plan.) In other words, children are grouped under a given age-designation whose age is within three months in either direction of that designation. For the years following, the early growth period of the present grouping by whole ages is probably satisfactory.

What has been said above applies to all kinds of norms: it must be emphasized that the norms required are not merely physical and anthropometric, but also psychical and pedagogical.

3. The establishment of thoroughly reliable psychological norms of development for normal children. Everything that has been urged in respect to the need of establishing normal anthropometric norms and indices applies to the establishment of normal mental age norms of the important intellectual, motor and emotional functions. It will be impossible to make strictly reliable tests until these norms are available on a much larger scale than we now have them. It is also important to establish reliable objective pedagogical age-norms: but this work is large enough to demand the services of a special division of pedagogic research.

4. The psycho-clinical laboratory, in the fourth place, should serve as a clearing-house for all types of mentally and educationally unusual children–a function which it should discharge jointly with the special schools or special classes. At the present

time the special schools serve this function very inadequately; they have become rather a dumping ground for the neer-do-wells, the offscourings, of the schools–a place to which they may be relegated indiscriminately in order to relieve the regular rooms of an intolerable incubus. After the backward child has been examined in the laboratory, he should be sent to a special class (one in charge of a teacher specially trained for special-room work), with specific recommendations, for further careful pedagogical observation and psychological study. He should be given a well-planned try-out for a while, the results of which should be sent to the laboratory. On the basis of these results–the clinical examination and special-room observation and testing–the director should recommend the transfer to, or the placing of the child in, his proper place–the special class for the feeble-minded, the special class for the backward, the ungraded class for the retarded (those merely retarded in one or more of the academic branches), the classes for the blind, deaf, crippled, tuberculous, anemic or speech-defective, or the institutions for the feeble-minded or epileptic. Most elementary pupils who are mentally retarded more than four years are suffering from very serious permanent arrest, and are institutional cases. They should be separated from the merely retarded and the backward. The recommendations of the director should not be subject to reversal, except through action by the board or the superintendent. As a clearing-house for mentally unusual pupils, the laboratory would render an important service to the schools not performed by any existing agency. It is evident that to perform this service in the best possible manner the laboratory must be directed by an authoritative specialist and have available full data from the other sources which we have already discussed. Where there is no complete bureau of school research, the psycho-educational laboratory would logically assume the functions of such a bureau.

5. A fifth function of the laboratory is the psychological examination and efficiency appraisal of some of the applicants for vocational guidance. As already stated, it is preposterous to assume that the mass of children can be scientifically guided into vocational pursuits without such an examination. The director of the vocational bureau should be a psycho-educational expert, or the services of such an expert should be available to the bureau for the examination of at least all the candidates whose educational record indicates that they are mentally exceptional.

6. The laboratory may also undertake the training of special-class teachers in the psycho-clinical methods of testing pupils. If it were feasible, the teachers might assist in giving some of the tests in the special schools under the supervision of the laboratory director. The percentage of retarded children is so large that it would probably be beyond the means of the laboratory to examine all the pupils who should be examined in a large school system. To apply merely the Binet-Simon tests thoroughly requires from forty minutes to an hour. However, a distinctly better plan is to specially train one or two adaptable teachers in the methods of psychological testing, and let them devote all their time to giving some of the simpler tests. The more difficult tests and the final review of the cases should invariably be made by the expert clinical psychologist.

7. Finally, another function of the laboratory might be the supervision of the curricula of the special schools and the offering of courses in the training school on the psychology and pedagogy of the various types of mental deviation or deficiency. No teacher should ever be assigned to special class work who has not received special

training. It is obvious that to perform all these functions the laboratory would have to be organized on a comprehensive basis.

The Qualifications Of The Clinical Psychologist Or Psycho-educational Examiner

1. He must be temperamentally adapted for the work. I do not know that this is first in importance, but mere knowledge of the methodological technique peculiar to psycho-clinical work does not necessarily make a successful examiner. The examiner must have the ability or knack to draw out the best the child has to give; if he is obliged to force it out he is lacking in the very essentials of the work. Psycho-clinical examination is not a forcing-out process. The examiner should, through word, action, demeanor and bearing, be able to calm, pacify, set at ease the nervous, excitable child; and to encourage, incite, stimulate the phlegmatic, timid, taciturn, obstructed child. He must be genial, friendly, sympathetic, quick to praise and slow to criticise, and must be able to win the confidence of all. He must possess an unlimited reserve of patience with the frivolous, the resistant and the snail-like plodders. He must be versatile and resourceful, so that he can change his attitude and method of attack to suit all types of persons. There are persons who will respond only to pressure and with whom stern measures will produce the best results. But they are entirely exceptional.

2. It is not enough that he has a thorough grounding in the methods and results of analytical, descriptive, experimental, child, social, physiological and educational psychology; he should have a definite, technical preparation in clinical psychology. He should be conversant with its methods, standpoints, aims and results. Knowledge of structural psychology is not sufficient; the best structural and experimental psychologist may make the sorriest clinical psychologist. Often the paramount need is the ability to tear loose from the abstractions, schematizations and viewpoints of the structuralist. The clinical worker must use the case method of procedure; he must be familiar with the clinical method; he must be able to individualize each case (a capacity that is likewise needed by the special-class teacher), to study it in the concrete, to frame a clinical picture of it—in a word, to examine clinically. To do this requires more than a mastery of the framework of psychology or of the technique of laboratory experimentation; it requires ready powers of observation, keenness of insight, power to interpret, ability to notice signs and symptoms, a knowledge of symptomatology and of the best available methods of psycho-clinical diagnosis, and an extensive first-hand acquaintance with educationally abnormal children—three to four years of observation and testing in and out of institutions of a considerable variety of child deviates, such as the feeble-minded, backward, retarded, accelerated, epileptic, incipient and developed neurotics and psychotics, speech defectives, moral imbeciles. Until recently it was impossible to obtain adequate training in clinical psychology except through an apprenticeship with one of the few experts in the field. Now a few universities—although very few—are able to offer satisfactory didactic and clinical courses in the psychological and educational examination of children.

3. A knowledge of anatomy and pathology, of public and personal hygiene, of the common physical defects, of nervous and mental diseases, of psychopathology and psychotherapy, of pediatrics and normal physical diagnosis, is essential for a clinical psychologist working on juvenile cases in the medical school; I incline strongly to the

opinion that the psychological and educational examiner of mentally unusual children in the schools should also have a working knowledge of these specialties.

4. The clinical psychologist should be thoroughly grounded in the science and art of normal pedagogy. He will certainly be able to render a higher type of service if he has had practical teaching experience in the elementary grades of the public schools, so that he has had the opportunity to come directly in touch with the problems of the training, growth and development of the child mind, and so that he is thoroughly conversant with the normal pedagogy of the elementary branches (particularly the methods of teaching handwork, reading, spelling, number and writing). He will likewise be better prepared for his work if he has taught educational psychology or the principles of teaching in training schools for teachers, so that he is alive to the vital educational problems concerning pedagogical methodology (questions regarding methods of studying, learning, instructing, drilling, memorizing, initiative, working efficiency, hours, rests, alternation of subjects, etc.) and so that he may thus turn his investigations to wider pedagogical use.

5. He must have made a very exhaustive study of all phases of corrective pedagogics. He must be thoroughly grounded in the differential pedagogy which applies to the types of cases he expects to handle.

This may seem like an extremely exacting course of training but it is not more exacting than the training now demanded of the various medical specialists and it will certainly only make a reasonable demand on the time of the student who from the outset—at least from the baccalaureate—shapes his work towards the career of a psycho-educational examiner. Certainly the work is so varied, complex and technical that complete mastery is out of the question without three or four years of preparation. Eventually the well-trained specialist in this field must command the respect and the emoluments accorded to the specialist in the allied medical fields.

References 1. Bobertag. Uber Intelligenzpriifungen (nach der Methode von Binet vmd Simon). Zeitschrift fur ange-wandte Psychologic, 1911, 5: 105ff.

2. Boehne. Special Classes in the Rochester Schools. Journal of Psycho-Asthenics, 1909-10, 14:88.

8. Cattell. A Further Statistical Study of American Men of Science. Science, 1910, N. S., 82: 672f.

4. Dearborn. Medical Psychology. Medical Record, January 80, 1909.

6. Dubois. The Psychic Treatment of Nervous Disorders. New York, 1906.

6. Foster. Physiological Age as a Basis for the Classification of Pupils Entering High Schools—Relation of Pubescence to Height. The Psychological Clinic, 1909, 8:88f.

7. Franz. On Psychology and Medical Education. Science, 1918, 88: 555f. See also the statistical study of Abbot, Psychology and the Medical School. American Journal of Insanity, 1918, 70:447f.

8. Gayler. Retardation and Elimination in Graded and Ungraded Schools. The Psychological Clinic, 1910, 4:40f.

9. Gayler. A Further Study of Retardation in Illinois. The Psychological Clinic, 1910, 4: 79f.

10. Goddard. The Grading of Backward Children. The De Sanctis Tests and the Binet and Simon Tests of Intellectual Capacity. The Training School, November-December, 1908.

11. Goddard. Binets Measuring Scale for Intelligence. The Training School, 1910, 6: No. 11. Revised edition, 1911.

12. Goddard. Two Thousand Normal Children Measured by the Binet Measuring Scale of Intelligence. Pedagogical Seminary, 18:282f.

18. Gulick. Causes of Dropping Out of School. Worlds Work, August, 1910, 18285f.

14. Huey. Backward and Feeble-minded Children. Baltimore, 1912.

15. Huey. The Present Status of the Binet Scale of Tests for the Measurement of Intelligence. Psychological Bulletin, 1912, 9: 160f.

16. J. Progress and Retardation of a Baltimore Class. The Psychological Clinic, 1909, 8: 186f.

17. Jones. Psycho-analysis in Psychotherapy. Montreal Medical Journal, 1909, 88: 495f.

18. Kuhlmann. Binet and Simons System for Measuring the Intelligence of Children. Journal of Psycho-Asthenics, 1911, 15: Nos. 8, 4.

19. Kuhlmann. The Present Status of the Binet and Simon Tests of the Intelligence of Children. Journal of Psycho-Asthenics, 1912, 16: No. 8.

20. Macmillan. The Physical and Mental Examination of Public School Pupils in Chicago. Charities and Commons (now The Survey), December 22, 1906.

21. Meumann. Sammelreferat iiber die Literatur der Jugendkunde. Archiv fur Psychologic, 25:85f.

22. Munro. Psychotherapy in Relation to the General Practice of Medicine and Surgery. The Medical Herald (St. Joseph), June, 1910.

28. Munsterbero. On the Witness Stand, Essays on Psychology and Crime. New York, 1908.

24. Munsterbero. Psychotherapy. New York, 1909.

25. Mcnsterbero. Psychology and Industrial Efficiency. Boston, 1918.

26. Schmitt. Retardation Statistics of Three Chicago Schools. The Elementary School Teacher, 1910, 478f.

27. Taylor. The Widening Sphere of Medicine. The Harvard Medical School, 4: (Quoted under The Doctor and the Public), Science, 1910, N. S., 82: 664.

28. Terman and Childs. A Tentative Revision and Extension of the Binet-Simon Measuring Scale of Intelligence. Journal of Educational Psychology, 1912, 8: 61 f.

29. Town. Translation of Binet and Simons A Method of Measuring the Intelligence of Young Children. Chicago, 1918.

80. Wagner. Retardation, Acceleration and Elimination in Mauch Chunk Township, Pennsylvania. The Psychological Clinic, November, 1909, 8.

81. Wallin. Experimental Studies of Mental Defectives. Baltimore, 1912.

82. Wallin. The Rationale of Promotion and Elimination of Waste in the Elementary and Secondary Schools. The Journal of Educational Psychology, 1910, l:445f.

88. Whipple. Manual of Mental and Physical Tests. Baltimore, 1910. Chapter 18. (Indispensable to examiners of children.) 84. Witmer. Clinical Psychology. The Psychological Clinic, 1907, 1: If.

85. Witmer. The Psychological Clinic. Old Penn, 1909, 7:98f.

86. Woolley. Charting Childhood in Cincinnati. The Survey, 1918, 601 f.

Additional references:

Groszmann. The Study of Individual Children. Plainfield, 1912.

Holmes (Arthur). The Conservation of the Child. Philadelphia, 1912.

Holmes (W. H.). School Organization and the Individual Child. Worcester, 1912.

Witmer (and others). The Special Class for Backward Children. Philadelphia, 1911.

CHAPTER III

CLINICAL PSYCHOLOGY: WHAT IT IS AND WHAT IT IS NOT1

On an occasion like this2 it would seem proper, representing as I do one of the newest of the sciences, that I address myself to some of the basic questions of this science. Perhaps the very first question with which one is confronted is simply this: In view of the rapid multiplication of the sciences, by what right does clinical psychology lay claim to an independent existence? That is a question which may perturb some sensitive minds, but it does not disconcert the clinical psychologist, for he regards the question as perfectly legitimate and capable of satisfactory answer.

1 Reprinted from Science, 1913, pp. 895-902.

2 Substance of an address delivered before the Conference on the Exceptional Child, held under the auspices of the University of Pittsburgh, April 16, 1912. Lest misapprehensions arise, it should be clearly understood that in this discussion I am concerned only with the relation of clinical psychology to mentally exceptional school children; and that I distinctly recognize a different type of exceptional children, namely, the phy/rical defectives. The physical defectives should be examined by skilled pediatricians. The clinical psychologist is interested in physically exceptional children when they manifest mental deviations. Moreover, while I hold that the psycho-clinical laboratories must become the clearing houses for all types of mentally or educationally exceptional children in the schools, nearly all mentally exceptional children should be given a prior physical examination by consulting or associated medical experts. Physical abnormalities should, of course, be rectified, whether or not it can be shown that they sustain any causal relation to the mental deviations which may have been disclosed in the psycho-clinical examination. They should claim treatment in their own right.

It is just and proper that a new claimant to membership in the family of sciences should be required to present her credentials. It is a natural human trait to challenge or contest the claims of a newcomer. It has ever been thus. Every branch of knowledge before winning recognition as an independent science has been forced to demonstrate that it possesses a distinct and unique body of facts not adequately treated by any other existing science; or that it approaches the study of a common body of facts from a unique point of view, and with methods of its own. Psychology, bio-chemistry, dentistry, eugenics, historiometry and many other sciences have been thus obliged to fight their way inch by inch to recognition as independent sciences. It is not long since physiology claimed psychology as its own child and stoutly contested her rights to existence; nor is it long since medicine denied any right to independent existence to dentistry. It is no surprise that a number of sciences now claim clinical psychology as part and parcel of their own flesh and blood, and that they deny her the right to split off from the parent cell and establish an unnursed existence of her own. Just as nature abhors a vacuum, so science abhors the multiplication of sciences; just as the big corporation octopus in the industrial world tries to get monopolistic control of the sources of production and distribution, so the various sciences, naturally insatiable in their desire for conquest, attempt only too often to get monopolistic control of all those elements of knowledge which they may be able to use for their own aggrandizement, whether or not they have developed adequate instruments for scientifically handling those elements.

Clinical psychology, however, is quite ready to contest the attempts to deprive her of her inalienable rights to the pursuit of life and happiness. Fundamentally, she bases her claims to recognition as an independent science on the fact that she does possess a unique body of facts not adequately handled by any existing science, and that she investigates these facts by methods of her own. These facts consist of individual mental variations, or the phenomena of deviating or exceptional mentality. In other words, clinical psychology is concerned with the concrete study and examination of the behavior of the mentally exceptional individual (not groups), by its own methods of observation, testing and experiment.

In the study or examination of individual cases, the clinical psychologist seeks to realize four fundamental aims: 1. An adequate diagnosis or classification. He attempts to give a correct description of the nature of the mental deviations shown by his cases; he tries to determine whether they are specific or general, whether they affect native or acquired traits; he attempts to measure by standard objective tests the degree of deviation of various mental traits or of the general level of functioning; he seeks to arrive at a comprehensive clinical picture, to disentangle symptom-complexes and to reduce the disorders to various reaction types.

2. An analysis of the etiological background. His examination is bent not only on determining the present mental status of the case, but on discovering the causative factors or agents which have produced the deviations–whether these factors are physical, mental, social, moral, educational, environmental or hereditary. In order to arrive at a correct etiology, the psycho-clinician makes not only a cross-section analysis of the case, but also a longitudinal study of the evolution of the deviation or symptom-complex. Therefore, he does not limit himself merely to a psychological examination, but requires a dento-medical examination and a pedagogical, sociological and hereditary examination. The physical examination should be made by experts in dentistry and in the various specialties in the field of medicine. The psycho-clinicist, however, should be so trained in physical diagnosis that he can detect the chief physical disorders, so that he can properly refer his cases for expert physical examination.

3. A determination of the modification which the disorder has wrought in the behavior of the individual. He should determine what its consequences have been: what effects it has had upon his opinions, beliefs, thoughts, disposition, attitudes, interests, habits, conduct, capacity for adaptation, learning ability, capacity to acquire

certain kinds of knowledge or various accomplishments, or to do certain kinds of school work.   He should seek to locate the conflicts between instincts and habits which may have been caused by the deviations.

4. The determination of the degree of modifiabuity of the variations discovered. Can the deviations be corrected or modified, and if so to what extent and by what kinds of orthogenic measures?   A clinical psychologist is no less a scientific investigator than a consulting specialist; he diagnoses in order to prognose and prescribe. His aim, first and last, is eminently practical.

Basis Of Selection Of Cases

The clinical psychologist selects his cases not so much on the nature of the cause of the deviations (whether social, hereditary, physical, pedagogical or psychological) as on the nature of the deviations themselves, and the nature of the treatment. He is interested in cases which, first of all, depart from the limits of mental normality. Exceptional mentality, or, if you please, mental exceptionality is his first criterion. In the second place, he is interested in those cases in which the nature of the treatment– the process of righting the mental variations, of straightening out the deviations, the orthogenesis–is wholly or chiefly or partly educational.   In the term educational I include training of a hygienic, physiological (in Seguins sense), pedagogical, psycho-logical, sociological or moral character.

Geouping Of Cases It is thus evident that the clinical psychologist may group his cases into two main classes.

A. Those in which the mental variations are fundamental or primary, and the physical disabilities only accessory or sequential. With these cases the treatment must be primarily educational and only secondarily medical. What types of children are included in this group?

1. Feeble-minded children. Feeble-mindedness formerly was regarded as an active disorder–a disease–and was accordingly treated exclusively medically. The theory of causation was wrong and so the results were unsatisfactory. Since the year 1800 (Itard, the apostle to the feeble-minded) and particularly since the year 1837 (Seguin, the liberator of the feeble-minded), it has become increasingly apparent that feeble-mindedness is an arrest of development; and accordingly since that time the condition has primarily been treated educationally instead of medically. This change in point of view has revolutionized the treatment of the feeble-minded. The person who did most to ameliorate their condition is Seguin, whose method, almost entirely educational, has served as the model for the effective institutional work for the feeble-minded done since his day, although we have outgrown various details of his system. Moreover, it served as the chief inspiring force for the constructive orthogenic work done for the feebleminded within the last decade or so by Montessori. She, herself a physician, but with special training in psychology and pedagogy, tells us that in 1898, as a result of a careful study of the problem of feeble-mindedness she became persuaded that the problem was primarily a pedagogical and not a medical one. It is granted without question, of course, that there is a medical side to the care of the feeble-minded just as there is a medical side to the care of the normal child. Nay, owing to the heightened degree of susceptibility to disease and accidents found among the feebleminded, the medical side looms larger in the care of the feeble-minded than in the care of normals.

Indeed, no institution for the feeble-minded can be properly organized without an adequate staff of medical experts; but fundamentally the problem of ameliorating the sad lot of feeble-minded children is an educational one—their hygienic, pedagogical and moral improvement, as well as their elimination by the method of colonization or sterilization.

2. Retardates, technically so-called—of which there are probably on a conservative estimate 6,000,000 in the schools of the United States. Some of these are retarded (1) merely pedagogically in a relative sense—relative to an arbitrary curricular standard. Many children do not fit the standard, because the standard itself is off the norm. It is largely a case of a misfit curriculum instead of a misfit child. So far as this class of misfits is concerned, the problem is simply one of correct adjustment of the pedagogical demands of the curriculum.

A considerable percentage of the retardates, however, are retarded because of (2) genuine mental arrest of development. They are as truly arrested or deficient as the feeble-minded, but to a lesser extent. The difference is a quantitative and not a qualitative one, and the problem of correction consists fundamentally in providing a right educational regimen.

Then there is (3) a smaller proportion of retardates who are mentally retarded because of environmental handicaps, such as bad housing, home and neighborhood conditions, bad sanitation, lack of humidity, lack of pure air or excessive temperature in the schoolroom, vicious or illiterate surroundings, frequent moving or transfer, emigration which may cause linguistic maladaptation, etc. With such retardates the problem is partly sociological, partly hygienic and partly pedagogical.

We have a final group of children (4) who are mentally retarded because of some physical defect. With children of this type the problem is partly medical and partly educational. The first efforts made in behalf of such children should be medical and hygienic. Undoubtedly the removal of physical handicaps will restore some pupils to normal mentality, while in the case of other pupils the results will be negative. Unfortunately many of the studies in this field (see Chapter XV) have a questionable value because of the obvious, but evidently unconscious bias of the investigators. Some desire to show favorable results and, therefore, unconsciously select only the favorable cases; others are swayed by the opposite motive and accordingly tend to select the negative cases. Hence, at the present time we find considerable diversity of opinion as to the orthogenic influences of the correction of physical disorders. The opinion of John J. Cronin, M. D., probably approximates the truth:

The successes simply mean that a large number of children were perfect except for some one abnormality The alleviation of any single kind of physical handicap is merely one step towards the successful result sought, and many other factors must obtain before some measure of success is assured.

Likewise A. Kmi! Schmitt, M. D.: It should constantly be borne in mind that if every physical defect has been successfully removed the mental unbalance or defi- ciency can remain unaltered, inasmuch as it was primarily a mental defect and can be reached only by methods of education or psychological treatment.

While I am quite convinced that all mentally retarded children should undergo a careful physical examination, and that such physical corrective measures should be applied as are indicated by expert medical opinion, yet it needs to be reemphasized that the removal of a physical disability is frequently only the first step toward restoration. If the child has fallen behind pedagogically or mentally, he will in many cases need special pedagogical attention if he is to catch step with the class procession; moreover, after a certain critical age has been passed, the removal of physical obstructions exercises only a slight orthophrenic influence, and the reestablishment of effective mental functioning, if it can be done at all, will require the prolonged application of a special corrective pedagogy.

3. The supernormals. Both of the above types of children come on the minus side of the curve of efficiency. On the other side we find the plus deviates—the bright, brilliant, quick, gifted, talented, precocious children. These children may present no peculiarities on the physical side, if we except the type of nervously unstable, precocious children. With the healthy supernormal child the problem is almost entirely an educational one: the introduction of schemes of flexible grading; of fast, slow and normal sections, and of supernormal classes; providing special opportunities for doing specialized work, and a special pedagogy, which should probably be as largely negative as positive. If there is any one child in our scheme of public education which has been neglected more than any other, it is the child of unusual talents. A nation can do no higher duty by its subjects than to provide those conditions which will rescue its incipient geniuses from the dead-level of enforced mediocrity.

4. Speech defectives, particularly the 2 per cent (approximately) of stutterers and hspers who encumber our classes. In few fields of scientific research is it possible to find such astonishing diversity of so-called expert opinion as on the question of the causation of stuttering (or stammering). It is claimed to be a gastric, pneumo-gastric, lung, throat, lip, brain, hypoplastic, nervous and mental disorder. It is said to be a form of epilepsy, a form of hysteria and a form of mental strife, or repression, between latent and manifest mental contents. Moreover, few writers show such a consummate genius for self-contradiction as writers on stuttering. Before me lies a reprint of a recent dissertation on the Educational Treatment of Stuttering Children. The writer begins by saying that stuttering is a pathological condition, a disease, and that, therefore, its treatment belongs to a specialist on diseases. The disease appears, however, on the second page to be merely a purely functional neurosis, while on the last page the trouble is nothing more than a mental one, caused by influences acting on the mind. As a matter of fact, the treatment which the writer recommends is, through and through, educational and largely psychological. It consists of certain physical exercises, designed not so much to strengthen certain organs as to win the patients interest and restore his self-confidence; and certain psycho-therapeutic and hypnotic exercises.

Waiving for the time being the nature of the cause, we can agree on one thing; namely, that the methods of treating stuttering (and lisping) which have been proved effective are almost exclusively educational. Many of the neurotic symptoms (functional neuroses) found in the stutterer are the results of mental tension and will disappear with the correction of the stuttering.

5. Incipient psychotics, or children who show developmental symptoms of mental disorders or mental alienation. Here we meet with the same controversy between

the advocates, on the one hand, of a somatogenic theory, and, on the other hand, of a psychogenic theory of causation. While it must be admitted that many of the psychoses are certainly organic, others almost as certainly are functional and are produced by idiogenic factors (a view entertained by such well-known psychiatrists as Meyer, Freud, Janet, Dubois, Jones, Prince). Now, irrespective of whether the cause is chiefly physical or mental, it is being recognized by a number of the leading present-day psychiatrists that drug treatment for the majority of the insane, whether juvenile or adult, is secondary to the educational treatment. Instead of merely prescribing physical hygiene for the insane, leading alienists are now prescribing mental hygiene. The cure is being conceived in terms of a process of reeducation. Moreover, so far as concerns the mentally unstable child in the schools, the chief reliance is obviously on hygienic and educational guidance.

B. Cases in which the physical deviations are fundamental or primary, and the mental variations sequential, but the remedy partly or chiefly educational. Here we include malnutrition, rickets, marasmus, hypothyroidism, tuberculosis, heart trouble, chorea and similar diseases. In all of these the treatment must be primarily medical, although there should be a special temporary educational regimen for these children. This group also includes the blind and the deaf. But here the treatment is almost wholly educational. The physical defects are incurable, but the mental defects can be partly overcome by proper compensatory educational treatment. The epileptic also must be added to this group. Epilepsy is evidently an active disorder or disease process, although the pathology is wrapped in the deepest obscurity. The epileptics appear like purely medical cases. The medical aspect certainly is important, but the records show that only from 5 to 10 per cent are curable, and that the attacks can be as readily modified or regulated in most cases by proper hygienic treatment as by drug medication or surgical interference. To quote Montessori:

Benedickt, and following him, the principal authorities among medical specialists, are at present condemning the use of depressing bromides, which hide the attacks as an anesthetic hides pain, but do not cure them. The cure, says Benedickt, depends upon hygienic life in the open in order to absorb the poisons, and upon work, rationally measured and graded, provided, however, that the malady is still recent and has not assumed a chronic form. The treatment consists in educating them.

Even with these unfortunates, it can be said that the best results come from a proper medico-educational regime–colonization, outdoor employment, industrial schooling, bathing, etc.

Summary Of Important Conclusions

We are thus brought to the two following conclusions: 1. There is a set of unique facts–facts of individual mental variation–which no existing science has adequately treated. It is with these facts that the work of the clinical psychologist is concerned. Just as psychology became an independent science by demonstrating that it possessed a legitimate claim to a unique world of facts, so clinical psychology is ready to make her declaration of independence and dedicate herself to the investigation of a body of facts–facts of individual mental variation–not hitherto adequately handled by any existing science. It is concerned with the study of individual cases of deviate mentality, particularly with those types which are amenable to improvement or correction by psycho-educational processes.

2. The proper handling of these cases, whether for purposes of examination, recommendation or prescription, can only be done by a psycho-educational specialist who possesses the training indicated in Chapter II.

The Relations Of Clinical Psychology– Some
Affirmations And Denials

There are a number of sciences with which clinical psychology is, will be or should be closely related, but which are not synonymous with clinical psychology.

1. Clinical psychology is not the same as psychiatry (and psychopathology). The typical alienist is concerned with the study and treatment of mental disorders (technically called psychoses); the clinical psychologist, on the other hand, is concerned particularly (though not solely) with the study of plus and minus deviations from normal mentality. The alienist works chiefly with adults, the clinical psychologist with children. Few alienists possess any expert knowledge of the literature bearing on child or educational psychology, mental deficiency, retardation or acceleration, stuttering or lisping, special pedagogy or psycho-clinical methods of testing. An alienist accordingly is not to be considered a specialist on the mentally exceptional child in the schools unless, indeed, he has supplemented his general medical and psychiatric education with a technical study of the psychological and educational aspects of the problem. The alienist of the future will certainly have to secure a different preparation from that now furnished in the medical schools, if he is to enter the field of pedagogic child study.

Before me lies the report of the department of medical inspection of a large school system. Six hundred retarded children were examined in this department, which is in charge of an alienist, who, as I am told, is an expert on the questions of adult insanity, but who has no specialized preparation in the psychology and pedagogy of the mentally defective child. Of these children 49.7 per cent are recorded as feeble-minded. Applying this figure to the 6,000,000 retardates of the public schools of the country, we get a total feeble-minded school population of 3,000,-000. This figure, it need scarcely be said, is monstrously absurd. It is fully ten times too large. Feeble-mindedness and backwardness in children, it must be said, are distinct problems from mental alienation, and require for their satisfactory handling a specialist on mentally deviating children. A high-grade feeble-minded child can not be identified merely by some rule-of-thumb system of intelligence tests. Feeble-mindedness involves more than a given degree of intelligence retardation. At the same time, lest I be misunderstood, it should be specially stated that psychiatry and clinical psychology will be mutually helped by a closer union. Clinical psychology has many important facts and a valuable experimental technique to offer to psychopathology, and psychopathology in turn is able to contribute facts of great value, and more particularly an effective clinical method of examination, to clinical psychology. As the idiogenic conception of the causation of various psychoses wins greater recognition, clinical psychology will become more and more indispensable to the psychiatrist and psychopathologist. It is also certain that the efficiency of the clinical psychologist will be greatly increased by a study of mental alienation–not a study of texts on psychiatry, but a first-hand study in institutional residence of individual cases. Any one intending to do psycho-clinical work with mentally deficient children certainly should spend at least a year or two in residence at institutions for feeble-minded, epileptic and alienated children. The clinical psychologist should be prepared to recognize cases of incipient mental disorder, so that he will be enabled to select these cases and refer them to a psychiatric or psychopathic specialist for further examination.

2. Clinical psychology is not neurology. There are important neurological aspects involved in the study of mentally exceptional children. Mental arrest can be largely expressed in terms of neurological arrest, and a clinical psychologist should have a first-hand knowledge of nerve signs and a practical acquaintance with the methods of neurological diagnosis. His knowledge of neurology should be sufficient to enable him to pick out suspected nervous cases and refer them for expert examination by a neurologist. However, it must be emphasized that neurology touches only one side–though an extremely important side–of the problem of exceptional mentality.

3. Clinical psychology is not synonymous with general medicine. The average medical practitioner certainly knows far less about the facts of mental variation in children than either the psychiatrist or neurologist or even the classroom teacher. This fact should occasion no surprise when it is stated that the study of psychology as a science has been practically ignored in medical curricula throughout the country. The clinical psychologist, however, as I have already said, should be able to detect the chief physical defects found in school children, so that if the laboratory of the clinical psychologist assumes the function of a clearing house for the exceptional child he may be able to refer all suspected medical cases to proper medical clinics for expert examination and treatment.

4. Clinical psychology is not pediatrics. To be sure, the pediatrician deals with children. But his attention is focused on the physical abnormalities of infants; his interest in the phenomena of mental exceptionality is liable to be incidental or per-functory. In fact, one may read some texts on pediatrics from cover to cover without so much as arriving at a suspicion that there is a body of unique facts converging on the phenomena of departure from the limits of mental normality which require intensive, specialized, expert study and diagnosis. So far as the physical ailments or disabilities of young children are concerned the pediatrician is in a position to render valuable service to the psycho-clinicist; likewise so far as concerns the mental deviations of children the psycho-clinicist is able to render valuable aid to the pediatrician. But one must not confuse pediatrics with clinical psychology.

5. Clinical psychology is not the same as introspective, educational or experimental psychology. It differs from these in its method, standpoint and conceptions. While the clinical psychologist should be grounded in introspective and, especially, experi-mental, educational and child psychology, expertness in these branches of psychology does not in itself confer expertness in practical psycho-clinical work. Such expertness comes only from a technical training in clinical psychology and from a first-hand prolonged study by observation, or experiment, or test of various kinds of mentally exceptional children, particularly the feeble-minded, the psychopathic, the epileptic and the retarded. The skilled specialist in experimental or educational psychology or experimental pedagogy is no more qualified to clinically examine mental cases, than

is the skilled zoologist, physiologist or anatomist able to clinically examine physical cases. Clinical work, both in psychology and medicine, requires clinical training. The assumption that any psychologist or educationist (and, forsooth, any physician or medical inspector) is qualified to do successful psycho-clinical work, after learning how to administer a few mental tests, is preposterous and fraught with the gravest consequences. Clinical psychology can have no standing in the professions as long as we permit this absurd notion to prevail.

CHAPTER IV

THE FUNCTIONS OF THE PSYCHOLOGICAL CLINIC1

The psychological clinic is a very modern American creation. The first clinic was started in a small way only eighteen years ago in the University of Pennsylvania. The growth of these clinics was at first very slow, but during the last three or four years they have rapidly multiplied (see statistics in Chapters II and XVIII). Besides the clinical psychologists there are a considerable number of teachers, nurses, physicians and others who are tyros or amateurs in psychology and psycho-educational therapeutics, who are testing children in schools, juvenile courts and institutions, but the work of most of these amateurs can scarcely be considered in speaking of clinical psychology or of psycho-clinical technicians. Professor OShea has recently predicted (School Review, April, 1913, p. 285) that within a decade there will be a psychological clinic in every community with 2,500 or more school children. That may be so if we agree to call any place in which mental tests may be given a psychological clinic. The psychologist, however, would probably just as strenuously object to having these testing stations called psychological clinics as the psychiatrists would object to having them called psychiatric clinics.

i Reprinted, with alterations and additions, from The Medical Record, September 20, 1913.

The development of the psychological clinic has come in response to a demand for more accurate psychological diagnosis—and this is the first function of the psychological clinic which I wish to discuss.

1. Expert diagnosis of mentally deviating cases and expert prescription and consultation. The central aim of the psychological clinic is psychological diagnosis and consultation and advice in regard to mental cases, particularly children. In other words, the aim of the clinic is essentially practical. The clinical psychologist is engaged in serious work and not mere play. His interests are not confined to the theoretical or academic. His efforts are in the field of human conservation, individual orthogenesis and remedial philanthropy. All the psychological clinics, so far as I know, are doing philanthropic work. The psycho-clinicist is concerned with the proper mental hygiene, the correct educational classification and the skilled pedagogical training of the mentally exceptional child.2 The aim, in one word, of his basic effort is orthogenesis (particularly that phase of orthogenesis to which I have applied the term orthophrenics).

It is rapidly becoming generally recognized that the nature and extent of mental variations or abnormalities cannot be adequately ascertained by the method of mere observation or inspection, or by the ill-adapted methods of specialists in the fields of medicine. Many mental deviations are so subtle that they entirely escape common obser vation. Common observation, moreover, rarely penetrates so far as to reveal the cause of the defect. Before the advent of experimental and clinical psychology, mental diagnosis was based almost wholly upon common observation, if we except the pedagogical tests of the schools and a few tests of the trained psychopathologists. Many mental variations or abnormalities, however, are harder to get at by mere observation than many physical disorders. Many of the latter can be detected by the methods of so-called inspection, auscultation, palpation, percussion or mensuration. Nevertheless, the skilled physician does not depend solely upon these methods of diagnosis, but has developed a more refined laboratory technique, consisting of radiographic and microscopic inspection, serum reaction tests, mechanical and electrical tests of nervous sensitivity and response, etc. Likewise the psychologist within the last decade or two has developed a new science, which is now usually called clinical psychology, and a delicate, controlled laboratory technique. This technique sometimes involves the use of the most delicate apparatus for precisely measuring the functional capacity of the various sensory, motor and intellectual processes. At other times it involves the use of less elaborate testing appliances. For purposes of practical mental diagnosis the tendency at the present time is to make a more extensive use of the simpler forms of testing devices, such as test blanks, form and construction boards, set questions and graded scales of intellectual, motor and socio-industrial capacity. The most popular of the developmental scales is the Binet-Simon scale of intelligence, which consists of a series of tests (sixty-two in the 1908 series if ages one and two are included) gradually increasing in difficulty and arranged in age-steps. There are from three to eight tests in each of the first thirteen years of life in the 1908 series. Many of these tests are extremely simple. To illustrate: a child who can follow visually a lighted match moved in front of his face, who can grasp and handle a block placed in his hand and who can grasp a suspended cylinder is credited with a mentality of one year. A child who can state his sex, who can recognize and name common objects, such as a knife, penny and key, who can repeat three numerals heard once, and who can designate the longer or shorter of two lines differing by one centimeter, is rated as four years old mentally. The scale is constructed merely to test the stage of the intelligence, and not emotional or motor development. The stimulus to the development of this scale was the enactment in Paris in 1904 of an educational measure which required the individual examination of all mentally defective children. At first this work was left to the medical inspectors, but it soon became evident that they could do no more than they already had done in the way of medical inspection–namely, detect physical defects and diseases. It became evident that there was no scientific method of examining mentally exceptional children in existence, and hence Binet and his assistant, Simon, set about to establish normal mental age-norms by examining certain pedagogically average children in the elementary schools of Paris (children of the working classes from the poorer sections). They arranged certain tests in age-steps, and it is this arrangement of the tests into age-norms that has made the tests so popular. This scale is of considerable value for grading intelligence, but it has recently been subjected, particularly in this country, to indiscriminate exploitation and popularization, so that many erroneous ideas have arisen in respect to its real function or the real function of psychological examinations in general. Almost everything that has been written about the Binet scale (until very recently) has been in the nature of praise–both judicious and extravagant, rather more of the latter. I think it is worth while, therefore, to call attention to some of the current misconceptions and to sound a few warning notes, regarding psychological examinations.

2 It would seem better to call the psychological clinics in the schools psycho-educational clinict, just because of the fact that the character of the diagnosis attempted is distinctly both psychological and educational, and because the aims of the diagnosis are distinctly the scientific pedagogical training, correct educational classification and mental hygiene of the educationally exceptional child.

1. Very many persons who are not trained mental examiners seem to think that the Binet testing is all there is to a mental examination; that it is the only serviceable method we have; that it is the Alpha and Omega of psycho-clinical work. Indeed, that is about all there is to the mental examinations conducted by amateurs. This is a preposterous notion. It is quite possible to give from one hundred to five hundred other valuable psychological tests in the examination of a case. Of any one single scheme of testing, the Binet scale is probably at present our most valuable instrument, but it is only one among many diagnostic devices at the command of the trained psychological examiner.

2. Another fact that needs to be emphasized again and again is that simply putting a child through the Binet scale does not tell one very much about his real mental idiosyncrasies, the peculiarities of his mental constellations, his particular shorts or longs. It does not give us a differential diagnosis of type or of cause or a prognosis of outcome, except in certain very obvious cases. What the Binet scale does is to give one a preliminary, rough or approximate rating of the childs mental level. If the child is in the schools and has been carefully classified, we already have, through the pedagogical tests and grading, an approximation of his mental standing–often inaccurate, to be sure, just as the Binet rating sometimes is. All that can be expected from the Binet testing by persons who are not expert psychological examiners is usually merely an independent confirmation of the pedagogical rating already assigned the child in the schools. This may be of value. Sometimes, however, the Binet rating will be at variance with the teachers rating, and I have known of cases in which teachers maintain that, because they have been coming into contact with the child and have been studying its mentality, day by day for months or years, their judgment in regard to the childs mental standing is more reliable than the judgment of a teacher, nurse or physician who has spent only a few minutes with the child in putting him through the Binet tests.

It is doubtful whether the Binet tests will afford to an amateur in clinical psychology deeper insight into the operation of the childs mind than the pedagogical tests afford to the observant teacher. Certainly the Binet testing of itself will not confer any remarkable insight or comprehension upon any person using the scale. If he already has accurate knowledge and deep insight into mental mechanisms, the Binet testing will better enable him to use his skill, but without prior erudition or technical skill, the Binet testing is not a magical something that will transform a person into a mental wizard and give him occult powers to penetrate into a childs mental peculiarities and reveal the treatment he requires. The Binet testing is not a device for supplying brains or a substitute for a technical university course. It is just as preposterous to think that one can become a skilled mental examiner merely by reading books on mental tests, as to think that one can become a skilled surgeon by simply reading books on surgery. A clinical psychologist uses certain formal tests merely as the physician feels the pulse or takes the temperature. A physician must know a good deal more than how to take the pulse or temperature in order to physically diagnose his cases. Because of the large number of mental defectives in the schools, we shall always need a number of assistants to give certain psychological tests, but their function is that of the nurse in relation to the physician (see Chapters IX and X).

3. In the third place, the notion has gotten abroad that the Binet scale is infallible or amazingly accurate. I have attempted to show that both of these statements are false, by minutely analyzing the results of the daily application of the scale for eight months to epileptics. Since these results have either been ignored3 or criticised because they have been based upon the testing of epileptics, I have used precisely the same method in giving the tests to public school clinic cases. Here there is space to give in briefest form the results merely of a threefold method of testing the scale with the public school cases which have been examined in the psycho-educational clinic of the School of Education, University of Pittsburgh. (For criticisms of the tests growing out of their use with epileptics, see Chapters VI, VII and VIII.)

First, I have compared the Binet rating or classification with the pedagogical classification of the consecutive cases which were thoroughly examined. Age six to seven was considered as the normal age for Grade I. Briefly, the Binet rating gave 80.5 per cent as retarded, 2.7 per cent as exactly at age and 15.7 per cent as accelerated (based on 184 cases), while the pedagogical rating gave 89.4 per cent as retarded, 8.5 per cent as on time, and only 2 per cent as accelerated.

3 One of my recent critics ascribes the inaccuracy of the Binet work to the testers and not to the scale. My investigations, which have revealed the inaccuracy of the scale, have not yet been experimentally refuted; they cannot be refuted by bare denial.

Second, I have determined in units of years the gross amount of mental and pedagogical retardation and acceleration of all those children tested whose school records were such as to make it possible to determine the degree of pedagogical deviation (134 cases). The mental variations were recorded in years and fractional parts of years by the point system used in the Binet scale; and the pedagogical deviations were determined more or less according to the age-grade method. The difference between the point in the course where the child was at the time of the examination and where he should have been according to his age was determined in years and fractions of years. Graph I shows that the gross amount of Binet retardation amounted to 343.3 years as against 359.3 years of pedagogical retardation; and the corresponding figures for acceleration were 24.4 years as against 6 years. By both of the above methods the retardation is seen to be less by the Binet than the pedagogical rating, while the amount of acceleration is decidedly more by the Binet than by the pedagogical rating.

These methods of comparison, however, are subject to criticism, and I shall, therefore, pass on to the third and more important method. According to this, all the consecutive cases which had been thoroughly examined (184 cases) were first classified strictly according to the Binet system, with the exception that only those who were retarded more than three years were classified as feebleminded, while children less than nine years chronologically, who were retarded two years or over or less than three years were not so classified. It is thus apparent that I have classified less cases by the Binet tests as feeble-minded

SIMOH flhD PEDAGOGICAL
TION SHOWH BY 154 PITTSBURGH
SCHOOL CASES.

Retardation. Acceleration.
GRAPH I.
fl-S.
Peda-yoyical.
24.4 yrs.
B-S.
6./r5.
Pedagogical.
CLASSIFICATION OF COr/SECUT/VE CLIn/C CASES.
Psychal Clinic, Univ. of Pitt. Based on the Binet Testing (1308 scale).
GRAPH II.
/and3X 11,4 7.0 3.2 1.0 17.3 9,2.
2.7,
Feeble -Minded,
27.7
Retarded 60.5
Accelerated
Normal
CLASSIFICATIOn OF CONSECUTIVE CLIHIC C/JSES.
Psijchoi Clinic. Univ. of Pin.

Based on all the Available Facts.
3ft 2 X
GRAPH III.
tl.6, a i/ ".
9.9X
e 8
C 64
.5 I i. iy.
-fri o " 2 11111
, S Q iijM
"

Feeble-Minded 17.0 p 3
Subnormal 77.3 than the Binet system permits. In the second place, I have gathered all available data on the cases by other psychological tests and by other inquiries, and have based my own diagnoses on a careful study of all the facts thus secured. A comparison of graphs II and III shows that there is a certain degree of correspondence between the two classifications. The Binet rating gives 4.7 per cent more super-normals and 2.6 per cent more subnormals. The most important difference, however, is in the number

of feeble-minded and backward cases. The Binet rating gives 10 per cent more feeble-minded and from 15 to 20 per cent less backward cases than the final estimate. If we also consider the pupils who were retarded three years (or two years if under nine years of age) as feebleminded, the discrepancy would be perceptibly increased. It is entirely clear to my mind that 27 per cent of these children (as shown by the Binet tests on the above basis) were not feeble-minded. I am entirely clear on the proposition that the Binet rating in the hands of mere Binet testers will give us entirely too many feeble-minded cases. This conclusion seems to be abundantly confirmed by recent reports from Binet testers in the public schools. To cite only two instances: In one city 49.7 per cent of 600 retarded children (unselected retardates so far as I can gather) and in another 80 per cent of about 300 admissions to special classes, were classified as feeble-minded. In the latter city, the astonishing statement is made that this number includes only 15 per cent of the subnormals in the school system who should be in special classes. What a terrible focus of feeble-minded degeneracy this city must be! Apply this same ratio of feeble-mindedness to the 6,000,000 retarded children in the schools of the country, and we get a feeble-minded school population of from 3,000,000 to 4,800,000. Of course, this is ludicrously absurd. Even if the cases examined were rather extreme, the figures are still entirely extravagant. Very probably not more than from one-fourth to one-half of these retardates were feeble-minded. I will venture the assertion after years of teaching in the public schools and clinically examining public school cases, that the oft-repeated statement, that 2 per cent of the general school population is defective (if by this is meant feeble-minded), exaggerates the real situation. The actual number is probably about 1 per cent. Incidentally I may say that the percentage of feeble-minded found among prostitutes by Binet testers is also too large.

It is important to emphasize that so far as concerns the diagnosis of individual cases (rather than the statistical classification of homogeneous groups of cases), no system of formal intelligence tests yet devised can be used as an infallible measuring rod of intelligence. It is quite certain that if the psychological diagnosis of school children is to be intrusted to laymen, whether teachers, nurses or specialists other than psychological experts, some very inaccurate and pernicious diagnoses will be made of individual cases. In my own laboratory my diagnoses of individual cases are often quite at variance with the Binet findings. I have sometimes diagnosed cases with only a slight degree of intellectual arrest as feeble-minded because that is the prognosis (one two-year old who will probably remain at two, tested normal), while I have sometimes diagnosed others with a very considerable degree of deficiency as merely backward.

Thus, to cite only two cases: A is a gentleman, twenty-eight years of age, who has spent five years in university work. He has been diagnosed as a moron, as a degenerate, as a case of constitutional inferiority, as a case with paranoid trends, etc. According to the Binet tests he was clearly feeble-minded, as he measured only 11.4 years in the 1908 series. Anyone knowing no more about the technique of psychological examination than the Binet-Simon scale would at once have classified him as feebleminded, but he did not impress me at all as being feebleminded. His appearance, speech and conduct suggested the polished and cultured gentleman. Accordingly, I put him through approximately thirty sets of mental tests (other than twenty-five individual Binet tests) and thirty moral tests. These tests demonstrated that there was a considerable difference in the strength of his different mental traits. Some traits were on the twelve-year plane, some on the fifteen-year, some on the sixteen-year, and some on the adult plane. In some mental tests he did as well as college men. He passed correctly practically all of the moral tests. Here is a case showing more or less deficiency in respect to various mental traits; but the man is not feeble-minded, contrary to the Binet rating (a sexual complex was at the root of his trouble).

B is an attractive girl of considerable culture, age seventeen, studying Latin, history, algebra and English in the tenth grade of a private school. She entered school at the age of seven, but has attended rather irregularly because of precarious health. Her school work is not very satisfactory. The most marked mental defect noticed by her teacher is her forgetfulness. By the Binet tests she would be rated as feeble-minded, since she graded only 11.4 years. But no one but a psychological tyro or a mere Binet tester would so classify her. (Her condition borders on psychasthenia.)

While intelligence defect is the most obvious trait of feeble-mindedness, there are other clinical and developmental phases which must be taken into consideration before a positive diagnosis can be pronounced in many cases. It is a hazardous and unscientific procedure to permit amateurs to brand children as feeble-minded solely because they show a considerable degree of intelligence retardation; it is a serious matter always to classify any child as feeble-minded. Parents ought to have a right to demand an independent examination by a competent psycho-educational specialist before a child can be placed in a special class. In London, parents, by statutory right, may demand an examination of children placed in special classes every six months. The London County Council has recently appointed an expert psychologist to mentally examine school children. In Paris, a special examination for mentally defective children is enjoined by law. But this examination, at least the final diagnosis, should be made by a specialist whose verdict is authoritative. It is certain that parents will be far more ready to accept a mental diagnosis if it is made by a competent psychological expert. In some cities considerable friction has arisen because parents and teachers have not always been willing to accept the diagnosis of feeble-mindedness made by teachers, nurses or physicians who are amateurs in psychological work. As already stated, learning how to give a few tests is no substitute for a prolonged course in psycho-clinical diagnosis. Mere tests, whether in psychology or medicine, are not always conclusive. Even positive or negative serum reactions sometimes prove nothing. The psychologist, just like the physician, must base his diagnosis on both laboratory and clinical studies. The tests used by the trained psycho-clinicist are invaluable in that they enable him to arrive at a more accurate clinical pic ture of the mental condition of his case. But once the mental condition has been determined, there remains the more difficult task of locating the causes of the trouble and prescribing a differential treatment for each case. The accurate determination of the causation can only be made by investigating the personal and family history of the case; the hereditary factors, birth condition, record of diseases, physical and mental development, school history, mental habits, social heredity, environments and present physical and mental condition. In order to secure all the desired data, the psycho-clinicist should be able to command the services of social workers, nurses, medical specialists, trained helpers to assist in some of the formal testing and record and filing clerks. Some of the university psycho-educational clinics have a physician on their staff; others have a staff of consulting physicians in the medical school or affiliated hospitals or dispensaries.

To repeat: the first function of the psychological clinic is to make an accurate diagnosis of mentally deviating children, in order to give expert advice in regard to the childs mental hygiene (and in regard to the physical treatment in so far as this is orthophrenic in its bearings) and educational care and training.

II. The second purpose of the psychological clinic is to serve as a clearing house for mentally exceptional cases. The psychological clinic has no special interest in cases which are not mentally or pedagogically exceptional or abnormal. Moreover, its interests thus far have been largely, if not entirely, restricted to juvenile cases. The psychiatric clinic, on the other hand, deals more largely with adult than juvenile cases; and technically these cases are psychotic or incipiently psychotic in character. The psychological (i. e., the psycho-educational) clinic aims to serve as a focal point where the data bearing on mentally and educationally exceptional children may be brought together for careful analysis and collation, and where the cases may be finally disposed of—some to institutions, some to special classes, some to hospitals or medical clinics or private practitioners and some to special courses of corrective pedagogics. Some psychological clinics also conduct medico-pedagogical schools. They conduct classes during the regular or summer terms and offer special work in corrective pedagogics (particularly in speech training). Many of the psychological clinics in this country which are properly organized have become clearing houses of this character for juvenile cases in the schools and courts. Thus in Seattle the university psycho-clinicist is also the consulting psychologist to the public schools and the juvenile court. He also spends part of his time examining cases throughout the state. In Minneapolis the university psychologists are doing work both for the public schools and for the juvenile court. Here the juvenile court has a room equipped for the examination work in the court house. In New Haven the Yale clinical psychologist, who is in the department of education, but who has his laboratory in the medical school, does what psycho-clinical work there is done in the city. In Baltimore the study of mentally abnormal children is undertaken by the clinical psychologist, who is (or was until his death) connected with the Phipps Psychiatric Clinic. The University of Kansas examines cases at Lawrence and elsewhere in the state. The clinic in the State University of Iowa also aims to do state-wide work. The clinic in the School of Education, University of Pittsburgh, is examining cases not only from Pittsburgh, but also from the surrounding towns and country.

III. The third function of the psycho-clinicist is research, particularly with a view to increasing and perfecting diagnostic tests and to extending our knowledge of the nature, causes and treatment of mental abnormalities. Owing to our ignorance in this field, the need for systematic research is paramount.

IV. A fourth function of the psycho-clinic comprises education and propaganda—the dissemination of reliable information and knowledge regarding the condition and needs of the mentally abnormal classes. This is done through the offering of lecture and clinical courses, the publication of memoirs and investigations, the conducting of demonstration clinics, etc. There is constant need, e. g., to develop a sympathetic and enlightened public opinion in regard to the needs of the unreached children in the public schools, in order that they may be properly classified and segregated, so that they may receive the pedagogical training which befits their peculiarities. There is need for enlightened public agitation right here in Pittsburgh, to the end that facilities may be provided for the large army of subnormal school children in our public schools. Over 10 per cent of all the elementary pupils in the Pittsburgh public schools are retarded three years or more. It is safe to say that one-half of this 10 per cent or about 3,000 pupils should be in special classes instead of in the regular, ungraded, anemic or tubercular classes. And yet Pittsburgh today does not have a single special class in which differentiated training is provided for feeble-minded and backward children. It is the one city of its class in the United States without special classes for these children. In March, 1911, there were 319 cities in the country which had established classes for mentally defective and backward children (the former including epileptic classes and the latter those in which special teachers are employed to assist slow pupils). This is an entirely new phase of educational work in Pittsburgh, where it must be organized from the very beginning. (See note following Chapter XIX.)

One special class was started during the school year 1913-1914.

CHAPTER V

THE DISTINCTIVE CONTRIBUTION OF THE

PSYCHO-EDUCATIONAL CLINIC TO THE

SCHOOL HYGIENE MOVEMENT1 It is only in the twentieth century that we have come to recognize that the conservation of school children involves more than inspection for physical diseases and defects, more than medical treatment and physical hygiene, more than the provision of school lunches, sanitary drinking fountains, schoolhouses properly regulated in regard to temperature, fresh air and humidity, open-air classes for the tubercular and anemic and special classes for the crippled, deaf and blind. It is only within the last few years that the laity, and also very many of the experts, have so much as suspected that there is a realm of mental orthogenesis (or orthophrenics) independent of, although supplementary to, the realm of physical orthogenesis (to which I have previously applied the term orthosomatics); that there is a psycho-educational type of school inspection entirely different from physical, medical or dental inspection; and that there is a sphere of corrective pedagogics and psycho-educational therapeutics paralleling the sphere of dento-medical care and the surgical removal or correction of physical handicaps.

1 Delivered before the session on Mental Hygiene and the Hygiene of the Mentally Abnormal Child, at the Fourth International Congress on School Hygiene, Buffalo, August 87, 1913.

How loath the human mind is to recognize or sanction new movements may be best indicated by the fact that while this International Congress has a section devoted to school inspection (or health supervision), it appears from the announcements that the connotation of the words school inspection is confined to physical inspection (medical and dental), although numerous theses2 have been presented in the public prints during a number of years to show that there is a psycho-educational type of inspection radically different from dento-medical inspection, and although this type of inspection is now an accomplished fact in many of the leading centers of educational endeavor throughout the country (see Chapters II and XVIII). It is evident, therefore, that we must extend the connotation of the term school inspection so that it will include three distinct phases: medical, dental and psycho-educational.

The clinical psycho-educationist performs certain functions which no other specialist had previously been trained to perform. The pedagogue, even though he be amply trained, was merely prepared to instruct, educate and discipline children, but had no qualifications for making anything but the crudest psychological and educational diagnoses. He was in no sense a clinicist. The pediatrician knew much about the physical diseases of young children and a good deal about the diseases of older children; but his knowledge of childrens mental and educational deviations was limited to the merest generalities, and his knowledge of the examination technique of the psychological laboratory and of educational methodology and corrective pedagogy was extremely meager or practically nil. The neurologists and psychopathologists were versed in the nervous disorders of children and adults, and they knew a good deal about the phenomena of disordered or alienated mentality; but they knew far less about the minor forms of mental and pedagogical variation which more frequently occur in exceptional school children, and they had made little, if any, technical study of educational, experimental and clinical psychology, of child study, of the principles of teaching and of the differential pedagogic treatment required by each type of mentally deviating child. Likewise the ordinary psychological expert knew a good deal about experimental and physiological psychology and more or less about educational psychology and child study; but usually he had no professional training in elementary methods or special pedagogics, he had no training in clinical technique and he lacked that first-hand experience with cases which is essential in order to become skilled in diagnosis.

2 Thus articles written by the author in 1909 (Medical and Psychological Inspection of School Children, The American School Master, p. 435), in 1911 (The New Clinical Psychology and the Psycho-Clinidst, Journal of Educational Psychology, p. 191, 191) and in 1913 (Clinical Psychology: What It Is and What It Is Not, Science, p. 895; The Functions of the Psychological Clinic, Medical Record, September; Re-averments Respecting Psycho-Clinical Norms and Scales of Development, Psychological Clinic, p. 89).

Here, then, was a field of diagnosis for which the existing types of specialists, whether medical, psychological or educational, had practically no scientific preparation whatever. But this gap, the existence of which is now quite obvious to the intelligent observer, is being rapidly filled by the development of psychological or psycho-educational clinics. To America belongs the chief honor for constructive achievement in this field of applied psychology. In America we are rapidly developing a new type of psychologist or educationist trained in psycho-educational diagnosis and orthogenesis.

With the rapid multiplication of the psychological clinics during the last few years, there has developed a feeling in the medical profession that the clinical psychologist is encroaching upon a field preempted by, and held sacred to, the physician. This fear, however, is entirely without foundation. The work of the clinical psychologist

(i. e., the psycho-educational clinicist) and the medical man are not competitive or duplicative, but supplementary and correlative. To be sure, the clinical psychologist (psycho-educational clinicist) wants his cases medically and dentally examined in order that he may more accurately interpret his findings, but he leaves this work to the medical and dental specialists. If his clinic is well endowed, he will have a medical specialist or a number of medical specialists on his staff; otherwise he will utilize medical consultants from the dispensaries, hospitals and medical schools. The educational clinicist seeks all the medical data available on his cases precisely as he seeks all the sociological, hereditary, pedagogical, psychological and anthropometric facts that he can secure. But all these data are merely contributory to his chief purpose: the interpretation of the mental and educational peculiarities, abnormalities, reductions or intensifications revealed by his psychological and educational tests and analyses. And the purpose of an accurate interpretation of the psychological and educational symptoms is, in turn, to enable him to prescribe appropriate orthogenic treatment. This may consist in giving advice to the parent or teacher regarding the proper mental hygiene of the child and regarding its proper educational classification and pedagogical training, or it may consist in referring the case to the dispensary, hospital or a private practitioner for medical, dental or surgical care. In any case, the function of the psycho educational clinic is distinctly orthophrenic; namely, the righting or correction of the mental functions which are deviating or abnormal, either by the removal of physical handicaps or by proper mental and educational treatment; the stimulation by appropriate stimuli of functions which are slowed down or retarded, and the placing of the child in the right educational classification or environment, so that he may attain with the least expenditure of energy and the least amount of friction to his maximal potential.

The clinic strives to determine what are the inherent mental and educational peculiarities and what the inherent strength of various mental functions in the child; whether he is only apparently or genuinely abnormal, subnormal or supernormal; in which mental planes he is deficient and in which functions he is talented. But always the purpose of this detailed psycho-educational analysis is to furnish that insight which will enable the psychologist to place his case in the right place in the educational system, or to so adjust the educative materials and methods that they will minister effectively to the childs peculiar needs.

From what I have said, it is evident that the interest of the psycho-educational clinicist is in children who are mentally and educationally unusual and who can be helped by special psychological or educational treatment. This group includes, among other types, supernormal, bright, backward, feeble-minded, epileptic, psychasthenic, neurotic, speech-defective and morally and emotionally unstable children.

At the University of Pittsburgh we are conducting a free dispensary psycho-educational clinic, to which the above and other types of children, including child prodigies, children with alexia, agraphia and motor defects but without corresponding intellectual impairment, have been brought by parents, teachers, nurses, physicians and social and settlement workers. Of a limited number of consecutive examinees (the first 184 who were thoroughly examined) which I have tabulated, 11 per cent were classified as bright or supernormal, 11 per cent as normal and 77.9 per cent as subnormal. Most of the subnormals were backward; namely, 39.2 per cent of the entire number examined. Seventeen per cent of all the cases were classified as feebleminded, 11.6 per cent as border cases and 9.9 per cent as merely retarded. Eight and eight-tenths per cent were classified as morons, 6.6 per cent as imbeciles and .5 per cent as idiots. While very few of the feeble-minded belonged to any special type, there were two Mongolians, one cretin, one paralytic and one case of infantilism. The average amount of time devoted to the study of these cases was about one and one-half hours, while the maximum time given to any one case was over twenty hours. This case had been variously and fallaciously diagnosed as a moron, a moral imbecile, a degenerate and a mild paranoiac, but the mental factors which were found to be responsible for his abnormal behavior pointed to an entirely different diagnosis.

Some of the advice which had been given to parents concerning many of these cases would be termed ludicrous, were it not that it was actually tragic. Parents had been told by so-called experts, not to bother about their child as he was all right; not to worry, because the child would outgrow his trouble when he attained the age of six or seven, or thirteen or fourteen. In consequence practically all of these cases, which proved to be utterly hopeless so far as concerns restoration to normality, had been educationally neglected for years. They had wasted their childhood in the regular grades in the vain endeavor to do work for which they were utterly unfitted. Because of their inability to advance they had either been neglected in despair by the teachers or they had unduly monopolized the teachers time and robbed the normal pupils of the attention which by right was theirs, or they had been promoted irrespective of their deserts merely to relieve the room of an intolerable burden. The crime was not the pupils or the teachers, but societys. Society still complacently tolerates many a school system which utterly lacks the requisite machinery for the scientific psycho-educational classification of its educationally exceptional children, but it also must be conceded that one of the stumbling-blocks to progess in work with mentally abnormal children is the schools themselves. During the past year I have had the interesting experience of having several teachers report to me that they wanted to send cases to the clinic for examination, but the principals refused permission. The principals said: The children are all right; we will leave well enough alone, and proceed as we have done before. The fault is not with the children but with the inefficient teachers.

And now an interesting point is this: two parents brought me two cases which the principal had refused to send. Both of these children proved to be imbeciles. And yet the omniscient principal had said that they were all right and that the fault was the teachers. As a general proposition the teachers who work daily with the pupils can gauge their mentality more accurately than many principals or superintendents.

The moral of my story is simply this: just as the schools now pedagogically examine children as a matter of course, of legal right and of routine, in order properly to grade and promote them, so must the schools as a matter of legal right and as a matter of fixed routine, psychologically examine all mentally unusual children, so that they may be more accurately mentally and educationally classified and diagnosed. Only thus can we economically and scientifically train all the children of all the people. Every large school system should employ a psycho-educational specialist who is as thoroughly trained in this work as the best medical, neurological or psychiatric specialists are trained in their work.

Discussion following the reading of the above paper.

In answer to Dr. Ira S. Wiles remarks:

Under ideal conditions we ought to subject every school child to a psycho-educational examination at the time that it enters school for the first time, and periodically thereafter in case it does not develop normally. But I do not advocate this in practice, because to carry out such a program of work would require larger staffs of experts than the taxpayers will be ready to support. I do say, however, that every child who is retarded not more than two years in his school work, and every child who is obviously or even apparently mentally peculiar or abnormal, should be given a special psycho-educational examination, in addition to the regular dento-medical examinations which are now regularly given in all large school systems.

The methods and aims of a psycho-educational examination are not the same as those of a medical examination. The psycho-educational clinic, while closely related to, is not identical with, the neurological or psychopathic clinic. I should say that the average physician would require three or four years of technical training in order to be able to learn skillfully to psychologically and educationally examine a mentally unusual child and skillfully to direct his educational development, just as I should say that it would require a similar period of time for the average psychologist to fully qualify himself to examine children medically (as well as psychologically). I do not think we shall soon reach the point where either the medical men or the psychologists (or the clinical educationists) will be ready to spend three or four extra years of prescribed study, in order to qualify themselves as double examiners (medical and educational). Therefore, I maintain that we need, as a minimum, two types of specialists for the work of examining and directing the care and training of mentally exceptional children; an educational specialist thoroughly trained in the art of psycho-educational diagnosis and in the differential, corrective pedagogics appertaining to the different types of educationally exceptional children; and a medical man who has had special preparation in the art of detecting physical defects and in pediatrics, neurology and psychiatry. The problems concerning the diagnosis, care, training and education of the many types of mentally and educationally exceptional children are so varied and complex that one type of specialist very probably cannot develop sufficient skill to satisfactorily handle them all.

In answer to the question: What do you do for your cases after you have examined them?

That depends entirely on the results of the examination. There is no specific of universal applicability. There are, indeed, certain cases which can profitably be subjected to the same educative processes, but many cases require differentiated educational treatment. In the case of a peda-gogically retarded child who rates normal mentally and whose school retardation is due to adventitious factors (frequent transfer from school to school, absence because of illness, disinterest, etc.), I should not prescribe a special curriculum of corrective work, but more individual attention. His is a problem for the ungraded teacher, and not for the special class teacher. On the other hand, speech-defectives, the feeble-minded, children weak in spelling or reading, etc., require special courses of corrective exercises. Moreover, every peculiar case should be carefully followed and subjected to later examinations so that the treatment may be modified to meet individual developmental needs.

CHAPTER VI
HUMAN EFFICIENCY1

A Plan For The Observational, Clinical And Experi-
Mental Study Of The Personal, Social, Indus-
Trial, School And Intellectual Efficiencies Of
Normal And Abnormal Individuals

The questions of first importance in the study of mental defectives are the questions of etiology, medical treatment, educational training and guidance and criminal responsibility. Etiology naturally claims a large share of consideration, because it is only after the etiological factors or agents of different abnormalities have been precisely determined, that we are in a position to prescribe effective remedial and prophylactic treatment, or to deal successfully with the educational problems affecting defectives.

The criminal and legal aspects likewise deserve a large measure of attention. Various forms of mental (and possibly anthropometric) abnormality predispose toward criminality. It is of vital social importance to determine what types or classes of defectives lack moral insight and appreciation of moral values, the ability to distinguish between right and wrong, or truth and error, the power of self-control, and the feelings of shame, obligation and guilt. What classes of defectives are incapable of living in a normal human environment? How do criminalistic tendencies and moral discernment vary with degree of defect, type of disease (e. g., delusional insanities, epileptic manias), duration of disease, transitory states (well known are the occasional or transitory states of moral irresponsibility in some forms of epilepsy and in delusional and manic-depressive forms of insanity, which show themselves in maniacal outbursts, and kleptomaniac, suicidal and homicidal tendencies) and environmental conditions? The obligation of the state properly to protect the lives of its subjects, renders the study of questions affecting the moral responsibility of various kinds of defectives of fundamental social importance. The solution of the practical educational, custodial and legal problems concerning defectives will hinge largely upon the answers which scientific investigation gives to questions of this nature.

i Read, in part, before the New York Branch of the American Psychological Association, February 4, 1911. Reprinted from the Pedagogical Seminary, 1911, pp. 74-84.

While the medical and legal questions are thus of great importance, it is also important to secure accurate knowledge concerning the personal, social, industrial, school and intellectual capacities and incapacities of various grades and classes of defectives, such as idiots, imbeciles, morons, laggards, epileptics and insane, blind, deaf, mute and crippled persons. There are thus five sides to the question of efficiency.

First of all, what is the personal efficiency of a given grade or class of defectives? What can the individual do for his own care and protection? Can he feed and clothe himself, avoid dangers and temptations, control the primal instincts of appetite, sex, love, hate, anger, fear, jealousy, pugnacity, etc.? Where does he stand in the personal efficiency scale? What is the amount of his personal efficiency retardation, as measured in terms of the personal capacities of a normal person of the same age? The answers to these questions involve the establishment of age norms of personal efficiency–a task that probably cannot be done with any nicety except for the first years of life.

In the second place, what is the nature of the social capacities or incapacities of a given defective, or a typical defective of a given class? Is the individual able to communicate his ideas or desires through written or oral language or through cries or gestures? Can he converse coherently or intelligently? Does he seek or avoid social intercourse, conversation, entertainments, games, etc.? Is he socially-minded or anti-social? Is he chummy, entertaining, generous, sympathetic, timid, retiring, fretful, suspicious, deceitful, quarrelsome, slanderous, brutal, murderous, lascivious, sexually immoral, subject to exhibitionism or negativism, lying, thieving, etc.? Does he fit into the social organism? Can he so adjust himself to the customs and rules of society that he will not become a public menace? In short, what is the character of the individuals social deviation? What is his social efficiency age? Is he on the level of the morally undiscerning civilized young child or in the stage of the brutal adult savage?

In the tfiird place, what is the industrial and vocational, or motor, efficiency of various defectives? What kinds of work can they do, and how well? How much can they do for their own support? What particular capacities are present or lacking? What special existent occupational interests may be utilized? What is the individuals attitude toward work and toward supervision and correction? What are his learning capacities? What working habits can he form? What new tasks can he master? To what extent are his industrial capacities improvable by training? What is his best line of work? How does his industrial efficiency vary from time to time? (Witness the striking variations in epileptics.) What is the productive capacity of a given defective in comparison with a normal person of like maturity, and to what extent can the productive capacity be increased? In a word, what is the amoimt of the motor or indiistrial defect, or what is the motor and industrial age, of a given defective? These questions demand solution before the pedagogy of the industrial and vocational training of defectives can be placed upon a satisfactory basis, and before the labor of the patients in institutions for defectives can be so organized as to afford maximal returns.

In the fourth place, what is the nature of the academic or school capacities of different grades and classes of defectives? What sort of lessons can be mastered? In which branches do they make progress? Which subjects are worth teaching? What methods must be employed to obtain maximal results? How does the rate of progress differ from the normal rate (the rate with normals)? What is the precise rate and character of the improvement from month to month or year to year, as measured by scientifically devised serial tests of equal difficulty, of those mental functions which are central in the learning process; namely, perception, attention, association, memory, imagination, linguistic construction and reasoning? What kinds of improvement prove to be permanent, what merely transitory? What are the special difficulties of a given defective? What are his native or acquired interests, attitudes, ability to observe, judge, reason, form habits, adapt himself to changed schedules and new conditions, to learn by instruction, or imitation, or hit-and-miss experimentation, or repetition (drill processes), or reasoning? How many years over-age is the child for his grade? That is, what are the nature and extent of his pedagogical retardation? What is his pedagogical age? We cannot hope to adapt our curricula to the varying needs of defective children until we have thrown the searchlight upon these vital school problems.

Finally, we have the basal question of the character of the intellectual disorganization and the degree of the intellectual arrest of various defectives. This question is fundamental, because all the other capacities depend more upon the intellectual integrity of the individual than upon the integrity of any other group of functions. Here we must ascertain, not so much the range of the individuals information or his erudition, as the degree and character of his native and acquired intellectual grasp, capacity or ability. Is his intellectual development normal, or has it been arrested from the start, or has it become atrophied with time? What particular intellectual functions have suffered the greatest impairment? Where along the intellectual highway from the low-grade idiot up through the imbecile, moron and laggard to the normal person, has the individual stopped? What, in a word, is the individuals intellectual age? Can this be determined in definite units, or by diagnostic age tests, more precisely than can be done by observation or by the use of school grades?

The above are fundamental questions which must be properly answered before we can presume to deal intelligently with the problems affecting the housing, segregation, care, treatment and education of public school and institutional types of defectives, or before we can deal intelligently with normal and supernormal children.

At the New Jersey State Village for Epileptics2 it was my privilege recently to inaugurate investigations of the above questions by observational, clinical and experimental methods, and to prepare a series of record blanks on which to record the data. These forms are uniform in size with the other forms in use in the institution and are so made that they can be gathered into book form and thus provide a case history for each patient.

2 A laboratory of clinical psychology was established by the Board of Managers at this institution in October, 1910, under the directorship of the writer.

In order to determine the patients intellectual status we have been giving the form-board test, which throws light upon the patients ability to visually identify forms, upon his constructive capacity and his power of muscular coordination; the hand dynamometry test, which roughly tests the power of voluntary attention and effort, and particularly the power of muscular exertion; the Binet-Simon tests of intellectual development (all of the above are on Form 7); and a set of six serial or consecutive controlled group tests (Form V3). The latter tests were given serially (one set each month) to somewhat over thirty of our brightest epileptic school children, and to somewhat less than 100 dull, average and bright pupils from the second to the third high-school grades in a nearby public school. Owing to our late start, and the writers removal from the institution, these tests could be given only during five months; it would have been better to have given them once every second month during the course of the entire year. These group measurements embrace tests of various mental processes fundamental to intellectual operations: accuracy of perception, perceptual discrimination, obser vation and reaction; the capacity to memorize and the power of immediate and prolonged retention; the rate of forming spontaneous associations with determinate antecedents, the ability to form such controlled associations as are involved in adding columns of ten one-place digits and supplying antonyms to a set of simple words; the ability to retain a list of logical and illogical sequents with determinate antecedents from one reading by the experimenter, during a period of a couple of minutes and during a period of four weeks; the capacity for visual imagination; and the capacity for linguistic construction as evidenced by the ability to construct a maximal number of sentences each of which must contain three supplied nouns or verbs. The aim has been to make each of the six successive tests in the same series different but at the same time equally difficult, and all so difficult that no one can make a perfect score, so that they may serve as an experimental measuring scale of the growth and improvement which various mental capacities or traits undergo from month to month or year to year as a result of normal maturation, education, training, familiarity, removal of physical defects, proper regulation of temperature and humidity, or abstention from tobacco or alcohol. By giving these tests to many normal children from season to season or year to year it is possible to establish normal rate norms of development for the traits tested, by which to measure individual retardations or accelerations, as well as the differences in the capacities of various classes of children (normal, bright, dull, backward, epileptic, feeble-minded). Several of these tests were originally prepared for use with a dental squad of Cleveland school children receiving special prophylactic and operative dental treatment, in order to measure in definite units the effects of such treatment upon mental efficiency. The use of these tests for this purpose gave very gratifying results. The twelve tests which I have worked out–two are repeated during the following sitting in such a way as to transform them into new tests–may not afford the best measuring scales, but they furnish an initial set which can be altered and improved as experience demands. The materials for these tests, together with the directions for giving them, may be secured from the C. H. Stoelting Co., Chicago, 111. The results of the experiment have been tabulated, but have not yet appeared in print.

Four of the forms were distributed at the meeting. Form I also contains a number of miscellaneous tests; Form II deals with the effect of convulsions on mental traits and capacities; Form III is a personal, social and industrial efficiency report; Form IV is a school efficiency report; and on Form V is recorded serial experimental tests of the growth and improvement of mental traits and capacities.

The Binet-Simon measuring scale, with which I have made a survey of the entire village, enables us to make a fairly satisfactory determination of the degree of intellectual arrest of the patients, although the tests are faulty in various particulars (see Chapters IV, VIII, IX, X). Here it may be pointed out that the aggregate difficulty of the tests for a given age may be greater than that for a higher age; some tests are of questionable utility, notably those for the higher ages; the tests need to be extended so as to include more of the teens, and this is more difficult because in the teens one year makes less difference in intelligence than one year during the early years of childhood. Moreover, it is not yet certain whether the scale is applicable to the higher grade adult dements or to slightly retarded adolescents (it seems to apply fairly well to most demented idiots, and particularly to amented idiots, imbeciles and low-grade morons); nor is it certain that the same tests are applicable to both boys and girls, except during the preadolescent period, owing to the difference in the physiological, psychological and pedagogical maturity of boys and girls of the same chronological age.

After some tests have been repeated sufficiently often in a given school or locality to render them familiar, it is possible for the higher grade examinees to compare notes and coach one another. This has happened in my experience both with public school and high-grade institutional cases. This will enable some pupils to pass the tests beyond their intellectual age, and will transform the measuring scale into a series of tests of the ability to learn particular facts or to acquire particular accomplishments, by dint of direct instruction. But the tests are not designed to try the momentary capacity to acquire a determinate tet of facts by special instruction, but to measure the capacity to solve certain problems without special preparation. They are intended to be a measuring rod of the intellectual capacity or strength which normal children of various ages and of a given type of civilization should have developed as a result of normal growth and development. They thus supply a series of age norms of native and acquired mental capacity; not of native capacity only, as has been assumed. It would be fatuous to attempt to construct a scale for the measurement of pure native capacity, for pure native capacity, after the first few months of life, is a pure figment of the imagination. Only by excluding the psychical and social environmental influences would there be any possibility of measuring native endowment independent of acquired capacity. A measuring scale will, therefore, measure both native and acquired capacity. Just as native capacity differs with individuals, so will the capacity to acquire differ with individuals; but there is probably a certain rate of acquisition which is fairly normal in a given order of civilization, so that it will be possible to establish norms which hold for the great mass of average or typical individuals.

Fortunately the difficulty of which we have just spoken, the possibility of being coached so as to pass some tests, can be met by devising substitute or variant forms of equal difficulty for some of the tests.

The basis of initial rating and the corrective formula or the method of giving advance credits (one year for every five points passed in higher ages) sometimes create difficulties. This is due to the fact that the number of tests in the various ages in the 1908 scale is not uniform, and to the fact that subjects may pass superior ages while failing on lower ones. In four ages in the 1908 scale the number of tests is four (ages four, five, ten and twelve); in two it is five (three and eleven); in two six (eight and nine); in one seven (age six); and in one eight (age seven). The consequence is that the subject sometimes receives too few and sometimes too many credits. To illustrate cases from my experience: if the subject passes age six by virtue of two failures in age seven, he can obtain one and one-fifth year of credit for age seven; i. e., one-fifth of a year more credit than if he were credited outright as having passed age seven. If he fails on age six but passes age ten he can still be rated as ten years mentally. The maximum discrepancies which I have found arising from different bases of rating have amounted to over three years, while for 39 per cent of 103 epileptic cases studied they amounted to one year or over. This difficulty, however, is not innate in the tests themselves, and can be overcome by equalizing the number of tests in each age, as has been done in the 1911 revision, by rearranging the tests, or revising the corrective formula as may be needed.

There are two methods by which to scientifically eliminate, revise, add or amplify tests in the Binet scale. First, by testing masses of physically and mentally normal public school children. But it is necessary to emphasize that the testing must be a thoroughgoing try-out. To examine five or six pupils in an hour at a given level in the scale, as has been done, means partial and perfunctory work, and will render the try-out essentially unscientific. We cannot hope to establish reliable norms for children by a slap-dash examination of wholesale quantities of pupils. It is better to try the scale out thoroughly with 1,000 pupils than partially with 10,000.

A second way in which to improve the scale, is to undertake a systematic survey of the intellectual capacities of normal boys and girls at different ages. What, e. g., can the typical six-year-old or twelve-year-old boy or girl do intellectually? To answer this question fully we need to gather and compile extensive observational data from classroom teachers, expert paidologists, parents and intelligent observers who come into direct daily contact with children.

At the Skillman institution I initiated an attempt to gather such data for the epileptic school children by preparing a syllabus on the school efficiency of the pupils. School efficiency depends primarily upon intellectual capacity and thus furnishes an index of intelligence. From the reports, made by the teachers, it should be possible to gain information regarding the characteristic intellectual capacities of epileptics of various chronological and Binet-Simon ages and of various degrees of mental arrest. The information thus gathered should possess a unique value when brought into correlation with other reports and the various experimental tests. As soon as we have extensive data of this character for large masses of normal children, we shall not only know something definite regarding the intellectual capacities of children of different ages, but we shall have taken an important step toward the construction of an adequate measuring scale of intellectual develop ment. Such a program of work as this can only be carried to a successful conclusion by a properly organized and a well-manned department of clinical psychology, or bureau of research, in the public schools, in a university or in an endowed private research foundation.

It is probably not necessary to hold a brief in this day for the necessity of undertaking such a survey as this. There is a vast army of repeaters in the schools which threaten to become a national menace. At the present time, our ignorance concerning, and our neglect of, the best care, treatment and education of arrested children, stand out as a national disgrace. We know little at present that is scientifically accurate regarding the degree or character of the physical and mental arrest of our repeaters. We do, therefore, stand in need of comprehensive serial graded tests of intelligence, so that we may determine, not only the intellectual age of deviating children, but the nature of the mental functions most seriously affected, and the character of the arrest (whether permanent or temporary). It is sheer folly to spend millions of dollars trying to educate for an intellectual career children who are permanently retarded. There are instances on record where arrested pupils have made practically no progress during a dozen years of schooling, or where they have actually retrogressed. We have with us nineteen-year-old epileptics who are doing second and third year work. We should be able to determine by means of a scientific diagnostic (intelligence) scale (aided always, of course, by comprehensive case-studies) whether a given subnormal is a custodial or institutional case, or a case for one of the special classes in the public schools (for retarded, blind, deaf, mute children, etc.). Binet has given us a first-aid-to-the-sick device, just at the time that we are awakening to a realization of the magnitude of the problem of mental deficiency.

While the intellectual measuring rod is fundamental, we stand in need of a motor or industrial scale of development, or a combined intellectual-motor scale. This need arises from the fact that a sixteen-year-old child chronologically may have a twelve-year-old intellect and a fourteen-year-old musculature. Such a child is fairly strong muscularly; he is able to execute and coordinate his movements with skill; he can perform quite complicated manual operations; he can master fairly difficult industrial tasks; he can retain motor acquisitions and form stable muscular habits. Although he may be accounted an intellectual laggard, he ranks quite high in motor capacity and manual dexterity—a fact which is being demonstrated day by day in the manual training and industrial classes in the public schools. Such a child would, then, be fairly normal on the motor side.

Since, therefore, the intellectual and the motor developments will not in all cases coincide, we need a series of motor diagnostic tests arranged in a graded scale, in order that we may know what a normal girl and boy can do industrially, or in motor performance, at different ages. It should be possible to construct such a scale for, at least, the periods of childhood and early adolescence. Having both the intellectual and the motor scales, separate or combined, we shall be in a position to say whether the childs defects involve in equal measure the intellectual and the motor functions, or which of these two have suffered the most impairment, and to what extent the arrest has set in. The pedagogical value of such a differential diagnosis is obvious. Instead of allowing teachers to consume their energies and the energies of the pupils for years, trying by some sort of intellectual legerdemain to fit round boys and girls into square holes, we shall be able to prognosticate by means of standard tests (together with accompanying exhaustive clinical studies) the probable future pedagogical development of the arrested child, and thereby be able to plan a course in which he will make the greatest progress. This will not only redound to the good of the child, but prevent much pedagogical blundering, loss of time and money, and vexation of spirit.

Unfortunately there is no existent motor or industrial scale of development for normal children comparable with the Binet-Simon intellectual scale. At Skillman I had the pleasure of launching an attempt to construct such a scale for epileptics, by collecting extensive observational data from the officers, supervisors, attendants and employees of the institution, bearing upon the industrial capacities of the patients who are employed in various forms of indoor and outdoor work. From the results thus obtained it should be possible to construct a motor scale of development for epileptics for each Binet-Simon age. (Information is not now available as to whether these inquiries are still carried on.) It is evident that such a motor scale would possess greater value if we were in a position to turn, for purposes of comparison, to a motor scale for normal and supernormal individuals. The need of a normal industrial scale is felt as keenly by the student and trainer of the special child, whether subnormal or supernormal, in the public schools, as by the student and trainer of institutional types of defectives. Departments of child study in the public schools and research departments in institutions for defectives should make an attempt to gather extensive industrial or motor data by some such means as those we are now using.

Finally, we must make a survey of the personal and social traits and capacities, the moral characteristics and criminal tendencies of our patients. The data on the personal capacities will supply additional material for our comparative measuring scales. There is need of a similar systematic study particularly of the moral and criminal traits of the abnormal, mischievous and delinquent pupils who people our schools, and of the criminals who menace our civilization. These data should be secured, in the first instance, for the socially maladjusted child in the pre-adolescent years, before the criminalistic tendencies have become confirmed. Only when we have in our possession extensive facts of this character will we be in a position to place our pedagogical and moral training and prophylaxis, and our custodial care and treatment of abnormal and criminal individuals upon a satisfactory basis.

When we have given the same amount of careful, expert study to our normal and abnormal human population that the government is giving to the study of Indian corn or the American hog; when we have devoted the same scientific attention to the production of superb brain crops that experts, under government subsidy, are now giving to the growing of superior grain crops: then we may hope to make education a genuine science, and the school and institutional training, care, treatment or penalization of defectives, dependents or criminals a real art. The view that public institutions, in addition to their recognized duties, should function as research laboratories, is rapidly gaining acceptance. Just now we stand in great need of extensive mass studies: a broad survey of the total field of human capacity. It is with this idea uppermost that the set of efficiency blanks at Skillman were prepared for the systematic recording of observations. Our methods of inves tigation must at present necessarily be somewhat crude. But in time we shall have just as refined a technique for studying the human animal as we now have for studying chickens and pigs.

CHAPTER VII

EIGHT MONTHS OF PSYCHO-CLINICAL RE-
SEARCH AT THE NEW JERSEY STATE
VILLAGE FOR EPILEPTICS, WITH SOME
RESULTS FROM THE BINET-
SIMON TESTING1

The functions of a clinical psychologist in an institution for defectives, in a public school system, in a university, in a psychiatric institute or in a juvenile court is twofold: first, that of theoretical investigation, or the increase of knowledge under controlled and verifiable conditions. This is essentially the field of the research psychologist or of pure science, so-called. Second, that of practical application, or the utilization of the truths discovered for the educational, hygienic, medical and custodial treatment of the sufferers. This is the work of the consulting psychologist as distinguished from the pure researcher, and constitutes the sphere of orthogenesis, mental hygiene or applied clinical psychology. While the line of demarcation between these two aims should not be made too fast and hard, logically the work of investigation in an infant science naturally takes chronological precedence to the work of consultation, as, indeed, science logically precedes art. The art of righting defectives cannot rise above the empirical until it is based upon a foundation of assured facts. Until we thoroughly understand the different types of nervous and mental abnormalities our treatment cannot be made maximally effective. For these reasons the work in the psycho-clinical laboratory at Skill-man during the past eight months has been devoted entirely to investigation.

i Read at the tenth annual meeting in St. Louis, Mo., of the National Association for the Study of Epilepsy and the Care and Treatment of Epileptics, and reprinted from the Transactions of the Association, 1911, pp. 29-43, and from Epilepsia (Amsterdam), 1912, pp. 366-380. A volume of studies, based on my Binet-Simon testing of epileptics, will be found in Experimental Studies of Mental Defectives: A Critique of the Binet-Simon Tests, and a Contribution to the Psychology of Epilepsy, Warwick and York, Inc., Baltimore, 1912.

During these eight months a number of lines of investigation have been started, some of which have been concluded. Among the surveys of the village which have been completed (completed as far as testing each patient is concerned) are the following: Measurements of standing and sitting heights, of weight, of lung capacity, of the strength of right and left hand grip, of station or body sway, of the speed of performing the form-board test (replacing ten blocks of various forms in corresponding holes in a board), of intellectual capacity or the extent of intellectual retardation, as evinced by the Binet-Simon scale, and of the rate of growth and development, as well as the character and extent of the deviation or disorganization of a number of particular mental traits and capacities which play a basic role in mental development. The latter tests (described in Chapter VI) when given to normal children are intended to supply normal rate curves of mental development.

The desirability, or even the feasibility, of establishing psychological rate norms of development has, strangely, scarcely dawned upon us until recently, although the practical value of such norms is probably greater than the value of the corresponding anthropometric standards of yearly development during the growth-period of standing and sitting height, weight, chest perimetry, dynamometry and vital capacity. The importance of a set of anthropometric norms, arranged on the grade or percentile basis, has been eloquently set forth by the lamented Francis Galton, to whose comprehensive intellect many sciences have become indebted. Thanks to the labors of a few of Galtons followers, notably Bowditch, Porter and Smedley, and to the labors of the Italian anthropologists, we now possess a set of fairly reliable physical development norms and indices for certain ages, by means of which we are able to determine the physical station of a given child of a given age, and by means of which we can say whether his physical progress is normal or satisfactory as measured by the percentile grade for the age to which he belongs (using height as the basis of comparison), and by means of which we can determine the character of his anthropological indices. But we are now beginning to realize that we cannot properly diagnose developmental defects of the mind until we have constructed a similar set of psychic norms of development of various traits and capacities. When we have such norms for specialized capacities we shall be able to locate the mental station of a given child at a given time, and determine whether his rate of mental evolution is normal for the grade in which he classifies. These norms will possess fundamental value for purposes of developmental diagnosis, in the study of not merely the lesser deviations but also the more profound mental abnormalities. To supply these mental developmental scales is chiefly a matter of time, labor and ingenuity; the instrumental and technical difficulties are secondary. Such scales will not, of course, attain the accuracy of refined physical measures, but they will be far superior to our present common sense judgments. The fair degree of success attained by the simple Binet-Simon tests of intelligence justifies the belief that this problem, baffling as it seems, is not insoluble. By means of the serial group tests which I have been giving during the past year, I am hoping to make some little addition to our knowledge in this largely unexplored, but inviting and important, field of inquiry. Aside from the value which the data from these tests will have for developmental diagnosis, the results may also be used as a means by which to check up the Binet-Simon tests, which have recently come into wide use in institutions for defectives and in the public schools in our country.2 I turn now to a consideration of some of the results of our Binet testing. The space at my disposal permits only a brief reference to a few of the more obvious facts, particularly those which concern the characteristics of the curve of distribution, or the classification of the epileptics at Skill-man by this method.

Taking the gross or group classification, the 333 patients3 included in the curve (Graph IV) classify as follows: 5.7 per cent are idiots (mentality of one and two years), 27.3 per cent are imbeciles (mentality of ages three to seven), 61.5 per cent are morons (mentality of ages eight to twelve), 5.4 per cent have a mentality of thirteen years or over (see the table and the curve), and 82.8 per cent have a mentality of less than eleven years. The idiots and thirteen-year olds are about equally infrequent, while the morons are decidedly preponderant. These results will attain a new significance if we compare them with the Binet curve for 378 feeble-minded inmates at Vineland.4 2 For other studies undertaken in the psycho-clinical laboratory at Skillman during the same year by means of the printed questionnaire or syllabus method, see Chapter VI.

3 Those epileptics were excluded from the tabulation who had not had a convulsion within a period of two years, and a few others who were not thoroughly tested because of certain sensory defects. The patients were in their normal condition during the tests. The grading in all cases is based upon the highest age passed, plus the advance credits provided for in the scale, irrespective of whether or not the patient failed at a lower level. Patients who passed in two of the thirteen-year tests were credited with this age, provided they also passed at least five tests in ages eleven and twelve. Drawing one triangle was accepted for the first of the thirteen-year-old tests.

In this 19.2 per cent grade as idiots; 54 per cent as imbeciles; 26 per cent as morons; none as thirteen years of age; and 96.4 per cent less than eleven years of age. The feeble-minded idiots are about three and one-half times as numerous as the epileptic idiots, but the epileptic morons are more than two and one-half times as numerous as the feeble-minded morons. While the great mass of epileptic and feeble-minded defectives have a mentality of less than eleven years, the proportion is 13.6 per cent greater among the feeble-minded than among the epileptics. The typical epileptic category is that of the condition of moronity, which contains five-eighths of the entire number of the epileptics, while the typical feebleminded station is that of imbecility, which includes more than one-half of the feeble-minded. It is apparent that there is a marked difference between epileptic degenerates and feeble-minded retardates in the matter of intelligence. Graph IV goddard. Journal of Psycho-Asthenics, 1910, 15: Nos. 1 and 2. The per cents for each age for the feeble-minded are as follows: Age I, 9.5 per cent; II, 9.7 per cent; HI, 10.5 per cent; IV, 9.8 per cent; V, 11.1 per cent; VI, 10.9 per cent; VII, 12.4 per cent; VIII, 11.6 per cent; IX, 7.9 per cent; X, 3.7 per cent; XI, 1.3 per cent; XII, 1.8 per cent. Age X in the curve is placed somewhat too high.

Classification of 888 epileptics (Skillman) and 878 feebleminded (Vineland) by tbe Binet-Simon method.

Epileptics

Feeble-minded

The thirteen-year-olds may be classed as deviates, retardates or normals.

The intellectual superiority of the epileptic defective is conspicuous. This superiority will attain added prominence if we constitute the thirteen-year-olds into a separate class above the feeble-minded line, which we may regard as normal, or as retarded or deviating but not sufficiently to render them feeble-minded. We should then have to add to this class all the children who are retarded less than three years (certainly many adolescent children retarded less than three years would not be feeble-minded). There are nine of these, five boys and four girls. These with the thirteen-year-olds, make a total of twenty-seven normals, or deviates, which is 8.1 per cent of the entire group.5

This figure we are justified, I believe, in regarding as a lower limiting value for two reasons. First, the tests in the higher ages are very probably too difficult for the typical American child for the ages to which they are assigned.

To get a line on these higher tests I made use of the following means. A few of the supervisors and officers at Skillman who had known the patients intimately for a considerable length of time were asked to prepare estimates of the number of patients whom they regarded as ranking above the feeble-minded station. Three made identical estimates, unknown to each other, for the total population, namely 10 per cent. Five men made separate and independent estimates of the total male population, as follows: 11, 11,13,14 and 20 per cent. With one exception, these estimates agree fairly well. With the tests as at present constituted, it is a question whether the line of feeble-

B It is interesting to note, that among these twenty-seven there is only one who can be regarded as supernormal, a boy somewhat less than twelve years who grades as thirteen years.

mindedness should be drawn (if indeed it can be definitely drawn anywhere) between twelve and thirteen, as has been tentatively done by the American Association for the Study of Feeble-Mindedness. A number of our twelve-year-olds are certainly very slightly, if at all, feebleminded.

A second reason why the percentage of normals may be too low is the fact that the institutional cases at Skill-man may not be representative. Our curve in general is valid on the assumption that the epileptics tested are typical. According to the theory of the probability surface we are justified in regarding them as typical if the selection represents a chance distribution. But it is possible that two selective processes have operated in a way to distort both extremes of the curve. The reason that the idiots are so few may be due to the fact that the higher-grade epileptics have received preference in admission to the institution. The introduction of a constant factor of this sort would skew the frequency curve in the direction of the upper limit. This tendency would probably stop short, however, before it reached the extreme end of the curve, because it is likely that the highest grade of epileptics from the better social classes are very rarely found in public institutions. We shall not be able definitely to settle this point until other institutions have undertaken similar studies on a large scale. But three general conclusions seem assured: first, that the great mass of epileptics fall below the feeble-minded line; second, that they do not fall below this line to such an extent as the class of amented feeble-minded; and third, that the curve of distribution is markedly different for the two classes. Just how much inferior the high-grade epileptics are to those persons, taken at random in the general population whose schooling and training are about of the same character, cannot now be said.

One of the most striking peculiarities of the epileptic curve is its decidedly skewed or anomalous character, noticeable particularly between ages eight and eleven. The curve presents a marked contrast with the curve of feeble-mindedness in this respect. The latter is characterized by a fairly uniform rise up to and including age seven, and by a rapid and uniform fall after age eight. It has more or less of the normal bell-shaped appearance. But in the epileptic curve there are two irregular drops in the ascending portion, a minor at five and a major at nine. The former does not possess much significance, because of the small number of subjects tested in the lower ages. It may be regarded merely as a fortuitous phenomenon. But in a typical curve of frequency the rise from age six should have been continued without any marked break at nine to the apex at ten. It is, therefore, apparent that the accidental factors which normally operate to produce an unskewed or bell-shaped curve of frequency, were interfered with in our testing by some constant factor or factors. These factors can only reside in the method of giving the tests, or in the nature or arrangement of the tests themselves, or in the peculiar mental organization of the epileptics resulting from their inborn constitution or from processes of degeneration."

There must either be certain defects in the mentality of epileptics, that is, at the nine-year level, for we find 24.9 per cent of epileptics grading ten years old as against

Another factor may have to be considered, the relative proportion of children among the epileptics and feeble-minded. One-third of the epileptics were under twenty-one years of age; the corresponding figure for the feeble-minded is 54 per cent.

only 8.4 per cent grading nine years old; or we must consider the ten-year-old tests as normally too easy and the nine-year tests as too difficult; or otherwise some factor extraneous to the tests themselves has been operative.

The method of testing possibly plays a minor role, for while the method used has followed that in vogue at Vine-land, there is this possible difference: my testing has been done with great thoroughness in this respect, that instead of confining the testing of the patients to the ages immediately beneath or above the ages in which they grade, I have tested the majority throughout the greater part of the scale. This was done, not merely to arrive at a more complete clinical picture–to reveal the peculiar mental lapses, gaps and remnants which may be assumed to accompany degeneration changes–but in order to test the reliability of the scale itself. For this purpose nothing but a thoroughgoing try-out will suffice.7

This thorough testing has given some interesting results, which we cannot enter upon here further than to say that scores of low or medium grade epileptics were found who passed one or more tests in a half dozen higher age levels, and who received from ten to twenty (in a few cases from twenty-five to thirty) advance points from the first age actually passed. Certain mental remnants from higher psychic levels remained to tell the story of the wreckage wrought by the disease. At the same time, scores who passed the higher age tests failed in individual tests at lower levels. Two years particularly proved veritable ponies asinorum, namely ages six and nine. No per cent of those who are classified in age six passed the tests of this age (that is, all the tests or all but one), while only 10 per cent of the Binet-Simon nine-year-olds passed the tests of this year. Only 29 per cent of the groups of patients who grade six, seven, eight, nine and ten years old passed the six-year-old tests, while only 40 per cent of the nine, ten, eleven, twelve and thirteen year olds passed the nine-year tests. But what is of special interest to the question at issue now is the fact that the method of extensive testing used made it possible for patients to attain a different or higher classification on the basis of advance credits from numerous higher ages. That is why there is no fall in the curve at six, e. g., although not a single one of the six-year-olds actually passed all of the tests but one of that age. While this factor is thus of some importance, it does not explain why there is such a large number of ten-year-old patients, because the greater number of these (94 per cent) passed the ten-year-old tests while 84 per cent of them failed on the nine-year tests. There is some evidence to confirm the belief that the nine-year tests are too difficult: the first obvious break in the curve of feeble-minded-ness comes at this age, while Katherine Johnstone," testing a considerable group of normal girls in the Sheffield, England, schools, found this year to be the most difficult. After making due allowance for these two factors–the thoroughness of the testing, and the intrinsic difficulty of the tests themselves–the facts would seem to force us to include a third factor. A detailed analysis of the records, and particularly of the failures at various levels, shows that the inability to pass ages six and nine (eleven may also be included) is due, at least partly, to certain inherent defects in the epileptic mind. These defects, so far as pertains to these ages, arise: first, from a fundamental deficiency in memory span, as shown by the inability to repeat a sentence of sixteen syllables heard once, to recall six units or facts from reading a short passage once, and to correctly state their ages in years; second, from an inability to define common objects in terms of description or classification, or to define simple abstract qualities in terms of the essential idea; third, from a blunting of the muscular sensibility, or a raising of the threshold of muscular sensory discrimination of weight; fourth, from a failure to grasp the essentials of a simple situation, as evidenced by the inability to execute a simple triple command, or to arrange shuffled words into an intelligible sentence; and fifth, from a marked obstruction or retardation of the stream of thought, as evidenced by the inability to utter sixty words in three minutes.

7 Such a try-out must be made, of course, primarily on large masses of normal children.

8 Katherine L. Johnstone. Journal of Experimental Pedagogy, 1:24f. (She also finds that some normal children pass higher levels while failing at inferior levels.)

From the very fragmentary account which we have thus given of certain aspects of our Binet work, we are able to frame a picture of an interesting spectacle: a case of mental wreckage, whereby the integrity of various mental functions has been impaired in various levels of mental development, and whereby various lower psychic levels have been swept away while higher levels remain intact. The mentality of epileptics makes up a constellation that is extremely irregular. To what extent the minds of the epileptic males differ from the females, and the children from the adults, as determined by the Binet scale, time does not permit us to discuss. Nor can we detail the interesting results obtained by plotting age curves (for the thirteen Binet ages) for various individual tests by which it appears that, although the scale surely does not accurately measure every individual, it is, in the hands of the expert, a surprisingly serviceable means of classifying homogeneous masses or groups of individuals. These can all be graded relatively by means of a uniform measuring rod. To this statement we must except the highest grade epileptics, however. The capacities of a considerable number of these lie outside of the range of the scale. Altogether, the Binet-Simon scale offers an ingenious but simple, practicable, objective and rapid device for estimating and classifying defectives. No other available scheme gives such a satisfactory preliminary survey. It can tell us in one hour facts regarding new admissions which would otherwise come only after weeks of observation and experience. To an audience of this kind, the great need of a practical and simple means of grading and classifying institutional cases, and the conspicuous present lack of a generally accepted or satisfactory method need not be emphasized. It is pertinent to lay stress on the fact that the Binet method marks a decided advance step, in spite of all its imperfections. Supplemented by corresponding scales of person-al, mn-itil and hiihixlritil efficiencies, this scheme of graded intelligence-tests offers considerable aid in the solution of a vexing problem.

 I

S

 f O

 a, O

 d Z

 COrh

rh to to to vo Ov rh rh rh CM to toOOrhO vo 00 t Tf-(Tf -t to to , o a fo rh t O O voOOCM Ovo r- tv f o h

 CMOv–vo vo

 Ov vo ro H t tmrhTf CM roo voooto n to vo vo t 00 00 Ov Tj-CM r oo to to i- vo rh 00 fo t 0 Ov 00 to

 OOvo voto -tovoOOvo to 00 to 00 to

 Ov vo vo voCM

 OOOvorhCM

 ,3-2 rt

 P;.

 S S

 CHAPTER VIII

THE PRESENT STATUS OF THE BINET-SIMON GRADED TESTS OF INTEL-LIGENCE1

The Binet-Simon graded tests of intellectual development, or similar amplified and standardized tests, give promise of making so large a contribution to the methodological technique indispensable in the scientific study of all sorts of mentally deviating and defective individuals, that too much time cannot be devoted to the critical examination of the tests, in order to determine the accuracy and relevancy of the scale. It is no less necessary in psychological than in medical or biological investigations to rigorously adhere to the accepted rule in the physical sciences, that before making any measurements whatever it is necessary to determine whether the instruments of research are accurate, and if not what the amount of the inaccuracy is.

There are at least four methods available by means of which we may test the accuracy of measuring scales of intellectual capacity.

The first method is to test masses of supposedly normal children, and determine the percentage of passing for each test in each age-norm or for each collective age-norm. At the present time we have the returns from a number of scattered surveys made by the Binet-Simon method in France (Binet and Simon), Belgium (Decroly and De-gand), England (Katherine Johnstone), America (God-dard) and Germany (Bobertag). These studies represent much painstaking work, and are valuable contributions. But they are more or less unsatisfactory for various reasons. The number of children tested in each age, at least in some ages, has been rather limited. In the absence of any definite criterion by which to select a normal or typical or average child, the children tested have been largely selected at random. And the testing has usually been of the narrow-range type. By a narrow-range type of testing I refer to surveys which are limited to the childs chronological age and one or two higher and lower ages. Such limited surveys made on a small number of children are practically worthless for the purpose of arriving at an adequate clinical picture of the childs mental condition, or for determining his mental status, or for the purpose of trying out the accuracy of the scale, because from all that we know about human nature from a number of psychological and pedagogical investigations, mental traits, whether original or acquired, differ very considerably in children of the same chronological ages or of the same school classification. The defectiveness of restricted testing has been forcibly brought home to me from my own wide-range testing of a colony of epileptics, and from a less extensive testing of certain types of insane patients. From the wide-range method of testing epileptics with the Binet-Simon scale it appeared that dozens of those who were only able to pass one of the lower age-standards passed one or more tests in a half dozen higher ages, and several of those who failed on the age standards between six and nine passed age ten. It is necessary to remember in the later discussion that the surveys thus far made on public school children have usually, perhaps nearly always, followed the narrow-range method of testing (the writers have given little information to the public on this important point).

i Read before the American Psychological Association, at the Washington meeting, December 27, 1911. Reprinted from The Alienist and Neurologist, May, 1913.

It is important to raise the question as to whether a try-out of the tests to prove thoroughly satisfactory must not be based on fairly normal or typical children, and not on mixed groups of normal, subnormal and supernormal children. Even among normal children, so-called, we shall always find a considerable amount of variation in the strength of any trait or capacity; but if we include both dull and bright children the variation becomes so large that the survey can scarcely be used for the purpose of testing the reliability of the scale. It may be frankly conceded that we have no fixed standard of what constitutes the normal child in any age, but we are in a position to use a fairly satisfactory criterion by which to select average children, namely, the degree of pedagogical arrest or progress which the child has shown in his school work and the number of physical defects found by careful medical inspection.

A second method by which to test the accuracy of scales of mental development is to test the same groups of normal children annually. If the scale is measurably correct the children should gain approximately one mental age with the passing of each calendar year. No detailed studies of this sort, on normal children, made by the Binet-Simon scale, have yet been published, so far as I am aware.

A third method is to classify by mental ages all the members of homogeneous groups of individuals, such as entire colonies of epileptics or entire institutions for the feeble-minded or the insane. The curves of distribution or surfaces of frequency from such surveys should, from the theory governing distributions controlled by chance factors, assume the normal, bell-shaped appearance. In a homogeneous group (at least of persons who have reached maturity) the mental stations of the individuals should cluster around one mode. From this mode approximately equal negative and positive departures would occur. The frequency of the departures would depend upon their size; the larger the departure, the smaller the frequency. The curve, accordingly, will taper off in the form of a bell; and if any marked skews occur it is evident that the group in question is not a typical group–the group is, so to say, a loaded group because, certain factors having received undue emphasis in its selection, the law applying to chance distributions does not hold–or the size of the group is too small to furnish reliable data, or there are inequalities or irregularities in the measuring scale or in the method of testing, or the group is so peculiar or anomalous as not to be in accordance with Gauss curve. Two Binet-Simon curves of distribution have been constructed for homogeneous groups of individuals, and are available for this study.

A fourth method of evaluation is to plot efficiency or capacity curves for each separate trait in all the mental ages in which the given trait has been tested. If the individuals of a given group, whether normal or abnormal, have been classified with approximate accuracy by the scale, then we should expect a gradual rise in the efficiency or capacity curve with each higher mental age, or at least with every second or third higher age. Thus the children classifying as of six years of age ought to be able to repeat more detached words in three minutes than the children grading five, and the seven-year-olds more than the six-year-olds, etc. Moreover, instead of testing the relevancy of the scale by plotting efficiency age curves merely for the traits which are tested in the scale itself, we may employ extraneous tests. Thus if the children have been properly classified by the scale we should expect those who grade eight mentally to replace the blocks in a form-board more rapidly than those who grade six or seven, and so on. This would not hold true, of course, for every individual, but it should hold for masses of individuals. The gradual increase of efficiency or capacity may be expected to continue up to the point where the trait in question reaches its maturity or maximal development. This will be followed by a period of stationary efficiency which will continue to the beginning of the period of decline or of involution changes.

In the case of curves which are based on abnormal persons, such as epileptics, the feeble-minded and the insane, the validity of this method of testing the accuracy of the scales may be questioned. But it seems reasonable to suppose, and the supposition is in accordance with such evidence as we have, that if, say, fifty epileptics grade eight mentally, fifty grade nine and fifty grade ten, the average efficiency of a given trait will be less for the eight-than the nine-year group, and less for the nine-than the ten-year group. Hence the legitimacy of the method can scarcely be questioned so far as concerns the testing of the reliability of the scale for classifying the individuals of a given homogeneous group. Moreover, if we grant the contention that the individuals of the human race (the idiots possibly excepted) are not classifiable into disparate groups or classes, separated by distinct gaps, but that they differ merely in degree–quantitatively, not qualita tively–so that all can be ranged on a common surface of frequency in respect to any trait or combination of traits which may be tested, then we may assume that the strength of different mental traits in a group of abnormal individuals who classify, say, as nine mentally, should be approximately the same as in a group of normal persons who classify as nine. This would not hold for every possible trait, but probably would hold for the average of the various traits tested in the same age. It has been necessary thus to advert to these premises because no graded or age growth curves for individual traits have thus far been plotted with a view to testing the relevancy of the scale, save those to which reference will be made in this paper.

What, now, do the results of the surveys made by various workers indicate with respect to the correctness of the Binet-Simon scale? The space at our disposal makes it necessary to limit the discussion to a very brief recapitulation of a more extended monographic treatment.2 We shall take up first of all the curves of distribution.

In my plotting of a curve of distribution (Graph IV, p. 187) for a homogeneous group of mentally impaired persons (epileptics), two obvious skews attract the eye, a minor one at five and a major one at nine. The drop in the frequency at five is negligible, for reasons that cannot be entered into here, but the drop at nine clearly appeared to be abnormal. Only 8.4 per cent of the epileptics graded nine years while 24.9 per cent graded ten years mentally. A minute analysis of the data indicated that the irregularity at nine could be traced to four causal factors: the wide-range method of testing, the method of scoring, inherent inequalities or anomalies in the mental make-up of epileptics, and inherent inequalities or defects in the Binet-Simon scale itself. Of these factors the last two were far and away the most important.

2 Experimental Studies of Mental Defectives: A Critique of the Binet-Simon Tests, and a Contribution to the Psychology of Epilepsy, Warwick and York, Inc., 1919.

The above skews in the curve furnished presumptive evidence that the scale was not maximally correct. This presumption was abundantly confirmed by a further analysis of the data, which showed that several age-standards were entirely too difficult, more particularly ages six and nine. It was discovered, for example, that none of those who are classified as of age six were able to qualify on this age-norm (i. e., pass all the tests but one): they all made the six-year standard on the basis of advance credits. Only 29 per cent of those who grade six, seven, eight, nine and ten passed the six-year standard. Similarly only 10 per cent of the Binet-Simon nine-year-olds, and only 40 per cent of all those grading from nine to thirteen, passed the nine-year standard. These results for epileptics, taken by themselves, would be suggestive although possibly not convincing. But, unfortunately, similar inequalities in the age-standards appear in the published data based on the testing of public school children. In Katherine Johnstones testing of public school girls in England (Sheffield), twenty-four out of thirty nine-year-olds failed on the nine-year norms; and in Goddards testing of school children in our own country, the number of six-year-olds who were able to satisfy the seven-year norms was larger than the number who passed age six, a larger number of eight-year-olds stayed in age seven than made age eight, more nine-year-olds were able to pass the ten-than the nine-year norm, an unusually large number of ten-year-olds qualified on the standard for this age while a much smaller percentage of eleven-year-olds could pass the standard of that age, and more twelve-year-olds classified as ten than as twelve.

These relative disproportions in the collective difficulty of the different age-norms are, of course, ultimately dependent on inequalities or misplacements of the individual tests which make up a given age-norm. When the results are critically examined it is found, as a matter of fact, that there is an amazing lack of uniformity between the different tests of the same age. The extent of this inequality may be expressed in quantitative terms by the average mean variations between the percentages of successes for all the tests of the same ages. No mean variations have been computed except for a colony of epileptics. For the epileptics the M. V. s amount to over.20 in four ages (I-II, III, VII, IX), and less than.14 in six ages (V, VI, VIII, X, XI, XII), while the average for the thirteen ages amounts to.17.

Similarly the differences between the easiest and most difficult tests in the same ages, based on the performances of the epileptics who classify in the given ages, amount to as much as 62 per cent in age six, 57 per cent in age twelve and 56 per cent in age nine; while, correspondingly, the smallest ranges are 11, 21 and 24 per cent for ages four, eight and one, respectively. It is thus evident that most of the age-norms contain tests varying conspicuously in difficulty. Some are too difficult, some too easy and others about right.

Here, again, the findings among epileptics are paralleled in the results of the public school testing. Limitations of space render it quite impossible to indicate the status of all the tests in the scale. I shall, therefore, only take space to mention some of the tests which most obviously appeared in my own testing to be misplaced, and which likewise proved to be improperly located when judged by the testing of ordinary runs of public school children.

Among the tests which have proved to be too difficult for the age to which they have been assigned are the following:

Age V, rearranging triangles. Age VI, repeating sixteen syllables. Age VIII, copying a dictated phrase. Age IX, giving correct change, classificatory or descriptive definition, six memories and arranging five or six weights. Age XII, repeating twenty-six syllables. Age XIII, all tests.

The following tests, on the other hand, have proved to be too easy for the age to which they have been assigned. Age VII, counting thirteen pennies. Age VIII, naming four colors. Age X, naming money. Age XII, three rhymes.3 In the case of a number of tests (including some of the above) the results of different investigators are discrepant. The discrepancies are probably due, in part, to the fact that uniform testing conditions have not always been followed by different workers, and to the fact that there are national differences in the strength of various mental traits. Tests which are too difficult for children of one nationality may not be too difficult for those of another, but just right, or quite the reverse.

In considering some tests as too difficult and others as too easy, it is obvious that we have posited a norm or standard of normal variation for each age-norm. We have proceeded on the assumption that age-norms do not possess any scientific value unless a certain minimum percentage of so-called normal children pass the norms for their chronological age. It is evident that if, say, only 25 or 30 per cent of typical or average children pass the individual tests or the collective norms for their age that the norms are worthless. It is equally evident that the requirements are too exacting if the standard of passing were fixed at 100 per cent, since, as already stated, mental traits, even in normal children, will vary considerably from the mode or central tendency. A certain amount of variation in the capacity of average children of the same age must be regarded as perfectly normal. Mental measurements, at their very best, are variables and not fixed constants. Therefore the question, in the final analysis, reduces to this: What shall we regard as the maximal permissible amount of variation in the difficulty of age-norms in a measuring scale of intelligence which lays claim to the character of a scientific measure? The extreme limit may be fixed, I believe, at 25 per cent. That is, if 75 per cent of fairly normal children fail to pass the norms set for their age, the latter may be regarded as too difficult. Certainly, one of the problems for future investigation is the determination of the normal or mammal amount of variation allowable in normal age-norms–the establishment of normal norms of variation.

For figures which will substantiate the above conclusions consult the writers Experimental Studies of Mental Defectives: A Critique of the Binet-Simon Tests, and a Contribution to the Psychology of Epilepsy, Warwick and York, Inc., 1919.

Now, if we accept the 25 per cent criterion of variation as the limiting point, it is evident that the Binet-Simon scale is far from perfect, even altogether aside from the question as to whether the tests themselves are legitimate tests of intelligence or of intellectual development. The mere inequalities in the scale are, in fact, such as to suggest that it can be of little if any utility. But this con elusion cannot be justified, I believe. Even with all its imperfections tbe scale is a fairly serviceable objective instrument for determining the relative mental station of, or for classifying, homogeneous groups of defective individuals. This I have attempted to demonstrate by plotting efficiency curves for each of the following individual traits in epileptics: the time required to name four colors, to replace the blocks in a form board, and to read a given selection; the number of units or memories reproduced from the reading selection, the number of detached words mentioned in three minutes, the strength of the left and right hand grip, and the ataxiagraphic sway of the body. As already stated, if the patients were correctly graded by the scale there should be an increase in the strength of each mental trait with each successive Binet age. As a matter of fact, most of the curves thus constructed show an improvement from age to age. This improvement is fairly smooth or regular except in the color, dynamometry and ataxiagraphic tests. Such inequalities as appear in the other graphs are probably often due to the small number of subjects tested in certain ages. The strongest indictment of the scale furnished by these curves is supplied by the mean variations. These vary from 15 to 57 per cent for each age, with an average of nearly 30 per cent. While a variation of 10 or 15 per cent is regarded as quite considerable in various psychological measurements, we need to determine by experimental means, as has been said, what should constitute a normal or maximal amount of variation in normal age-norms. In any case, the maximal

See my Experimental Studies of Mental Defectives: A Critique of the Binet-Simon Tests and a Contribution to the Psychology of Epilepsy, Baltimore, 1912, 112f.

permissible variation would, as suggested, probably not exceed 25 per cent.

We may conclude, then, that this objective measuring scale, however imperfect, enables us to grade and classify defectives more accurately than can be done by unaided observation. The serviceability of the scale may be illustrated from one of my recent examinees, a male katatonic dementia precox case, age forty-two, a graduate of an agricultural college, now an inmate of one of the Iowa hospitals for the insane. According to the clinical and ward records made annually by the physician in charge, the patient had been gradually dementing for seven or eight years and at the time of my visit was thought to have reached a very low mental level. Certain observations made by the superintendent of the institution, however, had raised the presumption that this patient was in a better state of mental preservation than the records indicated. He was accordingly put through the Binet-Simon scale. The result was a surprise. All of the thirty highest tests in the scale were successfully passed with the exception of two, one owing to disorientation in time and one owing to a slight impairment of the weight sense. Not only so, the responses were nearly always prompt, decisive and well expressed. Twelve units were reproduced from the reading selection, which he read in twenty-seven seconds, the problem questions were answered in from three to thirty seconds, the words in the three shuffled sentences were correctly arranged in six, seven and thirty seconds, respectively, and the seven numbers and twenty-six syllables in age twelve were reproduced instanter. A wrong act committed in anger should be forgiven more quickly than one not committed in anger because anger is a disease. Evolution in mathematics occurs in connection with square and cube root and permutation, while revolution in society is disorder leading to war. Poverty is a state of being without riches, while misery is the absence of correct feeling. Pride is a state of mind in which we show elation over our possessions or certain attributes of ourselves, while pretension is deceit or false claim.

Here is a patient who had suffered from mental disease for about a dozen years. One hour of Binet-Simon testing was sufficient to show that he was practically normal intellectually (his obsessions excepted). And yet this fact had not only not been revealed by years of unaided observation by competent observers, but unaided observation had been completely misled. The scale, even as at present constituted, has undoubted value as a gauge for locating mental status.

Nevertheless, it is essential that we recognize the limitations and present imperfections of the 1908 scale. The scale is not, as some recent magazine and newspaper exploiters would have us believe, a wonderful mental X-ray machine which will enable anyone to dissect the mental and moral mechanisms of any normal or abnormal individual, a talisman which will transform any ordinary observer into a psychic wizard and enable him to infallibly measure mental status. Moreover, it has not yet been adequately shown that the later revisions are not also in need of extensive rectification and amplification (see Chapter X).

CHAPTER IX
CURRENT MISCONCEPTIONS IN REGARD TO
THE FUNCTIONS OF BINET TESTING
AND OF AMATEUR PSYCHO-
LOGICAL TESTERS1

Brevity is said to be the soul of wit, but it often subjects one to the charge of dogmatism. Because of the time restrictions imposed upon this paper, I fear that I shall appear somewhat dogmatic in the theses which I shall lay down in a more or less categorical fashion. But the conclusions arrived at have been formed as a result of the psycho-clinical study of a considerable variety of normal and abnormal mental types.

1. The first popular misconception to which I invite your attention is the idea that mere formal, stereotyped psychological testing by any system of tests whatsoever is all there is to a psychological examination. The fact is that formal testing is only one of the many phases of a mental examination. To be sure, it is a fundamentally important phase. The development of an objective controlled psychological testing technique has brought order out of chaos in the field of psycho-educational diagnosis, and has done more than anything else to render the work of psychological examination respectable and scientific. But, while this is so, it must not be forgotten that there are many important clinical and developmental aspects of mental deviations which cannot adequately be revealed by mechanical testing, whether by the Binet or any other system of tests.2 These conclusions have been sufficiently emphasized in Chapter IV.

i Delivered at the conference on the Binet-Simon scale, Fourth International Congress on School Hygiene, Buffalo, N. Y., August 29, 1913. Printed here in greatly abbreviated form.

2. Because psychological diagnosis involves more than the ability to administer a set of formal mental tests, it is preposterous to suppose that one may become a competent psycho-educational examiner by taking a short university course on mental tests or by taking a six-weeks summer course in a training school for teachers of mental deficients. There is no royal road either to psychological or physical diagnosis. There is no educational magic by which we can, in a five or ten weeks course, transform an ordinary observer into a psychic wizard and confer upon him extraordinary powers by which he will be able to divine or dissect the mental make-up of children.

Let me say here that the evils which have been creeping insidiously into clinical work in education and psychology may be partly attributed to the recent practice of psychologists, most of whom are in no sense clinical men, of offering courses on mental and physical tests to all comers, with the implication that anyone who takes the courses will be qualified to diagnose children in the schools. Unfortunately, those who take such courses usually make this implication, and believe that somehow miraculously they have become competent examiners, even though the instructor has taken pains to emphasize the fact that no one can become a reliable educational diagnostician without spending several years in the technical didactic study of psychology and education, and in the first-hand clinical study of different mental types. I have deliberately limited eligibility to my psycho-clinical practicum to three classes of students; first, to those who desire to fit themselves to become expert psycho-educational examiners and who are willing to spend sufficient time to make themselves thoroughly competent; second, to those who seek to develop skill in the technique of administering certain mental tests, in order to qualify as trained assistants to the expert diagnostician; and third, to those who, seeking a practical course in child psychology, desire to observe and study children in the concrete by means of tests, for the sake of gaining insight into childrens minds from a new viewpoint, and not for the sake of qualifying themselves as psycho-clinical examiners. I would no more regard the two latter classes of students as competent clinicists than I would regard students who had taken an introductory experimental course in psychology as competent university professors of psychology. My demonstration clinics are, of course, open to all who take the didactic courses.

2 The following confirmatory opinion is apropos: I do not think that we can label a child as defective in mind by any fixed test, or set of tests, no matter how carefully thought out. As a means of exploring the workings of a childs mind they are undoubtedly useful, but they cannot properly be regarded as standards. Judged by them alone, the minds of many children who are not mentally defective will be weighed in the balance and found wanting.–Frederick Langmead, M. D., School Hygiene, London, 1913, p. 18.

Departments of psychology and education in universities must be held accountable for maintaining higher standards of clinical work in psychology and education. They must raise their standards just as the medical schools have latterly been forced to adopt higher standards of work. Potential quacks should be kept out of the field of psycho-educational diagnosis no less than they should be kept out of the field of medicine.

To be sure, psycho-educational amateurs, whether teachers, nurses or physicians without extensive psychological or educational training, may be competent to administer formal psychological tests, provided they have been sufficiently trained. My experience indicates that it requires two exercises per week during a ten weeks summer course so to train teachers,8 principals, social workers and college graduates that they will be able to administer merely the Binet tests with accuracy and facility and with confidence in themselves. But although it is possible to prepare measurably competent testers in short courses on mental tests and on the psychology and pedagogy of mentally exceptional children, we must not, therefore, deceive ourselves with the thought that we are thereby training competent psycho-educational diagnosticians. A person trained in short psychological and educational courses can no more be considered a skilled psychological and educational clinicist than a nurse who has had even three full years of training can be considered a skilled physician or surgeon. The skilled psycho-clinicist would no more think of intrusting his diagnoses to the mental tester than the skilled physician or surgeon would intrust his diagnoses to the nurse. The role of the Binet tester and the nurse is precisely similar: their function is that of the assistant to the trained specialist. The medical nurse may serve as a

A recent critic avers that teachers can be trained to become perfect Binet testers during a five weeks term by listening to lectures and discussions on the tests, by observing ten testings (six of these by beginners) and by testing three pupils. Granted. But these claims can scarcely be proved by having beginners test feeble-minded children who have been tested again and again by the Binet tests, and who can, therefore, answer the questions in essentially the same way even though they may be improperly asked. However, the essential point is: Binet testing is one thing, diagnosis is another.

trained examining assistant, taking the pulse, temperature and respiration, assisting in the examinations and administering treatment. Likewise, the mental tester may serve as a trained examining assistant, gathering various data, administering certain tests, and supervising treatment; but neither the nurse nor the Binet nor any other psychological tester is a skilled diagnostician. The mental diagnostician must be able not merely to locate the mental level, but also to form a comprehensive psycho-clinical picture of his case. In order to prognose with measurable accuracy, he must be able to trace symptoms to causes, and correctly differentiate types. Mere psychological testing does not indicate whether we are dealing with cases of infantilism or simple imbecility, of cretinism or mon-golism, of moronity or backwardness, of aprosexia or dullness, of inherent or merely apparent mental deviation, of stupor or amentia, of permanent or recoverable impairment, of progressive chorea or paralysis, of psychotics or neurotics, of epilepsy or hysteria, of idioglossia or baby talk or partial aphasia, of stuttering or partial aphasia or tic speech. But a diagnosis involves the making of precisely such differentiations.

From what I have said it is evident that psycho-clinical diagnosis and prognosis must be based on the entire symptomatology of the cases and not merely on a few mechanical tests. Hence, let us disillusionize ourselves of the smug belief that psychological and educational diagnoses are easy or trivial matters. In many cases they are considerably more complicated and baffling than physical diagnoses; and in any case a skilled psycho-educational diagnostician will require a preparatory course of training not one whit less technical or elaborate than the course required by the skilled oculist, neurologist or psychia trist. If the science and art of psycho-educational diagnosis could be mastered in a summer course, or a couple of short university courses, it would be safe to set it down as humbug. Several teachers of more than average training, who have taken my courses and who have elsewhere observed or tested feeble-minded or backward cases during a six weeks summer term, have remarked that they have been unable satisfactorily to diagnose all cases which they have studied even under these very favorable conditions, and that they regard it as entirely improbable that teachers, nurses or physicians who have been trained to give a few formal psychological or educational tests have thereby acquired such a profound understanding of the childrens mentality that they are qualified to educationally classify them correctly and to direct their educational development.

The above reasons, among others, have lead me to affirm frequently that the department of psycho-educational diagnosis in the schools belongs in the educational division rather than in the department of medical inspection (see Chapter II). No medical inspector can make a satisfactory educational diagnosis and offer sane advice regarding the childs educational development unless he is a technically trained educationist.

3. A third set of misconceptions relates to the accuracy of the Binet-Simon scale. On the one hand, there are the exploiters or enthusiasts who claim that the tests are infallible, and certain serious and perfectly sincere students who, somewhat more modestly, claim that the tests are astonishingly accurate. On the other hand, there are able students who claim that the tests are utterly worthless or only of secondary consequence. During several years I have been making a study of the tests with

a considerable variety of cases, and have gradually formed the conclusion that the tests, in spite of their imperfections, are of considerable value to the trained examiner (see Chapter VIII). They provide a fairly impersonal and uniform method by which to grade or classify, with a fair degree of accuracy, institutional and school cases relatively to one another. Sometimes they enable us to locate the mental level of individual cases with surprising accuracy. But it is absurd to say that the tests are astonishingly accurate. The construction of the scale itself is by no means perfect (as has been shown in Chapter VIII). It is equally absurd to claim that the tests provide a means for making an infallible diagnosis. On the contrary, as already shown in Chapter IV, they may lead to utterly worthless, fallacious, monstrous or pernicious diagnoses, and they cannot be regarded as strictly reliable, not to say infallible, shortcuts for differentiating the backward from the feeble-minded, or the normal from the supernormal, or the psychasthenic from the asthenic, or the Freudian psycho-neurotic with retardation from the mentally deficient. Valuable as they are, they are not a diagnostic automaton which will serve as a satisfactory substitute for an expert examiner.

4. And finally: the impression prevails that adequate and reliable clinical norms can be established by group tests or by the random testing of limited numbers of children. This misconception is discussed in Chapter X.

CHAPTER X
RE-AVERMENTS RESPECTING PSYCHO-
CLINICAL NORMS AND SCALES OF
DEVELOPMENT1

Recent discussions seem to call for a reemphasis of certain conclusions at which I had previously arrived.

1. An expert experimental, educational or genetic psychologist is not, in any legitimate use of the word, a skilled clinical psychologist.2 The former has no more right to regard himself as an expert clinical psychologist than the professional anatomist or physiologist has to consider himself a medico-clinical examiner. The skilled psycho-clinicist will require just as prolonged and thorough a technical preparation as the skilled medico-clinicist.8 Just as the preparation of the physician necessitates more than a thorough grounding in anatomy, physiology and embryology, so the preparation of the clinical psychologist requires more than an expert knowledge of general, experimental, educational, genetic or abnormal psychology or of child study.4 He should have in addition a thorough training in psycho-clinical procedure, which should in-

clude not only work in a laboratory clinic but an interneship–a hospital year, so to speak,—spent in firsthand study of backward, feeble-minded, epileptic, psychopathic and disciplinary cases. These cases must be juvenile subjects if the examiner intends to work with children. He must have also a thorough training in educational therapeutics. By this I include primarily not the so-called psycho-therapeutics of the skilled psychiatrist or psychopathologist–suggestion, psycho-analysis, reeducation–but particularly the differential, corrective pedagogics of the educational expert on mentally deviating children. There is, however, no general scheme of corrective pedagogics. The methods will have to be differentiated to meet the needs indicated by a diagnosis of each case. It will be as different for the feeble-minded and for the stutterer as it is for the deaf and for the blind. Finally, the clinical psychologist must have some knowledge, didactic and clinical, of physical, orthopedic and pediatric defects, of neurotic and psychotic symptomatology, and of personal, family and heredity case-taking.

i Reprinted, with various additions, from The Psychological Clinic, 1913, pp. 89-96.

2 Science, 1913; Journal of Educational Psychology, 1919, p. 294. Journal of Educational Psychology, 1912, p. 924f; Science, 1913. Journal of Educational Psychology, 1911, p. 207f.

It is evident that there is no modern specialist who is equipped with all these elements of knowledge except the properly trained clinical psychologist. The general practitioner, pediatrician, orthopedist, neurologist, psychiatrist, educational, experimental, genetic or abnormal psychologist is lacking in some of the essentials which the expert psyche-clinicist must possess. The ordinary special-class teacher (or school nurse) is, of course, not to be considered for a moment as a trained psycho-clinicist.5 To be sure, well-trained classroom teachers can learn to administer a few tests, and may thereby be able to group some children with approximate accuracy into retarded, normal and accelerated classes, just as an intelligent layman may be able to classify, with some accuracy, people into sickly and healthy groups. But surely the skilled physician attempts to do more than roughly classify his cases. In the measure in which he is competent, he makes a differential diagnosis of each case and adapts the treatment to the diagnosis. The problem of the competent psycho-clinicist is precisely the same: he must attempt not only to measure the amount of mental deviation but to give a differential diagnosis of each case. The teacher or nurse may, indeed, be of considerable service as an assistant to the psycho-clinicist–provided, of course, that she possesses the requisite tact and the necessary technical training. To her (or him) may be entrusted a considerable portion of the formal, mechanical testing, and the collection of the data for the case histories. But her relation to the clinical psychologist is much the same as the relation which the trained nurse sustains to the skilled surgeon. The psycho-clinicist would no more think of entrusting the final diagnosis of a mentally abnormal child to the teacher or nurse, than the physician would permit a nurse to make a differential diagnosis of a physically diseased person. A teacher or nurse or physician, whose psychological training is limited to elementary courses and to giving the Binet or other mental tests, has no more right to the title of clinical psychologist, than a nurse who is trained to take the temperature, pulse or any other medical readings has a right to call herself a physician.

5 Experimental Studies of Mental Defectives, 1:110; Journal of Educational Psychology, 1912, p. 294. Medical Record, September 20, 1913. A similar view is evidently entertained by Bruner, Addresses and Proceedings of the National Educational Association, 1912, p. lllof It may always be necessary to utilize more or less unskilled, or only partially skilled, workers in the mental testing of deviating children, because we shall probably not be able for a long time in the future to secure a sufficient number of adequately trained specialists to examine the millions of pedagogically deviating children which clog the wheels of our educational machine. But this crude type of work–routine testing by amateurs–will probably not enable us to select mentally retarded children with markedly greater precision than can now be done by the ordinary classroom standards for determining pedagogical retardation. Nor will it give us any markedly superior insight into the peculiarities of the mental defects of the children. Extensive use of the tests on various types of children (normal, backward, feeble-minded, epileptic, insane, precocious) has convinced me that many diagnoses by teachers, physicians or nurses based purely upon the Binet tests will be very misleading, often humorously absurd, and at times pernicious. The diagnoses which I make after an exhaustive study of all the available facts are quite at variance with the Binet rating in a considerable percentage of cases. I am free to confess, however, that I have found the Binet scheme of more value than have the psychologists in the Chicago schools (judging by personal reports made to me by Dr. Bruner).

It should be remembered that mental testing is only one phase of mental diagnosis; the determination of mental status does not automatically include the determination of the causative factors. The function of the Binet-Simon, or any other graded scale of intelligence, is to give us a preliminary, and not a final survey or rating of the individual. The testing is merely a point of departure for further diagnosis.8 Grade teachers or nurses are unfitted

Experimental Studies of Mental Defectives, 109 for the two highest functions of the psycho-clinicist. First, they are incapable of giving a satisfactory diagnosis (the chief consideration in any examination) of individual cases; and secondly, they are unable to conduct research–to prosecute productive and constructive research.7 And I want to repeat with all possible emphasis that the real function of the amateur–the examining teacher or nurse or the physician unskilled in psychology–in the schools is not that of the clinical psychologist or the expert diagnostician, but that of the laboratory assistant to the skilled diagnostician, who, to far as mental cases are concerned, must be the specially trained clinical psychologist.

That there are only a few clinical psychologists who have an adequate conception of, and training for, this type of work it is almost needless to say–though unfortunately there are many teachers and psychologists who quite delude themselves (largely because of the prevalent fluid standards of what constitutes a skilled clinical examination) into the belief that they are prepared to function as competent consulting psycho-clinicists. It is, however, no matter for wonder that there are only a few competent clinical psychologists–persons who are qualified to act as professional or trustworthy consultants rather than men who, themselves lacking in clinical experience, may be able to write learnedly on what the clinical psychologist should do. For clinical psychology is just in its infancy. But I believe it is safe to predict that the type of training insisted on in this book will in future be demanded of the mental examiner of deviating children.

2. Norms of mental functioning established by experimental or educational psychologists by group tests on squads of children may have little practical value as clinical tests. There are various reasons why this is so.

i Journal of Educational Psychology, 1912, p. 225.

First–group tests require written responses. But the clinical psychologist must reduce written responses to a merely nominal amount, partly because children differ in the rate or skill of writing without evincing a corresponding difference in intelligence; partly because many abnormal children suffer from special motor defects of the hand, so that they cannot do themselves justice in graphic tests; and partly because written responses require too much time. A comprehensive psycho-clinical examination is a time-consuming ordeal, hence there is no time to waste on the mechanics of writing. There are, of course, many valuable tests which can only be done in writing, and these should be given in as brief a form as may be feasible.

Second–many of the best single group tests carried out by the experimental and educational psychologists cannot be given in less than from three to thirty minutes. It is quite practicable for the educational psychologist to give lengthy tests because usually during any one sitting he attempts to measure only a limited number of traits. But the psycho-clinicist, in order to get a comprehensive picture of his case, must test a very considerable number of functions. Hence the time of each test must necessarily be reduced to an irreducible minimum.

Third–experiments show that children do better when tested in groups than when tested singly.9 For this reason group norms may not be serviceable as clinical norms. Merely on a priori grounds, since the conditions of testing are different, we should always feel a certain amount of skepticism about the accuracy of clinical norms which have been derived from group results. As a matter of fact, nearly all norms now in practical use, whether mental or anthropometric, have been secured by individual and not by group testing.

8 Alienist and Neurologist, May, 1912. See Burnham, Science, 1912, p. 761f.

It is just because our clinical norms must be based on individual and not on group testing that the task of securing them is herculean. It is this fact that I had in mind in previously emphasizing that the establishment of extensive and reliable clinical norms requires a large staff of workers and an ample subsidy.10 The problem would be comparatively simple if group-norms could be used with assurance for clinical work: it takes no more time to test forty pupils at once in a group than to test one pupil alone. It is worth repeating, therefore, that it is probably not to the group results of the educational and experimental psychologists that we must look for our norms but to the clinical data of examiners of individual cases. At any rate, some one should make a comparative study to determine whether there is any difference between norms established by group tests and norms for the same tests established clinically.

3. So far as concerns the probing of the efficiency of mental functions by testing, the most serviceable clinical examining technique consists in the graded scales of intellectual, motor and socio-industrial (possibly also emotional) development.11 The high value which Thorndike" ascribes to the correlation formula probably is justified

so far as concerns the diagnosis of the school system or of a number of individuals of the same ages when tested in groups. But the most valuable contribution made thus far to the technique of clinical diagnosis–and fundamentally diagnosis means precisely clinical diagnosis–does not come from the correlation formula. If there is any professional psycho-clinicist whose constant reliance in the diagnosis of individual cases is the Pearson formula, I do not happen to know him. No one has yet selected tests for developmental scales on the basis of correlation coefficients, although it is probable that in the selection of tests for such scales preference should be given to tests which have been shown by group experiments to possess a high degree of correlation. Certainly the most important type of educational diagnosis done today, from the point of view of the practical good accomplished for the children, is clinical diagnosis; and the value of the technique of individual diagnosis would be little impaired if the correlation formula were non-existent.

10 Journal of Educational Psychology, 1911, p. 204; Alienist and Neurologist, May, 1912; Experimental Studies of Mental Defectives, 1912, p. 56ff.

11 Pedagogical Seminary, 1911, p. 74fl.

12 Science, 1913, p. 133.

4. The position I have taken in favor of the continued use of the 1908 Binet scale unttt an extensive mass of clinical data is available for a thoroughly scientific revision of the scale13 seems to me to be justified by the developments. The relocations of the tests do not always accord with the authors own findings, or with the findings of other investigators, and numerous contradictions and discrepancies have not been satisfactorily eliminated. The detailed analysis of the numerous revisions which have appeared in less than a year is here out of place. But it is well to remind the reader that Binet and Simons own 1911 revision, so far as I can gather, is largely theoretical. Evidently it was made to meet some of the criticisms lodged against the 1908 scale: viz., inequality in the number of tests for each age; the presence of scholastic or training tests; incorrect placing of tests, etc. It was not based, as it should have been to meet any justifiable scientific demands, on the retesting of large masses of normal children. Moreover, some of the changes introduced into the scale fly directly in the face of experimental warrant. Thus the date test is placed in Age VIII although the authors maintain that naming dates are facts that boys of nine are just able to retain (Towns translation). All the children at eleven years succeed in composing single sentences containing three designated words; children of eleven succeed in giving sixty words in three minutes; at eleven the majority succeed in giving abstract definitions; and yet, notwithstanding these findings, these tests are placed in Age XII. Here we have the absurd procedure of placing tests in an age in which they do not belong, in the interests of a theoretical reconstruction, and of leaving an important age vacant. It would be interesting to know the evidence on which the seven-digit and rhyme tests were placed in Age XV. As a matter of fact, the XV-year norms, not to mention any others in this revision as well as in certain other revisions, are practically worthless. Moreover, it is more important to have supplied reliable tests for Ages XI, XIII and XIV, than for Age XV and for adulthood.

i The Psychological Clinic, Vol. V, No. 7, December, 1911, p. 218; Journal of Educational Psychology, 1912, p. 224f; Alienist and Neurologist, May, 1912; Experimental Studies of Mental Defectives, 1912, pp. 55, 117.

Of the other revisions, particularly the American, which have appeared in rapid succession, it may be said that in no case are they based upon the performances of selected normal children (however, no one has yet demonstrated whether selected or unselected cases should be used); in one case a revision has been made on the performances of feeble-minded persons; in no case has an extensive number of cases been tested in every age that has been revised (the one possible exception is Goddards survey; this is entirely commendable from the point of view of the number of children tested, but it is vulnerable, I believe, because of the narrow-range scheme of testing employed); in no case have the revisions been based on the testing of children who have just passed their birthdays (some six-year-olds have been six years and one month, others six years and eleven months); in no case has the wide-range method of testing been used, which I have found essential for purposes of testing out the accuracy of the placing of the tests;" in gome cases revisions have been made in ages in which only fifteen or twenty children have been tested, while in other instances age-norms have been revised or supplied although not a single child has been tested in those ages. This manner of constructing measuring scales may be fascinating as an intellectual diversion, and the scales may indeed be suggestive and possess certain theoretical interests and values; but I must submit that the serviceability of scales thus constructed for the purpose of the practical reliable diagnosis of the cases which daily come to the clinic is questionable. Superficial work like this is misleading and tends to arouse contempt for the slipshod standards of scientific work obtaining in this field of applied psychology. Worst of all, these scales, because of the claims made as to their reliability, are appropriated and used by large numbers of uncritical Binet testers who are neither psychologists nor scientists, and thereby pupils are judged or stigmatized on the basis of unproved assump tions. Instead of glutting the market with measuring scales whose accuracy has not been sufficiently established by extensive testing to render them practically serviceable, it would be better if the investigator devoted his time to thoroughly testing out, standardizing and establishing age-norms for single tests. It is this type of extensive, detailed draft-horse work which is now most needed.

i Experimental Studies of Mental Defectives, pp. 21, 28, 55.

5. The improvement of mental measuring scales involves not merely the standardization of the administrative procedure, nor yet merely the establishment of reliable age-norms for the tests already incorporated in existing scales;" but it requires the addition of new tests in the various age-steps;1"the establishment of age-norms for half-years for younger children;" the establishment of various age-standards throughout the scale for the same type of test; the establishment of normal norms of variation in addition to normal norms of performance;1 and the elaboration not only of intelligence scales, but of scales, separate or combined, of motor, socio-industrial and possibly emotional development, as well as tests, graded or otherwise, of the characteristic types of mental disorganization which obtain in various disequilibrations and psychoses–tests of orientation, paranoidal or delusional trends, memory for remote

and recent happenings, etc., so that graded and standardized scales may better serve the purpose of differential diagnosis.

is Pedagogical Seminary, 1911, p. 70ff; Experimental Studies of Mental Defectives, p. 56 f.

i8 Experimental Studies of Mental Defectives, p. 56; Alienist and Neurologist, May, 1918.

i Journal of Educational Psychology, 1911, p. 206. The scheme there proposed should read as follows: The six-year group will include children from five years ten months (beginning of tenth month) to six years three months (end of third month), while the six and one-half year group will include children from six years four months (beginning of fourth month) to six years nine months (end of ninth month).

is Alienist and Neurologist, May, 1912; Experimental Studies of Mental Defectives, pp. 42, 104f.

The need for tests of conative capacity and emotional development is evident. A childs mentality includes more than the cognitive function: he is a being who feels as well as knows and his life-success often depends on how he feels and does. The most satisfactory single measure of a childs mentality is undoubtedly the test of his intellectual development. This furnishes the best preliminary working basis for diagnosing his mental age. But to fix a childs mental age fully, we must also have especially graded series of tests of motor-industrial performances.

The number of tests in each age should be increased to, say, ten rather than decreased to five, as has been done in the recent revisions. It is hazardous to attempt to use the scale to mentally diagnose defective individuals on the basis of a few deviations or abnormalities. Moreover, since individuals of the same age and training vary considerably in different traits, the scale must be so comprehensive that it will survey a maximal number of fundamental functions–so many that we shall be measurably certain of striking a fair average. Several of the tests eliminated in the 1911 revision have given such valuable insight into the mental condition of epileptic and insane defectives that it would be a misfortune to drop them simply because they are schooly, or because the capacities tested are influenced by training. Indeed, nature and nurture are mutually interacting and reciprocating factors in the developmental process, whence it is idle to attempt to sharply separate tests into those which measure natures dower and those which measure the contribution made by the environment. The environmental factors begin to influence the individual at the very portal of life, and practically no child of school age in this country succeeds in evading the formal educative influences of the school.

The standardization of the methodological technique is a fundamental prerequisite of all scientific work. Tests cannot be given or repeated under uniform and controlled conditions, particularly not by amateurs, unless the procedure is fully set forth, both as to what is permissible and as to what is expressly forbidden. Moreover, a standardized procedure for each test should be followed. I have found experimenters who read for the child the reading selection for ages eight and nine, instead of requiring the child to do the reading. Some tell the child in advance that he is expected to reproduce what he reads or what is read to him, while others say nothing about this. Some give the tests as group, instead of clinical tests, thereby both changing the conditions and omitting certain tests in each age-level which cannot be given group-wise. Discrepancies in results inevitably arise from such diversities of procedure. Fortunately attempts to standardize the procedure have recently been made by several workers.

Since emphasizing the advisability of testing identical traits at various age-levels by the same form of test, and thus determining the status of specific individual traits in different individuals in terms of normal age standards,19 this need has been recognized by other writers.20 As I have stated before:21 We know little at present that is scientifically accurate regarding the degree or character of the physical and mental arrest of our repeaters. We therefore stand in need of comprehensive serial graded tests of intelligence, so that we may determine not only the intellectual age of deviating children, but the nature of the mental functions most seriously affected. A series of consecutive tests, each differing somewhat from the others, which I have used with various groups of children and which can be given once annually for a period of six years, are now available.

i Pedagogical Seminary, 1911, p. 76f; Experimental Studies of Mental Defectives, pp. 8f, 56, 109; Journal of Educational Psychology, 1912, pp. 224f; Epilepsia, 1912, p. 368.

20SEA8HOEE, Journal of Educational Psychology, 1912, p. 50 j and 1vr i:. same Journal, 1912, p. 95.

The greatest present obstacle to genuine progress in psycho-clinical work is the lack of reliable normal mental age-norms for the fundamental mental capacities. Until these are supplied the work of routine inspection and consultation will be more or less blind or guideless. Therefore, in the present stage of the science, the first concern of departments of clinical psychology in schools, universities, psychopathic institutes or institutions for defectives should be the establishment of reliable psychical (and anthropometric) normal age-norms for individual traits. This, I judge, was essentially the view of Smedley, who devoted his energies, while he was connected with the laboratory of the Chicago schools, toward the establishment of developmental norms, particularly of an anthropometric nature. No one has yet made any systematic attempt on an adequate scale to give us normal mental development norms, Binet possibly excepted. Nor is it probable that reliable age-norms, whether psychological, pedagogical or anthropometric, will ever be supplied, unless the work is undertaken, intensively and systematically, by a large research foundation, or unless the work is properly parceled out among the various psychologists in universities, normal schools, public schools, psychiatric institutes and institutions for defectives. For we shall not be able to test existing scales satisfactorily except by wide-range testing (Chapter IV), nor shall we be able to establish thoroughly reliable norms except by testing multitudes of normal children,22 at the very minimum one hundred boys and one hundred girls at each age by years and also by half-years in the earlier ages. It would be better to set the number at five hundred or a thousand for each age. That would be a gigantic undertaking, however, requiring the concentrated attack of a large corps of trained workers, but the ultimate results which this research would yield toward the better understanding of children would well repay the toil and expense required.

21 Pedagogical Seminary, 1911, p. 82.

22 Pedagogical Seminary, 1911, p. 81; Journal of Educational Psychology, 1912, p. 225f; Alienist and Neurologist, May, 1912; Epilepsia, 1912, p. 376; Experimental Studies of Mental Defectives, pp. 21, 28, 56.

CHAPTER XI
INDIVIDUAL AND GROUP EFFICIENCY1

For ages, men waged wars on purely fortuitous or haphazard principles. Not until Bismarck and Von Moltke instituted, parallel with the line, a military staff organization composed of scientific experts, was warfare reduced to a science and conducted in accordance with the scientific principles of efficiency. The military supremacy attained by the German army, after it had been organized in accordance with staff efficiency principles, has lately been duplicated by the Japanese government through a similar organization of its military forces. The modern science of national efficiency in its broadest aspects may thus be said to owe its inception to the military application of efficiency principles in the empire-building campaign of Germany.

For four or five thousand years men have been building houses out of bricks. Successive generations of masons have probably laid the bricks in much the same uneconomical fashion. The thought that bricklaying could be done in strict accordance with a scientific standard of efficiency seems not to have dawned upon the world until an efficiency engineer of our own day, Frank Gilbreth, demonstrated by means of a simple experiment in psychological observation and chronometry, that thirteen of the eighteen customary movements in bricklaying were entirely superfluous and that, supplied with standardized conditions and standardized operations, the output of the average bricklayer could be increased from 120 to 360 bricks per hour, without any material increase in the amount of physical exertion or fatigue. The modern application of scientific efficiency principles to the details of shop management–to the utilization of labor, materials, equipment, the details of operation and distribution–had its origin in the time and motion studies of Frederick W. Taylor in the Midvale Iron Works, about thirty years ago, by means of which the maximal limit of efficient performance under normal and wholesome conditions was scientifically determined. This forward movement in human engineering deserves to be ranked with the introduction more than one hundred years ago of uncarnate power in the place of carnate forces, as the instrument by means of which the worlds labor was to be accomplished. For (although mechanical power is decidedly cheaper than man power–from 135 to 1,350 times cheaper) the scientific studies of occupational habits and task schedules have not only multiplied the producing capacity of human muscular power three-or fourfold, but they have led to the introduction of labor systems which have transformed devitalized, mechanical toilers into organizers, directors, administrators and constructive forces.

i Reprinted, with additions, from the Psychological Bulletin, 1913, pp. 390-397.

Begun as a scientific attempt at economic empire-building and profitable industrial organization, the efficiency propaganda has latterly become crystallized into a system of efficient psycho-technics, and has grown into a national philosophy, a philosophy of conservation and efficiency, single in its controlling aim (the elimination of waste due to human inefficiency), and all-inclusive in its scope. The philosophy is applicable alike to men and materials, methods and management, labor and capital, employer and employee, line and staff, rank and file, lettered and unlettered, producer and consumer, service and equipment, processes and plants, natural resources and manufactured products, factory and church, school and shop, charity and business, nation and state, city and corporation, individual and community, unit and group.

The results of the present-day widespread interest in the gospel of efficiency, human and material, are seen on every hand: in the incorporation of efficiency planks into the national party platforms (conservation of natural and human resources); in the establishment of national conservation bureaus (the Childrens Bureau); in the organization of municipal research bureaus (the Bureau of Municipal Research of New York City, Chicago Bureau of Municipal Efficiency, the Pittsburgh Social Survey and Morals Efficiency Commission, etc.); in the establishment of departments of heredity or psycho-clinical research in institutions for various kinds of mental defectives, juvenile courts, public schools and universities; in the organization in the public schools of departments of health supervision and child hygiene (unfortunately still largely restricted to limited systems of medical inspection); in the organization of staffs of consulting specialists or efficiency engineers in industrial and commercial plants; in the founding of efficiency societies (thus the American Society for Promoting Efficiency, April, 1912, the National Committee for Mental Hygiene, 1912, the American Association for the Study and Prevention of Infant Mortality, the American School Hygiene Association, etc.); in the launching of efficiency periodicals (thus Human Engineering, Cleveland, 1912; The Child, Chicago, 1912), and in the creation of a rapidly growing literature, dedicated to the objective, impersonal, scientific study of the factors or conditions which make or mar human efficiency, whether in the individual or in the group.

In the following pages it is my purpose to review briefly the efficiency literature which has appeared during the last two years, and which admits of summary under the heads which follow: 1. The conservation and increase of vocational (industrial-commercial) efficiency, by means of scientific shop or business management.

In two lucidly written and aptly illustrated volumes, Emerson has presented the ablest exposition extant of the philosophy of efficient industrial management (9), together with a codification of the practical scientific principles involved (10). He recognizes that efficient shop management—which depends on the establishment of scientific analytical motion and time studies, of time equivalents for every operation or task, and the adoption of a standard service or labor equivalent for a given wage—cannot be instituted without a staff of consulting experts, consisting not merely of efficiency engineers and wage specialists, but also of character analysts, psychologists, hygienists, physiologists, bacteriologists and economists. While absolute standards for chemical, physical and electrical processes can readily be set and enforced, human beings must be rated, classified and treated as sentient, moral beings. Properly to administer men on efficiency principles requires the expert services of the psychologist, physiologist, physician and humanitarian. Indeed, Emerson avers that, so far from being a purely material engineering problem, the highest staff standards are psychological. It is psychology, not soil or climate, that enables a man to raise five times as many potatoes per acre as the average of his own state (9, p. 107). Moreover, the science of industrial efficiency is an idealistic philosophy, and not merely a cold, brutal, calculating scheme for oppressing labor—a fact which has been emphasized by Brandeis (3), who argues that there is no inherent incompatibility between the claims of scientific management and the rights of organized labor. Scientific management means the square deal for the wage-worker: shorter hours, without speeding up; more regular employment and greater security of tenure; proportionately higher financial returns; instruction for the inefficient; and a heightened feeling of self-respect and interest in the work.

That the problem is in part both psychological and pedagogical is likewise emphasized by Gantt (the author of the bonus system of compensation, which provides extra pay for work satisfactorily done in a specified time: piece work for the skilled and day work for the unskilled). He (11) recognizes the need of a factory pedagogue, who must be a keen psycho-analyst as well as an efficient teacher. His duties will consist in instructing the workmen, in training them to form efficient vocational habits, and to acquire habits of industry and willing cooperation. The policy of the past was to drive or force the wage worker: in the future it must be to teach and lead. The whip must be replaced by stimuli derived from skilled instruction, merited promotion and a deserved bonus.

That the new science of industrial efficiency cannot justify itself solely by its economic fruits, but must also be judged by its ultimate physiological and social effects upon the workers, is emphasized by Goldmark (12a), in an able and comprehensive digest of the literature bearing on Fatigue and Efficiency in industry. (The best psychological researches, unfortunately, receive no mention in this voluminous compilation.) Owing to the strong tendency to exploit the workers which will exist under any kind of management, the interests of racial efficiency need to be protected by adequate labor legislation. Such legislation must, in the first instance, be based on scientific studies of fatigue. Scientific shop management will have to conform to the physiological laws (and psychological, forsooth) underlying the industrial life.

The psychological and pedagogical principles which may be utilized to increase business efficiency receive their most explicit formulation by the psychologist. Scott (19) considers that human efficiency is not solely dependent on inherent capacity, but on a number of mental factors which it is possible intelligently to utilize by becoming familiar with the principles of business and educational psychology. Scott discusses a number of psychological principles which can be practically applied to increase business efficiency, such as imitation, competition, loyalty, concentration, wages, pleasure, habit-formation find relaxation.2 2. The conservation and increase of the efficiency of eminent talent, by the scientific, impersonal, objective study and control of the conditioning factors of scientific, literary and artistic eminence, fame or genius.

After a lapse of seven years, Cattell (5) has repeated his statistical group study of the most eminent American men of science. He has undertaken an analysis of the changes which have taken place during these years, in the relative rank, and in the sectional, state, city, institutional, professional, sex and age distribution of scientific workers throughout the country. Among the more important furthering environmental factors are geographical location or institutional affiliation, and professional position (career). Massachusetts and Connecticut continue to maintain their scientific preeminence, while three-fourths of the leading scientists are in the teaching profession—only three medical men not teaching in medical schools find positions in the distribution.

2 For a recent statement of the relation of psychology to industrial and commercial efficiency see Milnsterberg, Hugo, Psychology and Industrial Efficiency, Boston, 1913.

Cattells explanation of the fact that only eighteen of our 1,000 leading scientists are women as due to an innate sexual disqualification, is rejected by Hayes (13) and Talbot (22), who find the cause in womans social and educational inequalities and handicaps.

Woodworth (32) finds six or seven factors responsible for the fact that the average American standard of scientific productivity is below the European level, of which the most important is our rapid national, industrial, economic and educational expansion. The fields of industrial, economic and educational promotion, organization and administration offer higher financial and social rewards, and have thereby attracted our best minds.

But the fact that Massachusetts and Connecticut have produced far more eminent men in proportion to the general population than Virginia, North Carolina or South Carolina cannot be accounted for, according to Johnson (15), on Woods hypothesis of the dominance of heredity over environment. It is due, as shown by the financial school budgets of these states, to the greater expenditure of money for educational purposes in New England than in the Southern States.

On the other hand, the Whethams (29), from an his-toriometric study by the space method of one-fifth of consecutive names in the British Dictionary of National Biography, reach the conclusion that able parents have able children, provided like-to-like matings occur, as is found to be the case among the English administrative and peerage classes. The comparative inferiority of the progeny of artistic, literary or scientific men is due to the fact that these classes of men form chance alliances: they do not mate with their likes. The like-to-like matings thus subserve an important evolutionary function: they create a super-class in the general population.

In this connection note may be made of Sterns recommendation (20) for the conservation of incipient talent, that special-talent classes and a special pedagogy should be provided for supernormal children; and of Kiernans contention (17) that the genius is a child potentially developed, biologically and psychologically, that he must be provided with a favorable environment, particularly during the psycho-biological stress periods, and that his potentialities must be aided by all-round development and not by one-sided stimulation, which will tend to upset the instable bio-psychological mechanism.

One sympathizes with the facts, which are emphasized and deplored in current discussions of the super-child or super-adult, that we lack at present any satisfactory standard of genius (the Whethams, 29), that misconceptions of precocity are widespread (OShea, 18), and that the necessity has not always been recognized of clearly distinguishing between merit and fame in historiometric discussions (Browne, 4). Woods claim (31) that his-toriometry (the objective statistical treatment and relative grading of the fame of historical characters) can be reduced to an exact science is denied by Browne (4), because this would-be science does not possess any historiometric functions of constant value. This is particularly true of the adjective method (the ratio of the number of adjectives of praise to dispraise), which does not give a constant differential value to adjectives of different quantitative importance. Browne considers the adj ective method inferior to the space and reference-frequency methods.

3. The conservation and increase of racial efficiency, through eugenical matings, and the elimination of the unfit by sterilization or segregation.

Among the significant studies of the hereditary factors involved in dependency, defectiveness and delinquency are the family history investigations of Davenport (7) and (i Di111; iril (12). Davenport voices his disapproval in no uncertain terms (Oh, fie on legislators who spend thousands of dollars on drastic action and refuse a dollar for an inquiry as to the desirability of such action!) of the legislative efforts to eliminate the unfit by the enactment of compulsory sterilization or anti-procreation laws. He favors the milder remedy suggested by segregation.

Notice should be taken of an attempt to standardize the methods of collecting, charting and analyzing hereditary data (8).

4. The conservation and increase of the mental efficiency of individuals, by means of the removal of physical defects (orthophrenics through orthosomatics),3 or by the administration of proper pharmaco-or dietetico-dynamic agents.

I would suggest the use of the word orthophrenie to designate any process or regimen by means of which deviate mentality may be made to function aright; the word orthoaomatic to designate any process or regimen by means of which any malfunctioning bodily organ may be made to work normally; and the word orthogenic as the generic term to apply to any orthophrenie or orthosomatic processes of restoring deviate human nature to normal functioning. All these processes are essentially and specifically pedagogico-or medico-corrective. Effectually to apply them presupposes the development of a number of highly technical orthogenic sciences.

Wallin has measured by serial psychological tests given throughout a school year the euthenical effects of oral treatment and prophylaxis on the working efficiency of school children (see Chapter XIII). The contention is made that the desirability of establishing dental clinics in the public schools for free inspection and treatment should present itself to the taxpayer as a simple business, if not a humanitarian, proposition—the paying of proper dividends on the capital invested in the schools, the elimination of preventable waste.

The elaborate series of psychological measurements of Hollingworth (14) of the influence of caffeine on various mental and motor processes and on the sleep and general health of a control squad of sixteen male and female adults will serve as a model for similar scientific investigations in the future of the somato-euphoric and psycho-orthogenic effects of the use of vanous drugs, foods, dietaries, etc. His results indicate that mental efficiency may be heightened, without reactionary after-effects, by the administration of judicious doses of caffeine in its pure form.

Closely related is 5. The conservation and increase of the working efficiency of the school population, of normal or abnormal pupils, in elementary, higher, special, rural, urban or state institutions, by the scientific study and control of the processes and agencies which directly or indirectly minister to psycho-pedagogical proficiency.

Perhaps we may agree with the eugenist that permanent racial improvement will come only by improving the inborn qualities of men (considered under 3, above). At the same time, we are obliged to deal with conditions as we find them; after the human misfits have been born, we must bring them to maximal efficiency by improving the environmental factors. The most important euthenical agencies are the schools, and the training or corrective institutions. And it is gratifying to observe that in no field of modern enterprise is the efficiency problem receiving greater scientific study than in the realm of education. Here the major studies have been concerned with the attempt to determine more accurately than was formerly the case the current rate of progress through the grades (thus Blan, 2; Keyes, 16; Strayer, 21); with the introduction of effective schemes of varying the rate of progress through the grades, so that the needs of the individual pupil may be properly conserved (for example, the Mannheim system of grade organization, Van Sickle, 25); with the attempt to differentiate curricula, so as to render them sufficiently varied to meet the needs of all types of exceptional children (witness the recent organization of special classes, occupational courses, elementary industrial, trade and continuation schools); with the effort to establish by diagnostic, psychological tests, developmental age-scales of personal, social, industrial, motor and intellectual traits for retarded, average and accelerated pupils, so that pedagogical or vocational tasks may be fitly adjusted to the level of functioning of each child (thus Wallins plan for gauging the efficiencies of a colony of epileptics, 27); with the task of establishing pedagogical efficiency scores, criteria or scales, by which to make an impersonal, objective determination of a childs proficiency in various branches of the curriculum, such as English composition (Thorndike, 23), handwriting (Thorndike, 24; Ayres, 1) and the fundamental operations in arithmetic (Courtis, 6); with the effort to determine the functional efficiency of various methods of teaching, such as the incidental or drill method of teaching spelling (Wallin, 28, who fails to substantiate the claims of Rice and Cornman, and who shows by tests that spelling efficiency can be increased by the utilization of a psychologically justifiable drill technique); and with the attempt to determine the best age at which to enter children in the schools (Winch, 30, who finds that there is no intellectual advantage in entering children at three rather than at five in English schools).

This survey of the literature on human efficiency—necessarily all too brief relatively to the importance of the subject—should leave a threefold impression in the mind of the reader: first, that the problem of conserving and increasing the efficiency of the race is many-sided, presenting many varied and complex phases; second, that the problem is soluble only through the development and application of a distinct scientific technique, sufficiently varied and specialized to fit any phase of the problem; and, third, that the problem is too large to be solved by any one type or class of existing investigators, but that it requires the development of a new type of scientific investigators, namely, a cooperative corps of efficiency experts in physiology, psychology, education, hygiene, medicine, anthropology, sociology, philanthropy, economy, chemistry, engineering and jurisprudence.

References 1. Ayres, L. P. A Scale for Measuring the Quality of Handwriting of School Children. Department of Child Hygiene, Russell Sage Foundation, New York, 1912.

2. Blan, L. B. A Special Study of the Incidence of Retardation. Teachers College, Columbia University, New York, 1911, pp. 111.

8. Brandeis, Louis D. Organized Labor and Efficiency. The Survey, 1911, 26: 148-151.

4. Browne, C. A. The Comparative Value of Methods of Estimating Fame. Science, 1911, 88:770-778.

5. Cattell, J. Mck. A Further Statistical Study of American Men of Science. In American Men of Science, New York, 2d ed., 1910, 564-596.

6. Courtis, S. A. Standard Scores in Arithmetic. The Elementary School Teacher, 1911, 12: 127-187.

7. Davenport, C. B. Heredity in Relation to Engenics. Henry Holt and Co., New York, 1911, pp. 298.

8. Davenport, C. B., Et Al. The Study of Human Heredity. Eugenics Record Office, Cold Spring Harbor, Bulletin No. 2, pp. 17.

9. Emerson, H. Efficiency as a Basis for Operation and Wages. The Engineering Magazine, New York, 1912, pp. 254.

10. Emerson, H. The Twelve Principles of Efficiency. The Engineering Magazine, New York, 1912, pp. 428.

11. Gantt, H. L. Work, Wages and Profits. The Engineering Magazine, New York, 1911, pp. 194.

12. Goddard, H. H. Heredity of Feeble-Mindedness. American Breeders Magazine, 1910, 1:165-178.

12a. Goldmark, Josephine. Fatigue and Efficiency, a Study in Industry. Charities Publication Committee, New York, 1912. Part I, pp. 288. Part II, pp. 565. (Briefs in defense of womens labor laws by Louis D. Brandeis and Josephine Goldmark.) 18. Hayes, Ellen. Women and Scientific Research. Science, 1910, 82: 864-866.

14. Hollinoworth, H. L. The Influence of Caffeine on Mental and Motor Efficiency. Archives of Psychology, New York, 1912, 22: 166.

15. Johnson, G. H. Dr. Woods Application of the His-toriometric Method. Science, 1911, 88:778-775.

16. Keyes, C. H. Progress through the Grades of City Schools. Teachers College, Columbia University, New York, 1911, pp. 79.

17. Kiernan, J. G. Is Genius a Sport, a Neurosis, or a Child Potentially Developed? The Alienist and Neurologist, serial articles from May, 1907, to February, 1912.

18. OSHEA, M. V. Popular Misconceptions Concerning Precocity in Children. Science, 1911, 84: 666-674.

19. Scott, W. D. Increasing Human Efficiency in Business. The Macmillan Co., New York, 1912, pp. 889.

20. Stern, W. The Supernormal Child. Journal of Educational Psychology, 1911, 2: 148-148; 181-190.

21. Strayer, G. D. Age and Grade Census of Schools and Colleges. Bulletin No. 451, United States Bureau of Education, Washington, 1911, pp. 144.

22. Talbot, Marion. Women and Scientific Research. Science, 1910, 82:866.

28. Thorndike, E. L. A Scale of Merit in English Writing by Young People. Journal of Educational Psychology, 1911, 2:861-868.

24. Thorndike, E. L. Handwriting. Teachers College Record, New York, 1910, pp. 98.

25. Van Sickle, J., Et Al. Provision for Exceptional Children in Public Schools. Bulletin 461, United States Bureau of Education, Washington, 1911, pp. 92.

26. Wallin, J. E. W. Experimental Oral Euthenics. Dental Cosmos, 1912, 54:404-418; 545-566. Also, Experimental Oral Orthogenics. Journal of Philosophy, Psychology, and Scientific Methods, 1912, 9:290-298.

27. Wallin, J. E. W. Human Efficiency, a Plan for the Observational, Clinical and Experimental Study of the Personal, Social, Industrial, School and Intellectual Efficiencies of Normal and Abnormal Individuals. Ped. Sem., 1911, 18: 74-84. See also Eight Months of Psycho-Clinical Research at the New Jersey State Village for Epileptics, with Some Results from the Binet-Simon Testing. Transactions of the National Association for the Study of Epilepsy and the Care and Treatment of Epileptics, 1912, 8:29-48. (Reprinted in Epilepsia, 1912.) 28. Wallin, J. E. VV. Spelling Efficiency, in Relation to Age, Grade and Sex, and the Question of Transfer. Warwick and York, Baltimore, 1911, pp. 91. Also, How to Increase Spelling Efficiency. Atlantic Educational Journal, 1912, 7: 225-226.

29. Whetham, W. C. D. and C. D. Eminence and Heredity. The Nineteenth Century, 1911, 69: 818-882.

80. Winch, W. H. When Should a Child Begin School? Warwick and York, Baltimore, 1911, pp. 98.

81. Woods, F. A. Historiometry as an Exact Science. Science, 1911, 88: 568-574.

82. Woodwohth, R. S. On Factors Contributing to a Low Scientific Productivity in America. Science, 1911, 88: 874-879.

CHAPTER XII

THE EUTHENICAL AND EUGENICAL ASPECTS OF INFANT AND CHILD ORTHOGENESIS1

The mental and physical health of children is a national asset which the state is under obligation to preserve and develop, for the indefinite improvement of humanity and the cause of the young child are inseparably interwoven. The problem of infant mortality, therefore, cannot be viewed apart from the larger problem of race conservation; and in the final analysis the problem of race conservation involves not only race preservation but a twofold process of human orthogenesis: first, a process of physical orthogenesis, or orthosomatics, by which I refer to any process through which malfunctioning physical organs may be made to function aright, or by means of which healthy organs may be continued at normal functioning, so that the physical organism may develop to its maximal potential; and secondly, a process of mental orthogenesis, or orthophrenics, by which I refer to any process, mental or physical, of righting any malfunctioning mental power, so that the mind may realize its highest developmental possibilities. On such a theory, the immediate purpose of a constructive community program–and only a community program will prove genuinely effi cacious–of race conservation or human orthogenesis, may be stated as irreducibly threefold: 1 Read before the American Association for Study and Prevention of Infant Mortality at the annual meeting in Cleveland, Ohio, October 3, 1912. Reprinted from Transactions of the Association, ISIS, 3:173-194, and from The Psychological Clinic, 1912, pp. 155-173.

First, salvation; i. e., the salvation of every born babe, fit or unfit, from a premature grave. Perhaps it were better to follow the example of the Greeks, a nation of ancient eugenists, and allow the unfit, provided they could be infallibly diagnosed, to perish by exposing them to death perils. But this expedient can be dismissed at once, because the very thought is abhorrent to the twentieth century mind.

Secondly, improvement; i. e., the maximal uplift or upbuilding, bodily and mental, of every surviving babe, whether fit or unfit, so that it may reach its maximal potential of social efficiency. The duty to preserve the unfit babe, once it is born, implies the duty to provide it with that nurture and protection which will bring it to its highest estate.

Thirdly, elimination; i. e., the eradication of the social misfits, not by the impossible expedient of enforced selective euthanasia, chloroforming or infanticide, but by the reduction of the birth rate of the unfit stock, and the increase of the birth rate of normal healthy babies.

If the immediate or ultimate aim of the infant mortality crusade cannot be reduced beyond the above triple minimum, it is evident that a scheme of constructive planning must include remedial, corrective and preventive work, by the control of environmental and hereditary factors. While much of the conflict between the groups of environmental and hereditary infant welfare workers is due to the paucity of demonstrated facts in this field, which enables one group to attribute all, or nearly all, the blame for infant mortality, or for racial depopulation and degeneracy, to environment, while the other group just as confidently holds heredity responsible;2 yet it is probably true that the greater part of the controversy is due to one-sided views as to the basal aims to be realized, and accordingly the methods to be employed in an infant mortality crusade. On the one hand, there are some euthenists who limit the legitimate scope of the work to the saving of life from premature extinction, and who underrate, if they do not entirely neglect, a program of subsequent diagnosis, care and training; while on the other hand, there are those who admit that a follow-up program of orthogenic reconstruction undeniably possesses value for the individual, but insist that it has no beneficent influence on race improvement, that permanent race improvement can result only from eugenical breeding, and that environment is of minor importance. The student of orthogenics, however, regards it as impossible of practical achievement and fatal to the realization of the highest orthogenic results in the work of race reconstruction, to attempt to divorce the above aims, to neglect one at the expense of either of the other two, and to create a wide gulf between the euthenical and eugenical factors of control.

In the space that remains I purpose to present a brief statement of the points of view, claims, evidence and the measures advocated by the two schools of infant conservationist workers, and to offer a few suggestions for a fairly comprehensive program of euthenical and eugenical work.

2 Few of the factors productive of infant mortality have been studied under thoroughly satisfactory conditions of analytical control; hence the value of many of the statistical findings is questionable. Yet these discrepant findings are constantly used in support of the most divergent claims. There is great need of genuine scientific research in this field. Too much of it has been quite pseudo-scientific.

EUTHENICS

The euthenist claims that the major percentage of infant deaths are due to a maladjusted environment, or to detrimental factors which are under environmental control. He tells us:

That the vast majority (some say 90 per cent) of babies are well born;

That adverse environmental influences are not more destructive of the biologically inapt than the biologically apt infant;

That since the hereditary factors exert a minor influence during early life, the eugenically fit will succumb during infancy quite as readily as the eugenically unfit;

That the high infant mortality rate is in part due to the circumstance that infancy is the period of most rapid development, and the powers of immunity are weakened during the critical periods of maximal development;

That most infants die of preventable digestive disorders caused by bad feeding, bad food, food infected particularly by the house fly, or by injurious drugs or beverages, and of preventable respiratory diseases, caused by bad air and dirt; and

That, in the final analysis, therefore, the causes of infant morbidity and mortality are chiefly sociological, psychological and economic, a combination of ignorance, carelessness, indifference, neglect, filth, vice and poverty.

Thus it was found in a study of 44,226 deaths under age one, in New York, Philadelphia, Boston and Chicago, that acute gastro-intestinal disorders were responsible for 28 per cent, and acute respiratory diseases for 18.5 per cent of the deaths (L. E. Holt); while the corresponding mortality figures in England and Wales during the period from 1892 to 1901 were 57.5 per cent and 25.3 per cent, respectively. Of the 49,000 infants who die under the age of two every year in the United States from cholera infantum, it is maintained that the majority are poisoned by flies.

Moreover, the euthenist contends that the real causes are often mistakenly or fraudulently reported. Thus premature births or still births, which constitute about 25 per cent of the mortality figures both in England and America, and which are alleged to be due to impairment of biological capital or neuropathic taint, are often due to abortion produced by abortifacients or criminal operations, or to infanticide, or to overwork and starvation of the mothers (as they are frequently found among factory mothers). Likewise in some cases in which the cause is reported as parental alcoholism, the inebriety is only indirectly responsible for the deaths. Often the real cause is overlaying–the crushing or smothering of the infant by the narcotized parent. This circumstance seems to explain why so many infants die between Saturday night and Sunday morning—42 per cent of 461 cases reported in an English study.

With the emphasis placed on such factors as the above, it is evident that the euthenist will look to the control of environmental factors for his orthogenic measures. Among the control measures which may be mentioned are the following:

The complete extermination of the house fly;

The establishment of scientific standards of ante-and postnatal maternity and infancy nurture and care;

Relieving mothers from excessive toil,8 hunger or emotional tension before, during and following the period of confinement,

Women who toil at wearisome work up to the final hour give birth to children inferior in weight to those born of mothers who have given themselves up to rest and quiet for some time before the expected birth.–Pinard.

by the establishment of expectant refuges, lying-in hospitals or maternity nurseries, or nursing mothers restaurants, where wholesome food may be dispensed to the mother free of charge or at small expense, or by the legislative pensioning or endowment of motherhood, or by the issuing of a form of motherhood insurance;

The compulsory registration and periodical inspection of baby farms or foundling homes;

The licensing and supervision of foster mothers;

The establishing of medically supervised milk stations or social consultation centers, where properly modified, pasteurized or sterilized milk may be supplied, and where mothers may receive instruction and witness demonstrations in the scientific care of infants; or the establishment of community educational health centers of the Milwaukee type, for the training of mothers, nurses, social workers, midwives4 and doctors in infant feeding, care and hygiene, and in home and neighborhood sanitation;

The establishing of public summer baby tents;

The development of measures to substitute breast feeding5 for bottle feeding;

The legal imposition of fines on mothers who can but will not nurse their sickly babies;

The substitution by legal enactment of bottle teats for bottle tubes;

The frequent systematic inspection of the mouths of young children adequately to control the disease of the people, dental caries;

The after-care or supervision of sick children during convalescence;

Our first municipal school for midwives was established in New York in 1911.

s Children fed at the mothers breast double their weight at the end of the fifth month, and treble it at the end of the twelfth month, while those bottle-fed double only at the end of the first year, and treble only in the course of the second year.

The expert community supervision of infants until they statutorily come under the supervision of school boards;

The systematic (annual or biennial) examination of pupils in the schools by medical and psychological inspectors, with a view to the discovery and correction of physical disabilities and mental deviations or abnormalities; whether developed or latent;6

The community supervision, regulation and socialization of urban recreation;

The education of the youths of both sexes in sex hygiene; and

The education of girls and young wives for motherhood in little-mothers classes or in continuation home schools.

Concerning the desirability of instituting systematic, organized plans for putting into effect some of the above measures, there ought to be little difference of opinion. There is, at least, little reason to doubt the efficacy of many of these measures. To cite merely four instances: by the employment of various corrective, remedial and preventive measures in New York City the infant death rate between 1881 and 1902 was reduced 62 per cent; by providing infant supervision by means of district nurses the mortality in New York City last year was reduced to 1.4 per cent among 16,987 supervised babies (the cost of the supervision amounted to about fifty cents per child per month–the same as in Milwaukee); by arranging to give mothers a ten-day rest period before confinement 10 per cent was added to the weight of infants in Paris; and 8 The last two measures are partly in practical force in New York City (and Boston), where a Division of Child Hygiene, of the Department of Health, has been established under municipal control with the duty of supervising the health of children from birth to the legal working age. It is some such community organization as this for which I shall plead, though I prefer to have it established as a part of the public school system, with various additions to its functions.

by the simple expedient of feeding infants from the breast instead of from the bottle the mortality in various cities has been reduced in amount varying from fifteen per cent to several hundred per cent.

Obviously, the first efforts of any organized plan of human conservation should aim so to environ every babe that it may obtain a decent fighting chance for survival beyond the cradle. By the proper control of environmental factors I believe that we can eradicate 75 per cent of infant mortality, provided the work is organized on a community basis instead of being left to individual initiative or direction. Individual effort, because of ignorance, caprice, poverty or inefficiency, will mean desultory or worthless action, or no action at all. Nothing short of organized community action will enable us to eradicate the preventable mortality of infants. My first plea, therefore, is for the development of comprehensive plans on a community basis for preserving and conserving the lives of infants.

But I shall equally lay stress upon a second desideratum, namely the organization of community development supervision of the child during the entire growth period. That there is need of such supervision in this day of disintegrating homes there can be no doubt. The problem of the individual child only begins after the battles of the first years of life have been won, and after the child has become more or less emancipated from dependence on his mother or caretaker. The momentous period of individual-ization which now begins is fraught with grave perils at every turn. All along, the child will have to cope with insidious destructive environmental influences which tend to abort, deflect or retard his normal development. Can we safely entrust the responsibility for normal development under modern urban conditions to the child or parent? Do not practically all children and most parents lack the requisite knowledge, insight and foresight? Is it not, therefore, the duty of the community or state to supplement the home care, and systematically to direct the childs development, so that he may come to a true knowledge and appreciation of the ideals which the state regards as essential to its perpetuity? Clearly it is in the interest of the state that the child be so safeguarded from injury and disease and so trained that he may reach his maximal physical, mental and moral potential, to the end that he may become a productive civic unit and not a social drag. That the state has already assumed a paternalistic function toward her children is shown by the general establishment of compulsory systems of public day schools and special institutions, and by the more recent establishment of systems of school medical inspection. While I am of the opinion that the public school systems are the communitys logical agency for accomplishing the orthogenic work required by the infant as well as the child, neither the public schools nor the school medical inspection systems have as yet been adequately organized to carry out a satisfactory program of orthosomatic and orthophrenic work. The public schools are making heroic attempts to adapt their machinery to the varying physical and mental needs of all pupils, but school officers and administrators have thus far failed to appreciate that the mental and educational problems connected with the mentally exceptional child cannot properly be handled until the direction of the work is taken out of the hands of the dilettanti and placed in the hands of psycho-educational experts, who are not only skilled in methods of psycho-clinical diagnosis, but who are also capable of functioning as consulting experts in the various branches of corrective pedagogy. Likewise school medical inspection has failed to deliver, partly (1) because many school medical inspectors have no specialized training in the diagnosis of the physical and nervous defects of children, and lack expert knowledge of school hygiene and sanitation and the prevention of defects and disorders; partly (2) because the work is confined almost entirely to mere inspection and tabulation of defects instead of including corrective treatment, with the result that in many schools the percentage of pupils who actually have their handicaps removed varies from 5 to 25 per cent;[7] and partly (3) because emphasis is placed almost entirely on the discovery and correction of existent defects, instead of on the discovery and prevention of the causes of the defects (that is, the conditions which produce adenoids, enlarged tonsils, carious teeth, etc.).

In order that the schools may serve as an organized agency for carrying out an effective program of ortho-genie work for every child of school age,[8] the following plan of work is proposed: 1. Every child on entering school should be given an expert examination for the detection of latent or manifest abnormalities of mental, moral and physical development, the mental examination to be made by a skilled clinical psychologist who is an expert in psycho-clinical methods and in the differential, corrective pedagogy adapted to various types of mental deviates; and the physical examination to be made by a physician specially trained in the detection of the diseases, the physical defects, the nervous disorders and physico-developmental abnormalities of childhood.

7 In a Chicago school the principal told me that in one of her investigations she found that only 5 per cent of the defective pupils had taken any measures to have their defects removed. It is said that in New York last year, as a result of visits to the pupils homes by inspectors and nurses, 86 per cent of the defects discovered were treated.

8 The schools may well care for the child from the time of birth, in the department of orthogenics which I propose. This would entail the employment of nurses, who would devote themselves to the care of babies and young children. All the records would be filed in the one central school bureau.

2. Children found in these examinations to be mentally or physically deviating should immediately receive appropriate orthogenic treatment, whether this be hygienic, corrective or preventive, or whether it be physiological, pedagogical or psychological. By thus securing diagnosis and treatment while the childs brain is plastic we shall be able to accomplish the highest orthogenic results. We shall be able to prevent the formation of injurious pedagogical habits which result from the malfunctioning of the psycho-physical organism and which, once established, are often hard to eradicate. To obtain maximal results, the child deviate must be classified early.

3. Specially trained teachers, and special classes or institutions should be provided for the mental and physical deviates. School medical and dental dispensaries should be established for the free treatment of all properly certified indigent cases. It is economic suicide for the state to pay for the education of pupils who are largely unedu-cable because of physical handicaps. To spend large sums of money in the discovery of physical handicaps without providing the machinery for the rectification of defects is also economic suicide.

4. Physical training should be systematically required of every child during his entire school course. Health education must be given the same emphasis as mental education.

5. Children shown by the expert examinations and the results of special training to be socially and mentally incompetent, should be segregated in colonies for permanent oversight. They should be sent to such institutions as soon as their incompetency is measurably certain, at least before they reach puberty. No mental incompetents should be permitted at large in society, unless the home situation is such as to insure adequate protective oversight for the child.

6. The medical and psychological work throughout should contemplate not only the discovery and correction of defects or deviations which interfere with normal development, but also the discovery and removal of the conditions, whatever their nature, which produce physical or mental disabilities. The keynote of the whole plan must be prevention rather than cure. The problem does not so much concern the excision of adenoids or enlarged tonsils, as the removal of the conditions which cause them.

There is not space to argue the practical efficacy of a comprehensive program of orthogenic work along the line indicated above, but reference may be made to the experiment described in Chapter XIII, which was undertaken to discover whether or not the mental efficiency of a group of children actually could be raised by orthosomatic mouth treatment. The bearing of this experiment–it showed that the mentality of children could be heightened by the proper care and use of the oral cavity–is not only economic (the financial waste resulting from trying to teach pupils whose capacity for development is partially blocked by physical disabilities) or moral and humanitarian (the inhumanity and cruelty of forcing children to battle through the grades against heavy physical handicaps) but also eugenic. There are probably few physi cal defects which do more to impair the constitutional vigor of the individual than the insanitary mouth. The damage done to the individual by an unhygienic oral cavity has been said to exceed the damage done by alcohol. Be this as it may, whatever impairs the constitutional vigor of the individual will probably, in the long run, impair the racial vigor.

I incline to the unorthodox view that there is a eugenical side to euthenical recla-mation work. It is possible, I believe, by the orthosomatic and orthophrenic work suggested above, gradually to elevate the vital index of the growing generation and thus eventually to improve the inheritable qualities of the race. Will not a slow ortho-genie transformation of the somatic protoplasm gradually produce a benefi-cent transformation of the germinal protoplasm, just as the continuous indulgence in alcohol is thought by some investigators to produce a gradual deterioration of the reproductive cells?

Whether or not this view is scientifically justifiable, I want specially to emphasize the following vital eugenical aspect of the above community plan of school orthogenic work, namely: the truth that the practical efficacy of applied eugenics largely depends on the systematic study of children in the schools, so that all eugenically unfit children may be identified during the prepubescent years. Only through systematic cooperative child study on the part of teacher, educator, psychologist, biologist and physician will we be enabled to distinguish with certainty between the transmissible and therefore eugenically important qualities and the non-heritable and therefore eugenically irrelevant qualities, so that our eugenic duty toward a given child may be patent certainly not later than at the dawn of adolescence. The urgent need for improved differential eugenical diagnoses will appear presently. But before proceeding further let us summarize the argument of the preceding pages: It is the inalienable right of every child born into the world, whether fit or unfit, to receive such parental and community care as shall remedy or prevent sickness and disease, and as shall correct or mitigate constitutional or acquired physical defects and mental and moral disabilities, to the end that he may be able to appropriate in maximal degree the instruction and training which the community bestows upon him, and to the end that he may become a fit progenitor of healthy offspring.

But if this proposition be true, is it not equally true that it is the inalienable right of every child to be well born, to be saved from impending death, premature decrepitude or inaptitude before instead of after birth? Otherwise stated, is it not the inalienable right of the state to demand that no socially unfit stock shall be born, and to enforce that demand by all the police power which it possesses? To these questions the eugenist makes affirmative reply.

Eugenics

The eugenist affirms that human beings, like the lower animals, breed true. Like produces like, fit answereth unto fit, unfit follows unfit. Therefore the problem of human orthogenics is fundamentally a problem of breeding viable, untainted infants by means of eugenically fit matings.

If the euthenist has unbounded faith in the efficacy of the environment, the eugenist has a no less religious faith in his heredity formularies. We are told:

That the influence of the environment is less than one-fifth, nay, less than one-tenth, that of heredity (Karl Pearson);

That most infant deaths are due to lack of biological capital, or to constitutional inferiority, and the resultant increased susceptibility to disease;

That the issue born of precocious marriages (before the parents organisms have attained their maturity) are biologically and psychologically inferior (Sterility often results, or children are born with lessened chances of survival. The greatest child mortality comes from unions contracted at sixteen or earlier, and the lowest from unions contracted from twenty-nine to thirty-two.–Quetelet. The heaviest infants are born of mothers between twenty-five and thirty.–Matherot Duncan. Mothers who at the birth of their first child weigh less than fifty-five kilograms and are under twenty years of age, have children of inferior weight.–Schafer. Most famous men have been begotten of parents between twenty-five and thirty-six years of age);

Short intervals between pregnancies interfere with the normal progressive increase in the weight of later births (Wernicke) and thus presumably lead to inferior stocks;

That 80 per cent of infant mortality is due to inherited or congenital syphilis alone;

That syphilis is the chief cause of abortion;

That syphilis causes tardy growth in the child (e. g., normal children regain their weight at the end of one week, syphilitics at the end of two weeks), and sometimes infantilism;

That the congenitally syphilitic child is far more prone to contract the various contagions diseases than the non-syphilitic;

That more than one-third of tubercular cases in institutions come from tubercular families, which it is assumed are tubercular because of inherited tubercular diathesis;

That from 60 to 90 per cent (Tredgold) of the amented feeble-minded are hereditary cases, and that a large percentage of the insane (16 per cent, Koch), epileptic (56 per cent, Barr and Spratling) and criminals and social offenders are the victims of heredity;

That alcohol is a veritable race poison, producing both individual and racial degeneracy;

That parental alcoholism causes atrophy or pathological changes of the reproductive mechanism;

That it is responsible for 5 to 20 per cent of feeblemindedness and epilepsy, 80 per cent of male insanity and a large percentage of pedagogical backwardness in school children, for a large percentage of mortality soon after birth, for infantilism, deformities, nervous disorders, deficiencies of weight and disease in children, and for the inabilty of mothers to nurse their offspring (Bunge found that only 2.1 per cent of daughters of confirmed drunkards were able to suckle their infants);

That female inebriety particularly is a prolific cause of the ruin of infant life, inebriety in the expectant mother being responsible for a large percentage of sterility, abortion, miscarriages, premature births and still births, and retarded and unsymmetrical growth in the embryo (W. C. Sullivan: only 42 per cent of 600 children of 120 female inebriates lived more than two years; 55.8 per cent lived less than two years. Lonnett: of 107 English women dying of alcoholism before twenty-nine years old, 8 bore no children, 99 bore 6 delicate and deformed children; but 29 vigorous children were born before the mothers became alcoholic. Some pregnant Swiss women alcoholize in order to reduce the size of the child, so as to avoid the pains of birth);

That the death rate is greatest for the later pregnancies of maternal inebriates (88.7 per cent of deaths among first born; 72 per cent among the sixth to the tenth born; still births among the first born, 6.2 per cent; among last born, 17.2 per cent);

That increase in national sobriety has actually been attended with a decrease in infant mortality (English study. Latenens study of 20,000 from 5,846 families indicated that the number of deaths and miscarriages decreased as the amount of alcohol consumed decreased);

But that both the number of premature and still births and the number of infants who barely escape these conditions are increasing in civilized countries (Kaye, whose finding is based on English statistics), while likewise our neuropathic stock is increasing faster than the general population, so that the army of dependents, defectives and delinquents threatens to engulf our civilization (one medical alarmist, Kellogg, predicts that in the year 2012 no children at all will be born!);

That the preservation of unfit babies by euthenical means materially augments the increase of the degenerates;

That state systems of granting annual bonuses or allowances for each child born are pernicious, because only that part of the population which is barely living above the poverty line would take advantage of them, and this would tend to augment the ranks of the lower social strata;

That material prosperity, eugenically considered, is no panacea for racial degeneracy, because it tends to produce alcoholism, premature debauchery and syphilis (as shown by a study of prosperity in the wine-producing canton of Luchon, France. See p. 272);

That the potential limits of every individuals level of functioning are quite definitely fixed by heredity; that since the limits cannot be radically altered or lifted by nurture or training, each individual will tend to achieve his maximal success only in so far as lie follows his initial aptitudes, propensities or bent; and that therefore the improvement of human capacity is primarily a matter of eugenical mating and only secondarily a matter of teaching and training.

What now are the measures which are proposed by the eugenist for elevating the standard of parenthood? The strictly eugenical measures have to do either with the regulation of reproduction or mating, i. e., scientific breeding; or with the protection of the germ plasm from injury or deterioration (and possibly with the safeguarding of the fetus from injury, starvation or infection). The specific measures most frequently advocated are the enforced limitation of marriages to the eugenically fit, as determined by statutorily required physical and mental examinations of applicants for marriage certificates; the compulsory sterilization, under legal safeguards, of all persons adjudged socially incompetent; the quarantining of all persons who are carriers of infectious social diseases; and the permanent sequestration in state colonies of all the epileptic, insane and feeble-minded, chronic inebriates, syphilitics, rapists and sexual perverts.

The student of orthogenics finds himself in sympathetic accord with the fundamental aims of the eugenic movement. In our efforts to fashion a race of human thoroughbreds nothing less than the eugenical ideal is wholly satisfying. Moreover, we have a right to judge any proposed euthenical measure in the light of the eugenical ideal. Any euthenical measure which is manifestly anti-eugenical should not be encouraged. Legislators may well pause before favorably considering those measures now being advocated in various civilized nations which are threatened with depopulation. The probable immediate effect of paying bounties out of the public treasury to mothers for the support of babies would be the increase of neuropathic stock, so that society would ultimately succumb under the ever increasing burden. But while the eugenical conception is impregnable as an ideal, the student who is seriously interested in the cause of eugenics must recognize that there are almost insuperable difficulties in the way of the effective application of its principles, and that progress in the work will depend upon the measure in which these difficulties are successfully overcome. We may group these difficulties into four classes: 1. Psychological and sociological difficulties.

Effective reform of human practices is scarcely possible without the aid of the emotional forces of human nature. But mans emotional development has not kept pace with his intellectual progress. Emotionally, human nature is very much the same today that it was in the days of primitive man. This is explainable on the assumption that the emotions are merely the subjective side of the instincts, and instincts are relatively fixed. Therefore, in trying to transform the sex life of the race we are obliged to deal with a set of emotions which are connected with one of the three oldest and most basal instincts of the race, namely the sexual instinct. Now, it is at least supremely difficult, if not utterly impossible, suddenly to change instinctive racial reactions by mere instruction, demonstration, exhortation or legal enactment. An instinct has become deeply imbedded in the very fabric of the psycho-biological life of the individual as a result of age-long racial conflicts, by slow and painful processes of elimination and survival. Therefore, instincts have acquired a degree of stability, pertinacity and emotional intensity which renders them almost invulnerable to merely rational appeal, and which leaves but one way to transform them, namely the evolutionary method of gradual elimination and survival.

To illustrate: as a result of thousands of years of painful tribal struggle and warfare those tribes were gradually selected for survival which abandoned the practice of consanguineous marriage and incestuous intercourse between near relatives. Through painful experience the inexorable truth was slowly forced into the consciousness of the race that such unions weakened the stamina of the tribe, and therefore must be rigorously interdicted. Not only did such practices arouse the disapproval, contempt and condemnation of the organization, but they gradually awakened in the individual a feeling of disgust which in time became instinctive. The intense repugnance which the normal mind today feels toward consanguineous or incestuous intercourse rests more upon an instinctive than a rational basis. The taboo pronounced on such unions as these is founded on the deepest psychic subsoil of the racial consciousness, and has become incorporated in the very habitudes, customs and traditions of the race, obtaining thereby a sanction which is more authoritative than that conferred by command or arbitrary legal enactment.

The eugenic problem would be easily solved if there existed a racial instinct of repulsion against anti-eugenical matings–if there were a universally instinctive taboo on marriages between the biologically unfit. It is a question whether such a feeling of disgust, instinctive in its elemental intensity, can be instilled into the consciousness of lovers by mere teaching, enlightenment or prohibition. Sexual attraction is an instinctive psycho-biological phenomenon less subject to regulation by scientific or legal prescription than by blind impulse, custom, tradition or convention. Most free matings will be determined by certain intangible secondary sexual characteristics, certain fetiches peculiar to each individual, while the restricted matings will be determined by the conventional requirements of social station and wealth–unless, indeed, the eugenic creed can be transformed into a vital, national religion.

Just as there are deep-seated psychological instincts or emotional forces which tend to frustrate the enforcement of eugenic marriages, so the racial instinct of sexual modesty will offer the hardest obstacle to the effective and universal enforcement of laws requiring health examinations before marriage licenses may legally be issued. Even if such laws were generally enacted, will not the forces of sex frequently overleap all legal restraints and defy prisons and chains?

In the same way, the chief obstacles to the legal enforcement of the practice of va-sectomizing the unfit are of a psychological nature–various sentiments and prejudices, and mans instinctive recoil against any interference with the processes or impulses of nature. If it were possible to vasectomize the whole army of misfits, and to stop entirely the manufacture of alcohol throughout the earth, the problem of eugenics would be largely solved. The chief obstacle against the total elimination of the liquor curse, again, is also psychological–the instinct of appetite and certain mental states which are induced by the consumption of narcotics.

Finally, there are the maternal instinct and filial ties to thwart any effective plan of colonizing without exception all degenerates or eugenical misfits.

It has been necessary thus to emphasize the fact that there are certain psychological forces, certain instincts, emotions, customs, conventions and folk ways, which are anti-eugenic in nature, and which must be reckoned with in any well-conceived plan of eugenics. The fact that these eugenically hostile forces exist in the very citadel of humanity makes it all the more essential that the eugenist wage a relentless campaign for the increase and dissemination of verifiable and convincing knowledge of heredity, so that eugenic truths may lay hold on the deepest feelings and sentiments of the race and become in fact a national faith, tradition or religion. Then will it be possible to make eugenic enactments on the statute books genuinely effective.

2. Administrative and legal difficulties.

The adequate enforcement of eugenical measures in the present stage of civilization requires much governmental machinery. But because of the facts which we have just considered, it is not probable that adequate laws can be secured, or can be enforced if secured. Public sentiment would not support the enormous legislative levies which would be needed to colonize the vast army of misfits (already in New York from one-fifth to one-seventh of the state revenues go to the support of the institutions for defectives); and the popular outcry, based on prejudice, blind emotion, impulse or instinct, against the sterilization of at least all those misfits who remained at large in society, would nullify the law. As a consequence, a large number of degenerates would always be found in society polluting the race stream. Compulsory physical and mental examinations of all parties to marriage contracts would serve a useful eugenic purpose; but the laws would be powerless to prevent a man or woman from contracting, say, contagious venereal diseases after the bill of health had been issued. After all, the problem is not so much to get proper laws enacted as to secure the public sentiment which will demand their enforcement. There is no remedy for these difficulties, except a campaign of discovery and diffusion of eugenic facts, so that the public conscience may eventually be stirred.

3. Diagnostic difficulties.

Our third obstacle is the lack of a reliable or infallible criterion of eugenical unfitness, or of anyone competent to pronounce infallibly on all but the obvious cases. Who is competent to decide whether or not a given individual possesses desirable or undesirable hereditable determiners? Who is able to say unequivocally that a given individual is eugenically defective and that he can only give issue to tainted progeny? Who can determine with scientific exactness that certain determiners are lacking in x and that the same determiners are likewise lacking in his intended consort? Who is able to determine whether a so-called normal person may not be the carrier of defective strains, just as healthy persons may be disease carriers, whereby unions between such normals may be just as non-eugenical as unions between obvious degenerates? It must be confessed, I believe, that the gaps in our knowledge of the laws of human heredity from the biological side are still deplorably wide. As far as concerns the psychological identification of mental defectives, our present technique enables us to locate the extreme types, but not the borderland cases. One of our best schemes of mental classification is the Binet-Simon scale. But after having personally used this scale almost daily for three or four years in the study of the feeble-minded, epileptic, insane, juvenile delinquents and backward children, I am free to confess that while the great utility of the scale cannot be questioned, it is not by any means the marvelous, unerring machine which it is claimed to be by certain overzealous exploiters, even for the purpose merely of measuring the degree of mental arrest. Nevertheless, with improved measuring scales of intellectual capacity, supplemented by the scales of personal, social, motor-industrial and pedagogical efficiency (see Chapter VI), and by developmental and heredity case-studies, the difficulties pertaining to the accurate diagnosis of mental cases will probably not prove insuperable. The establishment of adequate, reliable mental development scales is a large task, which cannot be done within a reasonable time without liberal public or private subsidy. One of the reasons for supporting such work is the extreme feasibility of experimentation in heredo-psychology. In the psychological field it is easy to test and experiment on fit as well as unfit individuals, while in the biological field human heredity experimentation is almost impossible. This brings us to the statement of the final obstacle confronting applied eugenics, namely: 4. Experimental difficulties.

If it were possible to apply the principles of experimental genetics to human breeding as those principles are now applied to the breeding of domestic animals, many of the controverted problems could be brought to a fairly expeditious adjudication. Just because this seems impossible of achievement, the propagandist must beware lest he bring disrepute upon the eugenics movement by advocating precipitate, ill-advised or premature action. There is danger that zeal may get the better of wisdom, and that state and national laws may be passed which we shall later come to rue. In the absence of experimental demonstration, who shall say that the laws of human heredity are Mendelian and not Galtonian in character? What warrant is there for affirming that such socially significant complex mental traits as honesty, courage, virtue, initiative, concentration, perseverance, intelligence, judgment, reasoning, kindness and loyalty are unit characters and are transmissible as simple determiners? Woods affirms that they do not behave as unit characters and are not transmissible as such. But it is just such mental char acters as these that it is important to transmit, for fundamentally the difference between a social fit and misfit is a difference in mental qualities; the age of brute or muscular force has been superseded by the age of intellectual or psychic force.

Since the important question, therefore, is to determine whether socially significant complex human mental traits are heritable, and since this cannot be directly determined for man by the method of experimental genetics, what is to be done? The following brief outline of both practical conservational and eugenical research work is suggested:

1. Conservational bureaus or agencies should be established on a community basis, in the cities and commonwealths, for the purpose of scientifically supervising the health, growth, hygiene and educational development of the child from birth to the period of late adolescence. A community plan of this character has already been sketched in the earlier section of the chapter. I incline to the opinion that the work should be organized in connection with the public school systems, not merely because this public agency is already in existence, nor because it would prevent the duplication of material plants, nor yet because the people have confidence in the public school systems; but because I believe that the integral function of the public schools is not only instruction or training but also the conservation of the mental, moral and physical health of the children entrusted to their care.

2. One of the specific functions of this bureau, or of some other organization, should be the biographical charting of all babies born into the world, or at least of all infants of presumptively degenerate stock.9 The bio-

Mothers should be trained to keep maternal diaries of children from the time of birth.

graphical charts, on which the first entries should be made shortly after birth, should contain such facts as the following: date, order, circumstances, condition, weight and height at birth; the mental, socio-moral and physical condition, eating and drinking habits, overwork and accidents of the mother before and at the time of birth; the state of health, habits, etc., of the father at the time of the conception; a record of the hereditary factors in the direct and indirect ancestral lines; a statement of the housing and environmental conditions. Later entries would indicate whether the child was breast or bottle fed, and for how long, whether he was properly nourished, clothed, disciplined and protected from moral and physical injury during childhood, and contain a record of his diseases, physical defects, accidents, annual anthropo-metrical indices, developmental retardations or accelerations, mental and physical peculiarities or abnormalities. This card, or a duplicate, should accompany the child to school, where it would be properly filed and where it would be supplemented by annual entries made by the teachers, the school nurse or social worker, the school psychologist and physician. These entries would show the childs physical and mental condition, as determined by anthropometric, medical and psychological tests, and his pedagogical progress from year to year. The data thus secured (to be made available only to the officers of instruction, diagnosticians and research workers) would enable us scientifically to trace pedagogic facts and child problems to their real antecedents, they would be of value for the intelligent guidance, care, development and training of the child, they would enable us to locate and diagnose more speedily and effectively the social incompetents, they would contribute material of great value to the science of human eugenics, and would likewise possess considerable value for the guidance of the child himself after he has reached his majority.

3. A number of specific medical, psychological, pedagogical and anthropometric investigations, because of their practicability and the light which they will shed on various eugenical factors, should be prosecuted on a large scale. For example: what is the difference in the rate of mental and physical development between children of alcoholized or caffeinized or narcotized parents and children of abstainers from alcohol and caffeine and tobacco? If there is a difference, does it appear during early childhood, during early adolescence, or later? Do the differences gradually disappear, so that both classes of children eventually reach their normal type, just as some species of animals whose development has been artificially or experimentally retarded later recover their losses?

Likewise, what is the relation between narcotized parentage and mental and physical defects, deformities and abnormalities and arrested epiphyseal development in the offspring? To answer these questions extensive serial psychological, anthropometric, physiological and radio-graphic tests need to be made of children of alcoholized and non-alcoholized parentage.

A number of studies already made indicate that this is a fruitful field for protracted research. Thus in some of the special classes in London and Birmingham 40 per cent of the pupils are reported as having intemperate parents, while the corresponding percentage for pupils of the same age in the regular classes was only 6 per cent. Of like tenor is the reported fact that in some cantons in France the schools have been flooded with an army of laggards seven years after good wine years.

In an investigation carried out on the students of Mur doch Academy, in Utah, it appeared that the offspring of non-narco-stimulant parents were superior to those of the stimulant parents in all of the twenty-two mental and physical traits examined; that as the amount of caffeine consumed daily was increased there was observed a progressive deterioration in the height, weight and bodily condition of the offspring; that the mental and physical inferiority was increased when the parents used both coffee and tea, when they used tobacco and particularly when they used alcohol also; 79 per cent of the narcotized parents had lost one or more infants, while only 49 per cent of the abstainers had suffered such losses. It required from eight-tenths to one year longer for the narcotized progeny to graduate from the grades, and their average age was one year and seven months older in the academy.10 A parallel study11 of the effects of coffee drinking by children on their own development enforces a conclusion previously reached, that a sharp separation cannot be made between the eugenical and euthenical aspects of various environmental factors. Statistics were compiled for 464 children in two schools for a period of one month. The drinkers averaged from one and one-half to four pounds less in weight,12 one-half to one inch less in height, three pounds less in strength of grip, 2.3 per cent less in conduct as concerns those who drank one cup only per day, and 7.8 per cent less as concerns those who drank four cups or more. The rank in lessons was from 2.6 per cent less, up to 29.6 per cent less for those who drank four or more cups.

icf. J. E. Hickman. Journal of Philosophy, Psychology and Scientific Methods, 1919, 9: 234.

11 Charus Keen Taylor. Effects of Coffee Drinking upon Children, The Psychological Clinic, June IS, 1912, p. S6f.

12 In order to obtain light jockeys the practice is said to obtain in England of having boys indulge in liberal quantities of alcohol.

By prosecuting on an adequate scale standardized researches in heredo-psychology, heredo-pedagogy and heredo-biology, analogous to those to which reference has been made above, we shall eventually secure the groundwork of facts needed by both euthenics and eugenics in order that they may attain the dignity of authentic sciences.

CHAPTER XIII
EXPERIMENTAL ORAL ORTHOGENICS: AN
EXPERIMENTAL INVESTIGATION OF THE
EFFECTS OF DENTAL TREATMENT ON
MENTAL EFFICIENCY1

Little if any attempt has hitherto been made to measure by scientific, objective means the mental improvement resulting from the correction or removal of the various physical defects which are now generally known to afflict very many school children. We believe that adenoids, hypertrophied tonsils, nasal obstructions, defective ears, eyes and mouths interfere with normal mental functioning, but no one has attempted to determine experimentally the precise orthogenic effects which should ensue from a definite course of combined prophylactic and operative treatment.

In the present chapter we shall give a very brief sketch of the results of an attempt to determine by controlled, objective, mental measures the influence of hygienic and operative dental treatment upon the intellectual efficiency and working capacity of a squad of twenty-seven public school children in Marion School, Cleveland, Ohio (ten boys and seventeen girls), all of whom were handicapped, to a considerable degree, with diseased dentures or gums and an insanitary oral cavity.2 These children were the recipients of free dental treatment at the hands of the Cleveland Dental Society and the National Dental Association during the first few months of the experimental year, which began in May, 1910, and closed in May, 1911. The treatment included not only the carpentry of carious teeth (that is, the filling of dental cavities, the extraction of decayed roots, the cleaning of the teeth and correction of irregularities and malocclusion) and the sanitation of the oral cavity, but it also consisted in teaching the children how properly to brush their teeth after each meal and how to keep them free from deposits, how to harden the gums and how to fletcherize the food; for oral euthenics contemplates not only mouth sanitation and the repair and polishing of the teeth, but the thorough insalivation and mastication of the food. Verbal instruction and demonstrations relating to mouth hygiene and correct eating habits were given by the then chairman of the Oral Hygiene Committee of the National Dental Association during two demonstration meals which were served to the experimental class at the school. Follow-up work was done by an employed nurse, who gave individual advice and instruction to parents and pupils, and made it a point to ascertain whether the pupils were faithfully following the instructions.

i Read before Section L, Education, of the American Association for the Advancement of Science, Washington, December 29, 1911. Reprinted, with alterations, from the Journal of Philosophy, Psychology and Scientific Methods, 1912, 290-298.

This research was the outgrowth of the nation-wide school oral-hygiene campaign inaugurated in Cleveland in March, 1910, by the National Dental Association. My own connection with the movement consisted in suggesting, contriving and giving (in person or by proxy) five series of psychological efficiency tests at stated intervals during the experimental year. These tests were designed to measure any improvement or increase which might result from the practice of the oral hygiene regimen sketched above, in the power of immediate recall (immediate visual memory span), in the capacity to form spontaneous and controlled associations, in the ability to add, and in the ability to perceive, attend and react to, certain visual impressions.

A more complete discussion of this research appears in my Experimental Oral Euthenics, The Dental Cosmos, April and May, 1911, pp. 404ff. and 545ff.

In the memory test the pupils were required to memorize, during a period of forty-five seconds, as many figures as possible. Ten figures, each containing three digits, in large print on a cardboard were displayed before the class. Exactly one minute was allowed for writing. This test is thus based on the use of non-sense materials and furnishes a measure of the capacity to memorize digits.

In the spontaneous association test, the pupils were provided with a sheet of paper containing a column of thirty simple, everyday words. At a given signal they were told to turn the papers right side up and write opposite each word the first word suggested by it, irrespective of whether or not the suggested word was logically connected with the supplied antecedent or key-word. The time allowed was eighty-five seconds. The number of words written in a test like this furnishes an index of the speed of ideating or of forming free-word associates in connection with supplied antecedents—or, in other words, of the speed of thinking.

To measure the speed of forming controlled associations an antonym test was employed. In this, the pupils were supplied with a sheet containing a column of twenty-five key-words, opposite each of which they were instructed to write (during eighty-five seconds) only that word which has the opposite meaning: e. g., better–worse; sunrise–xtnikft. This test requires intelligent discrimination and demands a higher degree of associational efficiency than that required in the previous test.

In the test on the speed and accuracy of adding, the pupils were supplied with a sheet containing thirty-two columns of figures, each column consisting of ten one-place digits. They were told to add as many columns as possible within the time limits (two minutes) without stopping to re-add any of the columns. This test gives a measure of the ability to form controlled numerical associations.

In the attention-perception test (A-test) a sheet was provided containing twenty-six lines of capital letters. The letters were printed entirely promiscuously instead of in proper alphabetical order. The pupils were told to start at the left end of the top line and proceed to draw a line through as many of the As as possible within the time limits (100 seconds). They were specially cautioned not to skip any As or to cross out any other letters. This test gives a measure of the speed and accuracy of perceptual discrimination, of the power of sustained attention, and, secondarily, of the speed and accuracy of manual reaction.

These five tests thus explore some of the fundamental mental traits or capacities. In all tests, and in all sittings, the pupils were uniformly urged to do their very best. A system of quantitative and of combined quantitative and qualitative scoring was worked out for each test.

In order that tests of this character may be used as measuring rods for gauging the increased functional effi-

See reference on p. 276, and the instruction sheets which are supplied with the complete set of test blanks by C. H. Stoelting Co., 121 North Green Street, Chicago, 111.

ciency resulting from a given euthenic or corrective factor, or factors, a number of essential conditions must be supplied.

First, each of the tests must be constructed in sets or series, so that some of the tests may be given before the treatment begins, and some during the course of the treatment, or after its close. In this investigation each test was arranged in six sets, numbered from 1 to 6. Tests 1 and 2 were given before treatment began. The average of these two pre-treatment tests, therefore, represents the pupils initial efficiency, or his normal standard of performance. The last four tests were given during the course of the treatment, or after its close, so that the average of these represents the pupils terminal efficiency. The difference between the two averages accordingly represents the gain (index of improvement) made during the course of the experimental year. Or, instead of taking the average of the last four tests for the final efficiency, we may substitute the average of the last two. This plan seems preferable, because the last two tests were given from three to five months after the dental treatment had been completed for all the pupils, while tests 3 and 4 were given only one or two months after the beginning of the treatment for more than half of the pupils. Sufficient time had, therefore, not elapsed to allow the orthogenic effects to become operative, at least not in maximal degree, at the time of the third and fourth tests.

Second, the sets must be so constructed that all of the successive tests in the same set are uniformly difficult, although the material must be differently arranged. That is, tests number 2, 3, 4, 5 and 6 must be of the same difficulty as test number 1. Manifestly, if each of the successive tests diminishes in difficulty, the increased efficiency shown is spurious or largely exaggerated. Contrariwise, if each successive test increases in difficulty, the actual improvement will be minimized or counteracted. Considerable pains were taken to make all the tests of a given set equi-difficult. Elsewhere evidence has been adduced to show that the tests were fairly uniform in difficulty, while the material was differently arranged in every successive test.

Third, the conditions of giving the tests must be strictly uniform in all the successive sittings. These conditions refer to the character of the explanations, the use of incentives or suggestions, the constant putting forth of maximal effort by the examinees, the withholding of assistance or fore-knowledge of the test materials, the seating of the pupils, the hour of the day used for testing, the time allowed for the tests, and the employment of uniform supervisory conditions. Moreover, the pupils must continue their school work in their usual classrooms,4 and the school work should go on as before. A scrupulous attempt was made in this research to realize these requirements.

Fourth, to place the results upon a strictly comparable basis, a second squad of untreated children should be given exactly the same tests under precisely the same conditions. These children should come from the same social strata as the treated children, should approximately be of the same ages and suffer from the same degree of physical handicap. By means of the data obtained from such an untreated squad we should be able to determine the amount of improvement which is due to such contributing factors as familiarity, habituation, practice and natural develop ment (merely growing older), and the share which is solely due to the application of the orthogenic factor under consideration. Unfortunately it was not possible for me to get such a squad as this organized during the experimental year.

One of my critics assumes that the pupils were schooled in a small class. This assumption is entirely without foundation. The pupils remained in their regular classrooms.

Fifth, and finally, the factor, or factors, whose ortho-phrenic influence is to be measured must be investigated under controlled conditions. One must make certain that the factor is constantly operative in the treated squad, and that it is inoperative in the untreated squad. In this investigation the oral hygienic measures were subject to a fair degree of control. It was the duty of the employed nurse to see that the pupils conformed strictly to the requirements.

What, now, do the results show with respect to the influence of the dental treatment upon the working efficiency of the pupils? In attempting to answer this main question we shall also refer briefly to a number of accessory facts brought out in the investigation. One of these facts is the circumstance that while the boys manifested a higher degree of efficiency than the girls in all tests except the perception test, the indices of improvement were about the same for the two sexes, whence the boys manifest superiority in the efficiency scores is not paralleled by a corresponding superiority in the improvement indices. Similarly, the amount of improvement was about the same for the older and younger pupils, a result not entirely in accordance with expectation, for it is currently believed that the benefits derived from the correction of physical defects are greater the earlier the treatment is applied. This is believed to be true particularly as regards naso-pharyngeal obstructions. But so far as the mal-effects of dental defects are concerned we are unable to find any significant age differences. Pupils between the ages of eleven and fifteen appear to profit in equal degree, irrespective of sex, from the broad application of the principles of mouth hygiene.

On the other hand, the individual differences between the pupils in all tests are significant. The differences are quite as large as the differences frequently brought to light in other psychological and pedagogical experiments on pupils of the same age or school grade. Some pupils show a high degree, others a low degree, of proficiency; and some pupils make marvelous gains while others gain very little, or not at all, or actually lose in efficiency. It is therefore apparent that experiments of this sort, which are based on only a few pupils, are at best only suggestive, and that valid inferences or conclusions must be based on the central tendencies or average results of a considerable number of pupils.

Not only do we find these large individual differences in the efficiency scores and improvement indices, but the fact that a pupil gains much in one test does not warrant the belief that he will gain much in all the other tests. Quite the reverse may be the case. Thus a list of the five pupils who made the smallest improvements in each of the five tests, was found to contain nineteen of the twenty-seven pupils, while the list of the five pupils who made the greatest gain in each of the five tests, included thirteen pupils. But not a single pupil was enumerated among the five poorest in all the tests, nor was a single pupil enumerated among the five best in all the tests. On the other hand, eight of the pupils, ranking with the five poorest gainers in one test or another, also ranked with the five best gainers in one test or another. While two of these showed little improvement in two tests, they, nevertheless, made large gains in two tests. It is thus apparent that many pupils who gain little in some tests may improve remarkably in others. But it is worthy of remark that only one of the three pupils who were enumerated among the best gainers in three or more tests was included among the poorest gainers, while none of the three who were among the poorest in three tests took rank with the five best in any of the five tests, so that there is a certain amount of correlation between the indices of improvement in the various tests, justifying the conclusion that pupils who improve very slowly in several tests will not take place with the best ground-gainers in any of the tests. Such pupils are probably suffering from general impairment or marked retardation. But teachers must recognize that a child who gains little along one line of mental activity may be developing normally, or even supernormally, along other lines. His capacity for development cannot be determined from the improvement indices of one trait. Scientific pedagogy will make little progress until this fact is recognized, so that the educational activities may be adjusted to meet individual developmental idiosyncrasies.

Although there are these individual differences the character of the central tendencies is unmistakable: there is a decided gain in every test, and not only are the gains decidedly more frequent than the losses, but the largest gains are invariably emphatically larger than the largest losses. This may be seen from the following data for each test, based on the average scores of tests 1 and 2, and the averages of tests 5 and 6 (see also Graphs V to IX).

Graph V.

Memorizing Three-place Digitt.

Per cent of efficiency.

Sitting 1 2 3 4 561-23-61-6 Graph VI.

Spontaneous Association.

Per cent of efficiency.

Sitting

Graph VII.

Addition of One-place Digitt.

Per cent of efficiency.

Sitting 1 2 3 4 5 61-23-61-6

Gkaph VIII.

Antonym Tett.

Per cent of effic ency.

65 1

60 55 5O 45 40 S5 30 / A J

/ / / ,

r /

/ r

/ I

25 Sitting i

1 2 3 4 561-23-61-6
Graph IX.
    Cancelling At.
    Per cent of efficiency.
    Sitting 6 1-2 3-6 1-6
    Explanation of Graphs. The score for each test is shown in per cents along the vertical axis. The successive sittings are indicated by the figures under the horizontal line at the bottom. 1–2 is the average of 1 and 2, 3-6 of 3 to 6, and 1-6 of 1 to 6. Sitting 1, May 31, 1910; sitting 2, June 6; 3, August 31; 4, September 21; 5, May 4, 1911; and 6, May 10, 1911. For other graphs see Dental Cosmos, 1912, May, from which these curves are reproduced.

Memory: eight pupils lost in amounts varying from 5 to 15 per cent, while nineteen gained in amounts varying from 0 per cent to 116 per cent. The average gain for all pupils amounted to 19 per cent.

Spontaneous association: two pupils lost, the one 18 and the other 43 per cent, while twenty-five gained from 2 to 162 per cent. The average improvement amounted to 42 per cent.

Addition: one pupil suffered a loss of 13 per cent, twenty-six gained from 6 to 125 per cent, while the average improvement was 35 per cent.

Associating antonyms: all the pupils gained in amounts varying from 33 to 666 per cent, the average gain being 129 per cent.

Perception-attention: all gained in amounts varying from 19 to 101 per cent, the average improvement amounting to 60 per cent.

It is thus evident that the gains varied considerably in the different tests, and that the largest improvement occurred in the antonym, attention-perception and spontaneous association tests. The average gain for all tests amounted to 57 per cent, truly a remarkably large gain.

How large a percentage of this significant gain is due solely to the improved physical condition of the pupils, which resulted from the treatment? This question does not admit of a categorical answer in the absence of parallel data from an untreated squad. Because of the brevity of the tests, the length of the intervals between the tests and the counteracting effect of the growing monotony during the successive sittings, it is improbable that the practice effects were considerable. The improvement from familiarity would probably be larger, but, as a matter of fact, many lost instead of gained in the second test. The factor of novelty (in the first test) apparently was stronger than familiarity (in the second test). It is certain that children improve very little in their academic work from a similar amount of practice. But if we concede that one-half of the gain—and that is, I believe, a sufficiently liberal concession—is due to a number of extrinsic factors, such as familiarity, practice and increased maturity, the gain solely attributable to the heightened mentation resulting from the physical improvement of the pupils would still be very considerable. There is corroborative evidence to show that there was a general improvement in the mental functioning of these pupils. This evidence is supplied by the examination of the pedagogical record of scholarship, attendance and deportment. Most of the members of this experimental squad were laggards and repeaters, pedagogically retarded in their school work from one to four years, but during the experimental year only one pupil failed of promotion, while six did thirty-eight weeks of work in twenty-four weeks and one boy finished two years of work within the experimental year. Apparently the pupils physical condition had been so bettered that they were able to profit by the instruction, to form habits from practice and to improve mentally as a result of increasing maturity. They were making normal progress during the experimental year, while many had failed to do so during the preceding year. During the preceding year many of the pupils were quite irregular in their attendance owing to toothache, chronic weariness, bodily indispositions, irritability or distaste for school work, and five pupils were obliged to carry truancy cards; but during the experimental year the attendance was materially improved, the cases of truancy entirely disappeared, while certain boys considered formerly as incor

rigible now established new records for deportment and for tractability.

The improved physical and mental health of many of the pupils, which was noticed by the teachers, commented on by the parents and fully realized by the pupils, was also made manifest in a more buoyant spirit, a healthier complexion and an improved disposition and deportment.

This experiment, then, furnishes the first demonstration by means of controlled serial experimental tests, extending throughout a calendar year, of the psycho-orthogenic effects of the community application of the broad principles of mouth hygiene. The conclusions which follow from the results of the research are of far-reaching importance to the state and nation (see Chapter XIV).

CHAPTER XIV

THE RELATION OF ORAL HYGIENE TO EFFICIENT MENTATION IN BACKWARD CHILDREN1

My interest in the Oral Hygiene Movement springs largely from my interest in race amelioration and conservation. There are two fundamental methods by means of which we shall be able to conserve the best interests of the race: (1) by improved breeding, or eugenical mating. This is the more important of the two classes of measures, but it is likewise the more difficult to put into practical operation. We cannot escape the fact that there is a very wide chasm between theoretical and practical eugenics. (2) By improved bringing up, or the efficient control of euthenical factors. Among these factors I include not only improved methods of child training and education, but also improved hygienic and sanitary nurture and corrective and remedial care. While the problem is essentially one of prevention rather than one of cure, we cannot blind ourselves to the existence of defects already estab lished, but must make every effort to correct or remove these. Now, there is a general conviction that the application of the above two classes of preventive and corrective measures will improve the biological capital of the race, and thus make for race amelioration. Among other things, there are those who believe that by the removal of the physical handicaps which afflict our children we shall be able to elevate not only their health standard but also their mental standard. This is a question in which I have taken a genuine interest for a number of years. I have been particularly interested in obtaining demonstrated or demonstrable facts which would either prove or disprove the claim that the removal of physical handicaps will increase the mental efficiency of school children; for, fundamentally, in a state of civilization we cannot hope to fashion a higher type of humanity without elevating the mental index of childhood—although not, to be sure, at the expense of the body–for success in a state of civilized society depends more on strength of mental action than on force of muscular power.

i Substance of an address delivered before the Academy of Science and Art, Pittsburgh, Pa., February 14, 1913 At this meeting a moving picture film, Toothache, was shown. This film is being exhibited throughout the United States, in the interest of the Oral Hygiene Movement which has been inaugurated by the National Mouth Hygiene Association. Reprinted from The Child, London, 1913, pp. 27-32, and from Oral Hygiene, 1913, pp. 892-897, with eliminations and additions.

In looking through the literature, however, I found little direct or incontrovertible evidence that the mentation of school children could be elevated by correcting physical defects (I am not now speaking of diseases). To this general statement there is one conspicuous exception, namely, thyroid treatment in the case of cretins or persons suffering from thyroid insufficiency-To be sure, there were numerous observations– not to say extravagant claims–on record of the marvelous improvement made in individual instances from proper nose, throat, eye and ear treatment, particularly of the improvement resulting from the removal of adenoids. But this was not what I wanted. Instead of casual observation and opinion, I wanted expert mental evidence of a quantitative nature. But there was no such evidence available; no attempt had been made to measure by definite controlled objective tests the degree of mental improvement resulting from the correction of various kinds of physical handicaps. The nearest approach to an exact quantitative investigation were the few statistical studies made on the relation between pedagogical retardation and physical defects. But these studies suffered from serious defects of one kind or another (see Chapter XV). The necessity therefore appeared urgent to undertake an experimental inquiry, by which to measure by controlled objective tests the influence of the removal of physical defects on the working capacity of school children. It seemed to me that the best point of attack for such an investigation was the diseased and unhygienic cavity of the mouth, for two reasons: first, because there is no disease of childhood which is so prevalent as dental caries, in fact this defect is so common that it has been appropriately called the disease of the people; second, because, in accordance with the statement accredited to Osier, There is not any one single thing more important in the whole range of hygiene than the hygiene of the mouth. Accordingly, I suggested to the then chairman of the Oral Hygiene Committee of the National Dental Association (Dr. W. G. Ebersole) that a series of psychological tests be carried out on a squad of school children suffering from very bad conditions of the mouth, with a view to arriving at a definite, objective, impersonal measurement of the orthophrenic effects which might be assumed to follow proper dental treatment and mouth sanitation (for the description of the experiment and discussion of the results made at this point in the address, see Chapter XIII).

The significant positive results of this experiment suggest considerations of great practical moment.

There is no phase of the entire modern child conservation movement which merits deeper scientific study by qualified experts than the relation between the normal physical, mental and pedagogical health, growth and development of school children than a community plan of physical and mental orthogenesis. No phase of the problem of national conservation or racial euthenics more nearly affects the very fundamentals of human existence. Our greatest national asset is the normal, healthy child–the child originally sound in body and mind by virtue of a rich hereditary dower, or the child rendered sound by the removal of physical or mental handicaps through the application of the broad principles of human physical and mental orthogenesis. Instead of devoting their resources to the gathering of mere statistics, to making surveys of what this community and that city are doing to better the welfare of the child, or to treating results rather than causes, our child conservationists, eugenic enthusiasts and welfare foundations could make a larger contribution toward the permanent betterment of the race by undertaking on an adequate scale genuine scientific investigations of the physiological, psychological, hereditary and sociological causes of bodily and mental disability and inefficiency, and of the demonstrable effects of the broad application of orthophrenic and orthosomatic measures. The largest contribution to the permanent betterment of the race will be made by those workers who will undertake, on an adequate scale, genuine, scientific investigations into the actual, demonstrated effects of the application of various orthogenic measures of a physical and mental character. No such investigations are anywhere being prosecuted on an effective basis, notwithstanding that no one knows the actual, proven effects on the child of the application of various physical and psychological ortho-genie measures or various pedagogical methods and devices. Our knowledge in this field is largely pretense and illusion. In no field of organized modern enterprise has there been such a lame attempt made to measure results scientifically as in education. Indeed, we do not as yet so much as possess any strictly reliable scientific measures of educational results: the very conception of measuring results in education is a product of very recent industrial thinking. Is it not time that our large research foundations begin to treat more fairly the problems of human conservation and particularly those of child ortho-genics? A million dollars spent in orthogenic investigations–in the discovery of the psychological, dento-medical, social, hereditary, pedagogical and anthropo-metric factors of deviate development in children and in the ascertainment of corrective measures–will accomplish immeasurably more for the welfare of the human race than tens of millions devoted to the cataloguing of the stars of the heavens or exploring the trackless wastes of the polar regions.

The results at which we have arrived in this experiment by controlled objective quantitative methods emphasize anew the paramount importance of teaching the pupils in our schools proper dental prophylaxis, and of establishing dental clinics and dispensaries, and supplying free dental treatment in the schools to all certified indigent cases. But it should be specially emphasized that, owing to the enormous number of children suffering from diseased teeth, it is not sufficient merely to establish school dental clinics. There are not enough dentists in any community to treat the teeth of all the children who have oral defects. It is, therefore, imperatively necessary that the work of dental hygiene be so organized on a community basis that children may be systematically taught to care for their teeth and sanitate their mouths from the day that, as members of the schools, they become wards of the state or of the community.

Among the fruits which would accrue from the introduction of mouth hygiene instruction and the establishment of dental clinics in the schools may be mentioned the following: (1) Value to the afflicted pupils themselves. Dental hygiene furnishes a means of ridding the suffering pupil from the exciting cause of pain, disease, mental stagnation, moral deviation and irregular school attendance. It is one of the effective means available for raising the childs actual efficiency a little nearer to its maximal potential. Dental hygiene is a godsend to the individual child. The free dental school clinic must appeal to all lovers of children on humanitarian grounds. (2) Benefits to the school system. Dental hygiene is one of a number of effective means of combating the evils of pedagogical retardation, repetition, elimination, non-attendance and delinquency. It is a practical means of increasing the efficiency of the school system. It should appeal to the teacher, school administrator and school efficiency engineer. (3) Financial value to the taxpayers. The greater the return on the investment, the cheaper will be the cost of maintaining the schools; and obviously, the more proficient the pupils are made, the greater will be the returns on the investment. The provision of free dental inspection and treatment for indigent pupils is an economic measure of the first magnitude. In terms of dollars and cents, the annual saving in any school system would amount to a very considerable sum. For example, let us assume that those pupils who suffer from the very worst mouth conditions would improve only 15 per cent in working efficiency as a result of the application of a judicious system of mouth hygiene. This is a very conservative estimate; the improvement would probably be nearer 25 per cent. Now let us assume that at least 20 per cent of the 65,000 pupils enrolled in the elementary public schools of Pittsburgh suffer from very bad oral conditions, and that these pupils are in such impoverished circumstances financially that they would not obtain any dental treatment unless school clinics were established. The approximate cost of instruction for the elementary pupils in the public schools of Pittsburgh amounts to 30 per year, therefore if each of these 13,000 pupils gained 15 per cent in working efficiency as a result of dental treatment there would accrue a saving of 4.50 per year for each one of these pupils, or 58,500 a year for these 13,000 cases. This estimate, however, probably fails to do full justice to the benefits to be derived, because it is an undoubted fact that a very large number of this group of children who suffer from very bad dental conditions would fail in their school work, and thus have to be educated at least twice in the same grade. That would mean an additional cost of 30 per year for every repeater. Dental treatment would save very many of these cases from failure to make their grade, and thus save the cost of repetition to the taxpayer. According to the best estimates, it costs the country 27,000,000 annually to educate every sixth child two or three times in the same grade. That part of this enormous waste which is ascrib-able to the presence of those remediable physical defects in the children which exert a retarding influence upon the mental processes or which cause children to stay away from school is entirely preventable. (4) Benefits accruing to race conservation. Dental hygiene will improve the mental and physical health of the individual child, and this, in time, will lay the basis not only for a more efficient citizenship but also for a more efficient parenthood; for by elevating the health index of children we shall not only increase the health, happiness and productive capacity of adults but also elevate the genesic or reproductive index of the race. The application of the best euthenical principles of race amelioration will probably also produce the highest eugeni-cal results. This argument is perhaps one of the strongest arguments for developing community plans of child orthogenesis. Our most sacred duty is to the race, to posterity. Most of what we have we owe to our ancestry, and the best that we possess we should strive to bequeath to our posterity; and the most precious gift which we can bestow upon posterity is a normal, healthy progeny and an uncontaminated heredity.

Is it worth while to attempt to save the enormous annual waste in the schools due to the defective mouths of the pupils? Is it worth while to the taxpayer to eliminate, so far as possible, the necessity for the extra financial burden which he must assume for instruction that should have been done satisfactorily the first time? Is it worth anything to the child to enable him to attend school more regularly and thereby increase his chances of promotion? Is it worth while to the repeater to shorten his stay in the schools? Is it worth while to enable him to attain a higher level of academic efficiency? Is it worth while to remove physical obstacles which may lessen his efficiency for life? There can be none but an affirmative answer. One of the means for accomplishing these desirable results appears to be the establishment of departments of orthogenics in the public schools. But these departments must be given a broader scope than are the present departments of medical inspection, and must be under the skilled direction of health officers who are experts in educational, child and clinical psychology, corrective pedagogy and preventive and corrective hygiene. One division of these departments, orthosomatics, should include dental dispensaries.

CHAPTER XV

METHODS OF MEASURING THE ORTHO-PHRENIC EFFECTS OF THE RE-MOVAL OF PHYSICAL HANDICAPS1

The conviction that there is an intimate relationship between physical defectiveness and mental inefficiency or irresponsibility has become an accepted postulate of current educational, psychological, medical and criminolog-ical thought. But for the most part, this belief has been based on mere opinion, or favorable chance observations. It is only within recent times that any attempt has been made accurately or scientifically to evaluate the physical or mental influences of physical defects. And yet, our whole system of pupil inspection, whether medical, dental or psychological, must ultimately justify itself to the taxpayer by its demonstrated orthogenic results. The taxpayers have a right to know whether their systems of school medical, dental and psycho-educational inspection, clinics and dispensaries represent a paying investment. In a matter which assumedly so vitally concerns the conservation of our racial vigor, we cannot afford to rest our case upon the verdict of assumption, opinion, uncritical thought, a priori argument or on the unaided and favorable chance observations of physicians and teachers. Either physical defects do or they do not have a determinate retarding, deflecting or disharmonizing effect upon the physical and mental health, growth and development of the average child. If they do, this fact must be amenable to demonstration by the methods of modern science. The scientist rightly insists that the fields of physical and mental orthogenesis (orthosomatics and orthophrenics) must be subjected to exactly the same kind of investigation by verifiable, demonstrable, objective measures and the same critical scrutiny as any other field of modern inquiry.

i An address delivered at the third annual conference of the National Association for the Stud) and Education of Exceptional Children, New York, November, 1912.

In the present paper I shall attempt a brief survey of the six methods which have been employed to measure quantitatively the influence of physical defects on mental or pedagogical efficiency, and shall also very briefly resume and evaluate the findings with each method.

1. Computations have been made of the comparative per cent of pedagogical proficiency, in terms of average scholarship rating, attained by groups of physically defective and physically normal children. The comparison is based on the assumption that if physical defects exert a retarding influence the physically defective groups should rank lower in scholarship.

Of 219 boys and girls ranging from six to twelve years of age examined in one school in Philadelphia in 1908, it was found that the average grade attained was 75 per cent for normal children, 74 per cent for average children, 72.6 per cent for general defectives," and 72 per cent for pupils who had adenoids and enlarged tonsils (Cornell, Psychological Clinic, January, 1908). While the difference between the extreme groups amounts to only 3 per cent, the physically normal pupils, at any rate, rank slightly higher in scholarship than groups of physical defectives.

This method is subject to the criticism that it deals to some extent with an abstraction. The strictly physically normal child is largely a myth. This method, therefore, only enables us to compare the scholarship of children relatively free from physical defects with children quite obviously handicapped.

2. Enumerations have been made of the average number of physically defective pupils found in groups of pedagogically or mentally defective, retarded, normal and supernormal pupils. Here, again (because the method is just the obverse of the preceding), the argument is similar: if physical defects reduce the childs working efficiency or impair his mentality we should find more physical defects among the feeble-minded, backward and dull, than among the on-time, or the bright pupils. A number of investigations have approached the question from this point of view.

In Halle, it was found that only 26 per cent (or fifty-seven cases) of the 215 pupils (assumedly feeble-minded) enrolled in the auxiliary classes in 1901 were free from physical defects (exclusive of trivial disorders), while in 1903-1904 only 12 per cent of the 209 enrolled were in perfect condition. Unfortunately no comparative data for pedagogically normal children are given.

A study of 137 entrants in the schools of Princeton, 111., in 1901-1902 showed that those retarded only one year had no physical defects, while all of those retarded three years or more were defective (Gayler).

In Jefferson City, Mo., 37 per cent of the pupils investigated who had defective eyes did unsatisfactory work, while only 26 per cent of those who had good eyes did unsatisfactory work.

In Los Angeles, only 16 per cent of fifty markedly bright pupils were found physically defective, as against 86 per cent of fifty dull pupils.

In the schools of Camden, N. J., 8,110 on-time and 2,020 retarded pupils were given a physical examination in 1906. The percentages of defective vision and hearing were for the on-time (or normal-age) pupils 27.1 per cent and 3.7 per cent, respectively, while the corresponding figures for the retarded group amounted to 28.9 per cent and 5.8 per cent, a difference of merely 1.8 per cent and 2.1 per cent respectively. A special inquiry into the causal factors of the failure of the 2,020 retardates also indicated that physical defects were of minor importance. The causes were ranked as follows: late entrance, 21.2 per cent; slowness, 21 per cent; absence, 28.5 per cent; dullness, 12 per cent; ill health, 9.6 per cent; defects other than visual and auditory, 3.9 per cent, and mental weakness, 3.7 per cent (Bryan). A reexamination of 1,279 on-time and 573 retarded pupils, who failed of promotion, gave the following results:

On-time Retarded Difference

Per cent Per cent Per cent

Defective vision 51 40–11

Defective hearing 14 11–8

Bad health 21 21 0 Irregular attendance 80 40 10

Curiously, the normal-progress pupils were more defective than the retardates.

But among 203 Cleveland, Ohio, school children which were investigated, it was found that only 63 per cent with a scholarship mark of very good had physical defects, as against 73.1 per cent of those marked good, 71.1 per cent of those marked fair and 86.6 per cent of those marked poor.

In Philadelphia, physical examinations have been made of so-called exempt and non-exempt pupils. Exempt pupils include those who are advanced to a higher grade without examination, by virtue of superior attainments. Of 907 exempt pupils examined in five schools only 28.8 per cent were defective, as against 38.1 of 687 non-exempt (Cornell). In another group consisting of 3,587 exempt and 1,418 non-exempt pupils, only 49 per cent of the exempt were defective, as against 65 per cent of the non-exempt. The differences amounted to 0 per cent for defective vision, 2 per cent for defective hearing, .6 per cent for nose defects, –.1 per cent for throat defects, 1.1 per cent for orthopedic defects, 5.5 per cent for mental defects, 4 per cent for skin diseases and 3 per cent for miscellaneous defects (Newmayer). Singularly, the difference is considerable for certain defects which should have little bearing on mental efficiency, while it is negligible for those defects which are considered to impair mental action.

Another investigation in Philadelphia showed that in the general school population the percentage of physically normal pupils was 38 per cent, while in a primary school for dull pupils (William Mckinley) it was only half as large, or 19 per cent, and in classes for the high-grade or feeble-minded it was still less, or 12 per cent. This study no doubt also includes defects which can have little bearing on mentality; but it is significant that there were only 28 per cent of eye defects in the general school population, as against 80 per cent, 39.4 per cent and 42 per cent, respectively, in two schools for retardates and in the classes for the feeble-minded. Again, in one school the percentages of nose and throat defects in two bright classes were 12 per cent and 10.2 per cent, respectively, while in two of the dullest sixth and seventh grades the figures were 28.1 per cent and 31 per cent, respectively (Cornell).

On the other hand, if we turn to an investigation made in New York City embracing 7,608 pupils in the eight elementary grades, 6,084 of whom were on-time and 1,524 retarded, we find, curiously, that the percentage of physical handicaps was actually 4.9 per cent greater for the on-time than for the retarded group (79.8 per cent vs.

74.9 per cent: Ayres). Another investigation of 3,304 New York pupils ranging from ten to fourteen years of age seems to explain the curious discrepancies found in New York City and Camden. It indicated that comparisons in respect to physical defectiveness between over-age retarded and on-time normal children may be quite worthless, because of discrepancy in the age of the pupils. It was found that a marked decrease in the prevalence of some defects begins at eight, nine and ten, and that if the younger children are excluded from the study, a positive correlation exists between physical defects and the pedagogical rating. This may be seen from the following per cents of various defects among bright, normal and dull pupils:

Defect Bright Normal Dull
Enlarged glands 6 18 20
Defective vision 29 25 24
Defective breathing 9 11 15
Defective teeth 84 40 42
Hypertrophied tonsils 12 19 26
Adenoids 6 10 15
Other defects 11 11 21

Per cent defective. 68 78 75 It is noteworthy that the largest differences are for defective teeth, defective breathing, adenoids and enlarged tonsils.

In Elmira, N. Y., an investigation of repeaters in the second grade showed that 21 per cent of those who required three years, and 40 per cent of those who required four years to complete the grade had adenoids, as against only 19 per cent of those who required only two years to do the grade. Seventeen per cent and 27 per cent, respectively, of those who spent three and four years in the grade suffered from anemia, as against 15 per cent for those who required two years. The corresponding figures for defective vision are 24 per cent and 26 per cent, as against 21 per cent. Here there is a consistent positive correlation.

In 1907, a special study was made of 1,000 of the Cam-den repeaters (Heilman). The pupils were divided into five groups according as they were retarded from one to five years, and the percentage of pupils in each group having physical defects was computed. The correlation between pedagogical retardation and the percentage of physically defective children is given for the various defects in the following tabulation: 1 year Per cent Retardation 2 years 3 years Per cent Per cent 4 years Per cent 5 years Per cent

Defects
Health 16.5 18.4 6.8 5.2 15.5 8.2 21.8 28.0 8.9 17.2 7.8 8.1 5.1 4.2 15.9 18.2 6.7 4.9 19.0 87.5 17.5 7.5 20.0 22.8 10.0
Nutrition 20.2 9.6 10.5 22.8 6.1
Adenoids
Visual defects. Auditory defects.
Here there is a fairly good, although not uniformly consistent, positive correlation.

In spite of the discrepancies which we have found in the review of this method, the results, in the main, point to a positive correlation between physical defectiveness and pedagogical retardation. But the method itself, however valuable, is subject to various shortcomings. As usually applied, no cognizance is taken of differences of age, social and economic status, differences in the environment and other factors which are believed to influence both retardation (and acceleration)and physical defectiveness. For example, as already indicated, certain physical defects increase with age (viz., the visual, spinal and nervous), while others decrease (viz., the nasopharyngeal, auditory and dental). It is therefore evident that without a rigid control of conditions the results may be entirely misleading. Moreover, both the physical defects and the mental torpor may be merely symptoms of an underlying factor which is their common cause. They may not be independent variables, or even variables dependent upon each other, but both may be dependent upon a third factor or set of factors.

3. The average number of physical defects per child has been ascertained for groups of pedagogically retarded, on-time and accelerated pupils. This method differs from the preceding only in that instead of finding the per cent of defective pupils in the different pedagogical groups the average number of defects per child is found. It is, again, assumed that if there is any causal relation between physical defects and pedagogical stagnation, the more numerous the defects the greater will be the retardation in any given case.

Investigations made in Chicago from 1903 to 1905 showed that 1,600 boys in the regular grades had an average each of 4.6 to 5.3 of growth defects (these growth are not synonymous with the so-called physical defects), while the corresponding number of motor defects ranged from 2.9 to 4.3 per child. But in the parental school, in which most of the boys were peda-gogically retarded from one to five years, the number of growth defects averaged from 6.8 to 7.3, and the number of motor defects from 5.2 to 6.1. The deficiency for the parental school boys averaged about 25 per cent higher than for boys hailing from the better sections of the city. Not only were the defects among the disciplinary cases more numerous but they were more pronounced in severity (Bruner, 1906).

In the New York investigation, based on 3,304 cases, to which reference has already been made, the average number of defects for bright children was 1.07; for normal children, 1.30; and for dull children, 1.65, an appreciable difference as between the bright and dull.

The average number of physical defects per child for the 1,000 Camden repeaters, already mentioned, was as follows for the groups retarded one, two, three, four and five (or more) years:.65,.65,.82,.89 and 1.20 (Heil-man). Here there is a fairly consistent increase in the number of defects with each increasing year of retardation.

This method possesses the same virtues and the same defects as the preceding method. The results may be vitiated by the inclusion in the averages of physical defects which have no relation to intelligence, although they may multiply with increasing retardation, and by the fact that the physical defects may be no more truly causative of the mental deficiency than the mental deficiency is causative of the physical defects, because both may be only symptoms of an underlying lack of biological capital.

4. Pupils may be classified on the basis of psychological test of certain mental traits, into subnormal, normal and supernormal groups, and after being so classified the average number of physical defects per child, or the percentage of physically defective children in each group, may be ascertained. This method has elements in common with all the preceding methods, but the difference is that the pupils mental

status is determined by objective, controlled psychological tests rather than by the mere judgment of the teacher or by the less accurate pedagogical tests. Here the attempt may be made not only to determine the inherent strength of various mental traits, such as memory, imitation, perception, association, attention or reasoning, but also the relation of specific mental defects to specific physical defects.

No satisfactory studies of this type have been made. Two studies from the Chicago public schools may, however, be referred to in this connection. In 1900-1901 a study was made of the relation between deficiency in visual and auditory memory and subnormal visual and auditory acuity. A slight positive correlation was found. Of those who were superior to the average in auditory memory, 32 per cent had visual and 10 per cent had auditory defects; while the corresponding per cents for those who were inferior to the average were 41 per cent and 14 per cent. Of those superior to the average in visual memory, 32 per cent had visual and 10 per cent hearing defects; while for those inferior in visual memory the figures were 45 per cent and 15 per cent (Smedley).

In 1904-1905 a study was made of 256 delinquent boys in the parental school. The teachers made a careful study of the memory, reasoning and attention capacities of the pupils (but presumably not by controlled tests), and special investigators examined the boys for defects in growth, particularly for cranial anomalies. A correspondence between the physical and mental conditions was found in 77.5 per cent of the cases, and no correspondence in 22.5 per cent. The bright pupils had less defects than the normal, the fair about the average number, and the poor were decidedly below par.

It is regrettable that so little use has been made of this method, for there can be no doubt that valuable data for the scientific solution of our problem may be obtained by the application of mental tests, provided proper care be taken in the selection and control of the tests and in the selection of the control subjects.

5. The rate of progress through the elementary grades has been ascertained for groups of pupils suffering from various physical defects and for groups free from physical defects. How much longer does it take physically defective pupils to complete the eight elementary grades than physically normal pupils? What is the difference in the retarding influence of various kinds of physical defects? How long will it take the adenoid child to finish the eight grades? How long the child with enlarged tonsils, with teeth defects, etc.? It is contended that if physical defects exert a retarding influence on pedagogical efficiency the progress must be slower for physical defectives than for normal pupils.

Only one study of this sort has been made, namely the New York study of the 3,304 children whose ages ranged from ten to fourteen. The percentages of loss of pedagogical efficiency was determined for groups of these children suffering from different kinds of physical defects. The loss in time, based on the average number of years completed (4.94) by the pupils who had no physical handicaps, was as follows: for defective vision, 0 per cent; for seriously defective teeth, 5.9 per cent; for defective breathing, 7.2 per cent; for enlarged tonsils, 8.9 per cent; for adenoids, 14.1 per cent; for enlarged glands, 14.9 per cent, and for other defects, 8.5 per cent. On the average, the retarding influence of the physical handicaps appeared to amount to 8.8 per cent (Ayres).

This method marks some advance upon previous methods, but its crudity is apparent. It insures little, if any, control of conditions. It makes no attempt to isolate individual defects, except in a crude fashion. It is obvious that various defects may coexist in the same child, and that a variety of complications may exist. The method fails to evaluate the relative influence of the contributing factors, whether these be physical, sociological, environmental or mental. The physically normal children used as standards were probably only relatively free from defects. Moreover, if anyone should use eight years as the standard time required by the normal child to complete the elementary course he would be using a purely theoretical criterion. There are no direct data available to show that the average child, or even the child free from physical defects, is able to finish the eight elementary grades in eight years. In fact, the data we have indicate that the average child requires 9.34 years to finish the eight grades, for in an investigation of promotion in grades one to five in twenty-nine American cities it appeared that in no city did the average child finish the four years on time. The shortest was 4.08 years, the longest 6.22, while the average was 4.67. For every rapid-progress pupil there were found from eight to ten slow-progress pupils (Ayres). It is therefore apparent that the only legitimate basis of comparison is the number of years actually required to finish the elementary course either by the average pupil or by the pupil relatively free from defects, and not the theoretical eight years.

6. Finally, a sixth method approaches the problem from an entirely different point of view, namely from the orthogenetic standpoint. It consists in correcting the childs physical handicaps by proper orthosomatic treatment, and then ascertaining whether or not there is any improvement in scholarship, mental vigor, working capacity, classroom attendance, promotion or deportment. If we wish to determine whether adenoids interfere with mental development, let us remove them and find out what happens.

Of studies of this kind there are innumerable sporadic observations, and one psycho-experimental investigation.

In Philadelphia, seventy more or less retarded pupils in grades one to four were operated for adenoids. The reports of the teachers, based on sixty-three cases, indicated that 30 per cent improved considerably, 40 per cent improved, 25 per cent did not improve, 1.6 per cent deteriorated and 3 per cent deteriorated considerably. Of those who had two chances for promotion, 6.3 per cent were promoted twice, 16 per cent failed twice, while 33.3 per cent were promoted once and a like number failed once. On the other hand, of those with one opportunity for promotion, 11 per cent were promoted, while 31.7 per cent failed (Cornell). The promotion record was thus decidedly poor. It is possible, however, that the time for promotion came before the orthogenic effects of the operations had become effective.

In New York City, of eighty-seven cases operated for enlarged tonsils and adenoids, we are told that many (that exasperatingly vague term!) advanced three grades during the rest of the school year, and that only three lost time (Cronin).

In the same city, thirty-five pupils who were serious retardates in the regular or ungraded classes were fitted with glasses in January, 1912, to overcome hypermetropia and myopia. The teachers were asked to make estimates of the pupils work and conduct at this time, and again in June, 1912. The record of promotions showed that nineteen of the twenty-five pupils in the regular grades were promoted, one of the ten ungraded pupils was promoted to a regular grade, while seven made very slow progress and two made no progress. All were reported to have improved in habits, disposition and conduct.

A random examination in Cleveland, in 1910-1911, of the records of 224 corrected cases indicated that 24 per cent had improved decidedly in scholarship, 21.4 per cent had improved in deportment and 33 per cent in attendance.

In contrast with the above observational, deportment or promotion methods of estimating the orthophrenic effects of the correction of physical defects, is an experimental investigation by laboratory methods under controlled conditions undertaken to discover whether or not the mental efficiency of a group of children could actually be elevated by proper orthosomatic mouth treatment. The description of this experiment and the discussion of the results have been given in Chapters XIII and XIV and are therefore omitted here.

This brief review of the present status of the problem thus indicates that before long we may look forward to the creation of a genuine science of orthophrenics, so that we shall be able to say with greater accuracy than before what kinds of physical obstructions cause the greatest amount of retardation, what degree of defect is necessary to cause mental impairment, what mental functions are most affected by various disabilities, to what extent orthosomatic treatment will entirely remove the mental damage caused by various defects, and to what extent reliance must also be placed on differential orthophrenic or corrective pedagogic treatment. The problem is extremely complex, and its effective solution demands the cooperative efforts of the expert psycho-educational examiner, physician and teacher. Moreover, investigations should be made from purely disinterested scientific motives by private and public research foundations of the orthogenic effects of various orthosomatic and ortho-phrenic measures. These investigations should cover the various psychological, pedagogical, sociological, dento-medical, anthropometric and hereditary aspects of the problem. (One writer has already made an attempt to partially carry out this suggestion.2) 2 Kohnky. Preliminary Study of the Effect of Dental Treatment upon the Physical and Mental Efficiency of School Children. Journal of Educational Psychology, 1913, 4: S71ff.

CHAPTER XVI

MEDICAL AND DENTAL INSPECTION IN THE CLEVELAND SCHOOLS1

I. The Development Of Medical School Inspection In 1906, the Board of Health of Cleveland appointed twenty-six ward physicians, a part of whose duties consisted in inspecting, every other day, the public and parochial schools of their districts for the detection and exclusion-from the schools of pupils suffering from contagious and communicable diseases. But excluding children, in conformity with the law, with such communicable diseases as pediculosis, scabies, impetigo, etc., created serious school problems. Many children thus excluded remained out of school for days; they received no corrective treatment at home, hence when they returned they were often in a worse condition than when they left; their exclusion seriously handicapped the regular work of the classroom, for these pupils frequently stood in greatest need of the classroom processes, and they had to be excluded in large numbers owing to the enormous prevalence of some form or other of communicable disease. In a number of the congested foreign districts of the city, conditions were such that not only would exclusion result in a breakdown of the school system from the point of view of school attendance, but a large percentage of children were forced to labor under the handicap of needless suffering, owing to the ignorance, indifference or poverty of the parents.

i Reprinted, with alterations, from The Psychological Clinic, 1910, pp. 93-108.

To checkmate the evils due to those conditions and to demonstrate to the Board of Education the importance of a system of medical inspection that should embrace examination for physical defects, certain inspectors, working through the Sanitation Committee of the Chamber of Commerce, volunteered their services without compensation if the Board of Education would provide inspection stations in those schools in which the need was the most pressing. The Board established five of these stations in schools which drained large foreign populations, each station in charge of a graduate nurse of the Visiting Nurses Association. The first was organized at the Murray Hill School in 1908. School dispensaries or clinics, among the first of the sort in the country, were connected with two of these stations (Murray Hill and Marion). Three others were subsequently added. The equipment of these clinics, provided at the expense of the School Board, varies, but consists mainly of diagnostic appliances for examining the ear, nose and throat, eye test cards, instruments for removing adenoids and tonsils and for performing the simpler operations, ointments, solutions for treating communicable diseases, an instrument case, a metal stand for basins, glass top table, couch, enameled chairs, etc. While the primary aim has not been to supply free treatment at the clinic, emergency cases receive prompt attention, and at one of the schools, the Murray Hill (and in a measure, at a couple of the others also), all cases of infection, of wax and suppurating ears, atrophic rhinitis and all marked cases of adenoids and hypertrophied tonsils have received remedial or operative treatment.

The inspection work has been rendered practically effective through the follow-up work and the diversified ministration of the school nurse. She makes a record of the examination, and sends a copy to the childs parents. She visits the home to ascertain whether the physicians advice has been followed. If it has not, recourse is had to the gentle art of suasion, or in extreme cases of neglect the juvenile court is invoked. Indigent parents are advised to take the child to a free dispensary or hospital clinic. She looks after many of the minor troubles while the child remains in school, attends to ordinary dressings and the childs hygiene in general, inspects the rooms daily and treats at the dispensary the simpler infections of the skin and head, while referring the more complicated cases to the medical inspector. After treatment she follows the child home and instructs the mother how to continue treatment, or, in case the mother is employed, takes personal charge. She also teaches the older girls in school how to apply bandages and antiseptics, how to prepare common disinfectants and antidotes, and explains the importance of sanitation and personal cleanliness. She gives baths to the girls where showers are provided. Hers is a diversified calling, filled with noble achievement. In one month in the Murray Hill School, nurses aid was given to 680 cases, while 75 homes were visited. A monthly report of nurses aid in the Harmon School included 195 baths, 215 treatments for impetigo, 50 for pediculosis, 50 ocular cases were referred to the Humane Society and one to the Blind Institute. Similar cases from another school in a congested section (Eagle) are frequently referred to dental, medical and babies dispensaries, and family physicians. In 1907, through the cooperation of nurses, physicians, teachers, principals, parents, dispensaries, free hospital clinics and philanthropic organizations, over 3,300 pupils received aid of the following nature:

Number Per cent
Glasses secured by 990 29.2
Other eye treatment 1,016 80.
Ear treatment 228 6.7
Nasal treatment 879 11.1
Dental treatment 664 19.6
Unclassified-Ill 8.4
Total 8,888 100.

To the thousands of children and parents who have profited from this humanitarian and philanthropic ministration, the school nurse has become a guardian angel. There has been no frenzied outcry in Cleveland against this physical welfare work either on the part of ignorant or superstitious parents, or studied opponents of communism or socialism. Objections, so far as they have been heard at all, have been directed by parents against operations or by physicians against free treatment. Some parents object to the removal of tonsils, through the fear that this will injure the voice; and others to the wearing of glasses, because they fear that once worn they can never be discarded.

What a boon this work has been to the schools! Instead of ruthlessly excluding infected children from the schools and thereby clogging the school machinery, the district physician has been superseded by the school medical inspector and the school nurse, and the child has been permitted to remain in school without the danger of infecting his fellows. The statistics from one of the medical stations (Marion School) show most impressively how irregular attendance can be effectually counteracted. It has been computed by the principal that the school nurse and dispensary between January 1 and June 1, 1909, saved 1871 days for the child and the school. Without these adjuncts of the school, the following cases of exclusion would have been necessary: 48 infections for 5 days, or 215 days.

118 cases of conjunctivitis for 5 days 590 days.
28 cases of scabies for 5 days 115 days.
25 cases of ringworm for 10 days 250 days.
57 cases of pediculosis of head for 8 days. 171 days.
6 cases of pediculosis of skin for 10 days 60 days.
94 cases of impetigo for 5 days 470 days.
Total 1,871 days.

With a rigidly enforced exclusion law these children, and others who might have been infected by them, would have been deprived of the processes of the schools for about ten years in the aggregate, at a tremendous economic loss to the taxpayer. This enormous waste was obviated at a merely nominal cost to the community. This saving takes no account of the increased working efficiency which resulted from properly caring for the following 283 non-communicable ailments during the corresponding period: 79 cases of minor injuries.

65 cases of throat affections.

40 cases of burns.

20 cases of chapped hands.

19 cases of ear affections.

12 cases of nasal affections.

10 cases of foreign bodies in eyes.

10 cases of removed tonsils.

10 cases of eczema.

9 cases of adenoids.

7 cases of canker sores.

2 cases of cold sores.

To render this auxiliary work of the schools still more effectual, volunteer work in the direction of feeding indigent, anemic and underfed children has been started in some of the schools. The Philanthropic Committee of the Cleveland Federation of Womens Clubs regularly serves a simple breakfast in the Eagle School to an average of thirty-six pupils per day.

As a result of this hygienic and medical work the attendance records have reached unprecedented heights in these usually irregular districts. The principals estimate that 90 per cent of the affected pupils have remained in school who would in the absence of this service have dropped out for several days. This fact is of vital significance to the schools and the community in view of the contention2 that irregular attendance is the chief cause of backwardness and non-promotion, and that ill health is the chief cause of irregular attendance. It was found in New York that 43 per cent of the boys and 48 per cent of the girls of the 16,000 completing the eighth grade in 1909 were absent from school from illness. The net loss through inattendance to the girls amounted to 3.5 per cent of the length of the term, and to the boys 3.2 per cent. The causes of these absences were: measles, 2,108; scarlet fever, 1,550; diphtheria, 1,002; pneumonia, 621; whooping cough, 473; chicken pox, 387; mumps, 288; tonsilitis, 251; typhoid fever, 219; rheumatism, 200; malaria, 151.

Ayms, Leonard P. Irregular Attendance–A Cause of Retardation, The Psychological Clinic, Vol. Ill, No. 1, March 15, 1909.

Without any system of medical inspection and nurses supervision in the New York schools, these absences would probably have been increased from minor infections such as those which prevailed in the Marion School.

Since the work attempted in these stations has not contemplated a routine examination of every child, and since the form and completeness of the records kept have varied more or less with each inspector, it is impossible to state how many cases have been examined by the physicians since the work was launched, or how many defects (particularly the non-communicable, physical abnormalities) have been discovered, or what the relative proportions of different kinds of physical defects are, or precisely how the influence upon mental retardation differs with different defects, or what have been the subsequent effects upon the physical growth, the increase in body weight and the mental efficiency of the hygienic and medical treatment of the affected child. The magnitude of the inspection work may be inferred, however, from the records at the Murray Hill and Marion schools, where, during the months of January, February and March, 28,820 inspections were made. Moreover, I have been able to obtain three sets of reliable data, one from the printed records and two in response to a questionnaire. The first shows the ratio of the various physical defects obtaining among children in the better sections and congested districts of the city. During the academic year 1906-1907 the department of physical training of the public schools examined 30,000 children with respect to the conditions of the eyes, ears, nose and throat only, in grades three to seven. The following table is based upon the examination of 1,284 pupils in two schools, one in the East End and the other in a congested district:

	Congested East End District	
	Per cent	Per cent
Number examined	668	616
Wearing glasses	6.4	1.8
Defective vision	82.4	71.1
Other symptoms of eye trouble.	27.8	85.2
Defective hearing	5.2	1.8
Diseased ears	8.9	12.8
Obstructed nasal breathing.	45.1	57.1
Habitual mouth breathers	12.1	14.7
Teeth very defective	1.8	15.7
Teeth very dirty	27.8	46.4
Average	18.55	28.4

Dr. L. W. Childs has more recently made a routine examination of 425 pupils in the lower grades (from the second to the fifth) in the Murray Hill School, where 97 per cent of the school population is Italian, covering the ear, nose and throat, and has kindly supplied me with the results of his careful survey, to wit:

	Per cent
Retraction of drum membranes of both ears	82
Retraction of membrane of one ear 16 Impaired hearing	22
Enlargement of both tonsils	22
Enlargement of one tonsil	
Adenoids 18 Impacted wax in ears	18
Enlarged cervical glands	10
Goitre	7
Atrophic rhinitis	5
Deviated septum	4
Suppurating ears	2
Hypertrophied inferior turbinals	2

In a still later examination of 120 sixth, seventh and eighth grade girls in the same school, 32 per cent suffered from goitre and 16 per cent from anemia.

In a routine examination of the 972 pupils in the eight grades of Mayflower School (station opened March 25, 1909), the inspector, Dr. S. A. Weisenberg, to whom I am indebted for a full report, found the most prevalent troubles to be the following:

Per cent Pediculosis " 1
Defective eyesight 7
Miscellaneous eye cases 18
Eye troubles, total 20
Miscellaneous tkroat cases 8.4
Hypertrophied tonsils 4.5
Tonsilitis 2.7
Adenoids 2.2
Adenitis 1.8
Throat troubles, total 19.1 Impetigo 9 Injuries 8.2
Miscellaneous ear cases 4.5
Chronic rhinitis 1.6
Nasal defects 1.8
Nose troubles, total 2.9
Over 78 per cent of these children were Jewish, nearly half of these being Russian Jews (47.9 per cent).

That the conditions revealed by these medical surveys in Cleveland are paralleled in other centers of population has been shown in Chapter I. Of course, under the present indefinite standards of conducting school medical inspec tion, and under the rather chaotic methods of recording the findings, it. is not possible to state whether the nationwide figures exaggerate or minimize the true state of affairs. School medical inspection work cannot command the respect of scientific men unless it is properly standardized. There is urgent need for the adoption of more uniform and definite standards, practices and policies for conducting physical inspections in the schools. At present some inspectors record only serious affections or affections requiring treatment, while others record all sorts of minor or negligible defects. There is diversity of opinion as to the amount of deviation necessary to constitute sensory defects (e-g., of vision and hearing). Thus A. E. Taussig, M. D., maintains that the criterion of defective vision should be a degree of acuity less than 2 o-The methods of recording the results of the examinations differ widely in different systems. Many give no indication as to which are the principal defects discovered; many do not specify clearly the exact nature of the defects; some group the secondary troubles with the primary, the contagious diseases with the non-contagious physical deviations, the temporary and curable ailments with the non-curable or protracted defects; some give no individual records for visual and auditory acuity in comparative objective measures for each eye and ear separately (although such information is of paramount value to the teacher in enabling her to seat uncorrected children judiciously); others omit the age, sex, nationality, grade, home and community conditions of the child (although such details are of surpassing importance, to enable us to correlate physical defectiveness and disease with age, sex, nationality and environment); and practically all omit reference to the mental condition, disposition and behavior of the child prior to inspection and treatment, and nearly all lack a follow-up form of card on which to record the results of treatment upon the childs subsequent mental efficiency, disposition, deportment, health, increase in weight and physical growth and development. That the latter has received scant, if any, scientific study is no doubt due to the difficulty of obtaining pedagogical and psychological measures which shall be objectively and scientifically valid. The classroom registers and the judgments of the teachers surely have their values, but the grading and judgments of the teachers are so variable that to measure by them the childs increasing proficiency as the result of treatment in quantitative terms is out of the question. Nevertheless a follow-up system of recording the influence of various forms of treatment upon various kinds of pedagogical defects based upon the teachers marks and opinions is better than no system at all, and is imperatively needed unless we are content to be empiricists in this newly organized branch of community and school work. To develop this work aright we must have accurate knowledge of the influence of various abnormalities and of their treatment upon mental and physical development. Taussig has recently proposed a means of measuring the influence of physical defects upon school work; and the same means might be used to measure the effects of treatment. He would calculate the average grade of proficiency for each age for the normal and defective pupils by multiplying the number of children in each grade by the number of the grade. The average grade can then be secured by dividing the result by the total number of children. This gives a quasi-objective measure, but, again, it assumes the accuracy of the teachers marks and the correctness of the school classification. Assuming a fair degree of accuracy for the individual markings, the scheme offers an approximate criterion for gauging the scholastic influence of physical orthogenesis.

But a scheme by which to supplement the teachers grades and opinions by means of careful psychological tests of the pupils quickness of perception, rapidity of association, strength of immediate visual and auditory memory, strength of grip, ability to spell and add, etc., carried out a short time prior to treatment and subsequently at different intervals, will eventually command the attention of school medical inspection and psychological departments. Such tests are perfectly feasible and will enable us to quantify the influences of orthosomatic treatment upon the working capacity of the pupil (see Chapters XIII and XIV).

But to return from this digression to the medical inspection work in Cleveland. The conditions revealed by the volunteer inspections in the schools and the humanitarian work performed by the nurses and physicians in relieving needless physical suffering, which interfered with the working efficiency of both the child and the school, demonstrated to the Board of Education the urgency, on economic, educational and moral grounds, of establishing as an integral part of the schools a department of medical supervision and inspection. Such a department, under the administrative charge of the director of schools, was put into operation on the first of April. It has at its disposal an annual budget of 30,000. It has in its employ one supervisor at a salary of 3,000 per annum, fifteen medical assistants or inspectors at 100 per month for twelve months per year, ten nurses at 60 per month the first year, 70 the second, 75 the third and 80 thereafter, and one clerk at 1,000 per annum. The department contemplates the inspection of all the pupils to determine their state of health and the presence of diseased conditions and physical anomalies. Teachers and parents will receive advice on the diseases and defects found, with recommendations for their relief; the pupils and teachers will receive advice on the safeguarding of their health, and suggestions will be offered respecting the course of study, construction of buildings, etc. Records in duplicate will be on file at the schools and the headquarters of the department, and will be sent home to the parents. These records rtnll accompany the child throughout his course in the grades. It is expected that the records will be made unusually complete and accurate. The city will be divided into fifteen districts, comprising about six schools each, with one physician and nurse in charge of each, making each physician responsible for inspecting somewhat less than 5,000 children (each of the two hundred inspectors in New York has about 4,000 children under his care, while each of Chicagos one hundred has approximately 6,000). By thoroughly inspecting the first year entrants it is believed that the work will be materially lightened in the upper grades. Free treatment is not yet a part of the program. The rules and regulations of the department are made by the Board of Education and not by the Board of Health. School medical inspection should be under the administrative control of boards of education instead of boards of health. Actually in 1911 only 106 systems were under boards of health as against 337 under boards of education.

II. Opening Of The National Campaign On Oral Hygiene Under The Auspices Of The National Dental Association, The Ohio State Dental Society And The Cleveland Dental Society.

In 1908 the Committee on Education and Hygiene of the Cleveland Dental Society reported a plan for dental education in the public schools of the city, embracing among other matters a course of lectures to be given to the teachers. The plan was censored and criticised by the Dental Society and given scant consideration by the Board of Education. Nothing was accomplished beyond the issuing of a bulletin of information on the care of the teeth by the superintendent of schools to the teachers, who were directed to impart the information to the children. Somewhat over a year later a free dental clinic was established at the City Hospital. The venture proved largely unsuccessful, due to the unfavorable location of the clinic. Inspection trips were then made to Boston, New York, Rochester, Birmingham, Ala., and other places for the purpose of studying the methods employed for the dental education of school children. At this juncture, the chairman of the Cleveland Committee on Education and Hygiene became chairman of the Oral Hygiene Committee of the National Dental Association. With the oral hygiene headquarters established in Cleveland, and data available from the cities visited, the campaign began afresh. Permission was received from the Board of Education to conduct a dental survey in four representative schools. This survey was made in one day by about forty dentists. The detailed results are embodied in the following table. The table is not absolutely accurate, owing to the haste with which the work had to be done, and the occasional misinterpretation of the instructions by some of the examiners. Thus some examiners thought that good, fair or bad referred to the teeth only, and, therefore, some mouths were marked good when the oral conditions were unhygienic. The results thus rather minimize than overemphasize the actual oral conditions found. The figures from the Marion School are the most accurate.

Murray Hill Doan. Waterson. Marion. 1
Number of Pupils Examined. Condition of the Mouth: Good. 864 691 298 824 2677
346 381 134 132 135 99 63 244
Fair. 429 117 336 241
Bad

Condition of the Gums: Good 594 253 504 169 221 447 300
Bad 73
Use Tooth Brush: Yes. 101 762 524 161 193 243
No 100 456
Teeth Filled: Yes 9 843 275 404 102 191 72 707
No
Malocclusion: Yes 230 633 421 93 169 343 308
No 452
Teeth containing Cavities Teeth Extracted 641 257 14 745 125
Nationality: 69
25 657 198 20 45 116 73 11 420
Italian 4 4 828 1 6 1 7
Slavic 1 1 "i
Swedish 2 3
Irish i 9
Polish 7 49
Number of Perfect Mouths. Number of Defective Mouths 62–7.17 802–92.83 3920
20–2.9 14–4.69 13–1.5
671–97.1 4294 284–95.31 1342 811–98.43 5505
The 2,677 mouths examined contained 15,061 dental cavities, or an average per mouth of 5.6 (somewhat above the Worcester average, 4.85); in 2,145 mouths, or in about 80 per cent, the teeth were not filled; malocclusion affected 1,087, or somewhat over 40 per cent; in 1,479, or 55 per cent, a tooth brush–the instrument that is mightier than the sword in national human defense–was never used; the number of defective mouths ranged from 92 per cent to 98 per cent; and practically 97 per cent of the mouths required some sort of hygienic attention or dental service to render the mouth healthy and functionally efficient. As will be seen in the table, some of the defects are most prevalent in the schools with a preponderant Italian population–an indication of the relation of unwholesome environmental influences and unenlightened or poverty-stricken conditions in the home to unsanitary oral conditions.

It will be of interest to recount some of the results of dental surveys in other cities. One of the first, if not actually the first, inspection was made in Russia in 1879. Defective dentures afflicted 80 per cent of the inhabitants of St. Petersburg. Of Berlin school children, 90 per cent were similarly affected (Hitter), and of 100,000 school children examined in different states of Germany, from 81 per cent to 99 per cent had diseased teeth. In Ludlow, Mass., the 500 pupils examined (from eight to fifteen years old) displayed palpable neglect of dental cleanliness, very few used brushes, none had received any dental treatment aside from a few children who had had teeth extracted, bacterial deposits and malodorousness existed in varying degrees, some suffered from prolonged retention of the temporary teeth, while still more had lost these teeth prematurely, showing a disregard of the value of the temporary teeth. In New York, an expert examination was made of the teeth of 500 boys and girls from fourteen to sixteen who were applying for work certificates, on behalf of the Childrens Aid Society. Less than 3 per cent of these had sound teeth; 456 had 2,808 decayed teeth, or an average of about 6.1 each, 90 per cent of which could be saved by proper dental attention. Gangrenous pulps, or. decayed pulps exposing the roots, were found in 247 boys and 152 girls; and only 25 out of the 500 had received any dental care other than extraction. In an early inspection of all the pupils in Cleveland by the ward physicians under the direction of the Board of Health, 79 per cent of the children were reported as suffering from decayed or defective teeth (see also Chapter I).

With such distressing revelations as these–and the statistical data can now be multiplied a hundred-fold–it is little wonder that experts have come to regard caries of the teeth as the disease of the people, a world-wide affliction of civilized nations, and the unsanitary mouth, which is the gateway to the stomach, as the bodys chief breeding place for pathogenic bacteria, a hidden source of infection little attended to because of its hidden character. And with these revelations the modern propagandist of the body hygienic has rallied his forces about a new battle-cry: Keep the mouth with diligence, for out of it are the issues of life. Good teeth, good health–is the modern ortho-genie tocsin. In no branch of public hygiene are such decisive results obtained and with such small cost as in the dental treatment of school children.

The results of the Cleveland survey induced the Board of Education, in October, 1909, to grant the request of the National Dental Association, the Ohio Dental Society and the Cleveland Dental Society, to conduct dental examinations of all the pupils in the public schools during a period of one year, to treat gratuitously all indigent children so desiring, and to offer lectures in the school buildings to teachers, parents and pupils on the proper care and use of the teeth and mouth. On March 18, 1910, the formal opening of these clinics–four in public schools and one each in St. Alexis Hospital and the City Clinic–was signalized by a convention in Cleveland, at which addresses were made by the President of the National Dental Association, the Chairman of the Education and Oral Hygiene Committee of the Ohio State Dental Society, the Chairman of the Oral Hygiene Committee of the National Dental Association, the Commissioner of Health of Chicago, the Superintendent of Schools of Cleveland, the Dental Surgeon of the Naval Academy, the Mayor of Cleveland, the personal representatives of President Taft and Governor Harmon and others. The exercises included the formal dedication of the clinics and addresses on various aspects of school dental inspection. The convention marked the inauguration of a country-wide campaign for the organization of departments of dental inspection as integral parts of the public school systems of our cities. It is expected that one year of volunteer work in Cleveland will demonstrate that the work is one of the most needed and worthiest undertakings of the schools, whether viewed from an altruistic, educational or economic point of view. Special scholarship and deportment blanks will be kept on which records of the treatment will be made and of its effect upon the subsequent working efficiency and behavior of the child (see experiment described and discussed in Chapters XIII and XIV). Special blanks in triplicate, containing charts of diseased dentures, will be furnished to the Director of Schools, the Cleveland Dental Society and to the pupil or teacher for the parent. Parents who desire treatment for their children on the ground of poverty must make application upon a separate indigent blank. The clinic patient will be supplied gratis with a brush, tooth powder, antiseptic wash, plastic (not gold) fillings and pulp and root treatments. The examiners and clinicians will be certified and assigned to their respective schools by the director of schools and the supervisor of dental inspection. The material equipment of the clinics is furnished by the National and Ohio Dental Associations, and the dentists and assistants (each examiner will have a woman assistant) by the Cleveland Dental Society. Each examiner will donate one weeks services, or twelve half days. The lecture course will be in the hands of twenty men. The expense incurred by the Cleveland Society amounts, in cash equivalent, to about 3,491–1,866 for examination work, 1,500 for clinic work and 125 for the lecture and educational work.

Thus the year 1910 marks the introduction upon a volunteer basis of the first school dental clinic in the United States, six years after the first school dental clinic was established in Strassburg by Dr. Jessen. (It is stated that the first free dental clinic in the world was established in Rochester over twenty-five years ago and that the first school dental clinic was established in the same city February 23, 1910.) The Strassburg clinic is open to all school children without charge, and is manned by regularly registered dentists, under municipal control. School clinics of the same type have since been established in thirty-five or more German cities. With the better understanding which we now have of the effects of the unhygienic oral cavity upon the health, happiness, mental and physical efficiency and the morals of the child, it is predicted that the spread of the school dental clinic will be no less rapid in our own country. (At this writing, it is reported that over 200 American cities are providing dental inspection. In 1910, J. H. and Thomas A. Forsyth of Boston donated 500,000 for the establishment of a clinic to provide free dental service to any child from early childhood to the age of sixteen.) It is reported of a certain juvenile judge that he always has the teeth of his youthful culprits examined before he imposes sentence; and not infrequently the penalty imposed is a trip to the dental chair. Match manufacturers subject their employees to dental inspection and exclude all persons with decayed teeth. Phosphorous necrosis has thus disappeared among match workers. Some hidden cavity in a tooth or unclean surface is often a focus for bacterial deposits. Such foci serve as the breeding places for germs causing acute infections, scarlet fever, diphtheria and tuberculosis, and enlargements of the glands of the neck and throat may occur through absorptions from these cavities. The gases and poisons generated in an unsanitary mouth and the pain from toothache often produce general and gastric neurasthenia, indigestion, ill health, irritability, bad temper, mental inefficiency, inability to concentrate attention, bad morals, and, it is alleged, even insanity. The machinery for discovering these conditions in the schools– the only organized social agency with anything like police power–will come inevitably everywhere. Will we get the machinery for rectifying these conditions, the school dental dis pensary in addition to the school dental inspection station? Whether or not compulsory school clinics are desirable, some form of pressure cannot be dispensed with if this work is to realize proper returns upon the investment. In one of the German cities such pressure is secured by barring children with diseased teeth from the privileges of the recreation grounds, forest school and vacation colonies. Without good teeth there cannot be thorough mastication. Without thorough mastication there cannot be perfect digestion. Without perfect digestion there cannot be proper assimilation. Without assimilation there cannot be nutrition. Without nutrition there cannot be health. Moreover, without the retention and the wholesome development of the teeth there cannot be beauty of countenance.

REFERENCES.

Ayhes, L. P. The Effect of Physical Defects on School Progress. The Psychological Clinic, Vol. III, No. 8, May, 1909, p. 71.

Cornell, Walter S. The Relation of Physical to Mental Defect in School Children. The Psychological Clinic, Vol. I, No. 9, February, 1908, p. 281.

Mentally Defective Children in the Public Schools. The Psychological Clinic, Vol. II, No. 8, May, 1908, p. 75.

The Physical Condition of the School Children of the School of Observation, University of Pennsylvania. The Psychological Clinic, Vol. III, No. 5, October, 1909, p. 184.

The Need of Improved Records of the Physical Condition of School Children. The Psychological Clinic, Vol. III, No. 6, November, 1909, p. 161.

Ebersole. Report on the Proposed Dental Educational and Hygienic Work in the Cleveland Schools. Dental Summary, February and March, 1910 (reprinted in the Dental Brief and Dental Digest, same issue).

Elson, W. H. Annual Report of the Superintendent of Schools, Board of Education, Cleveland, Ohio, 1907, p. 88.

Emery. Medical Inspection in Two Worcester Schools. The Pedagogical Seminary, Vol. XVII, No. 2, April, 1910, p. 111.

Greene, Mary Belle. A Class of Backward and Defective Children. The Psychological Clinic, Vol. III, No. 5, October, 1910, p. 125.

Gulick and Ayres. Medical Inspection of Schools, 1918.

Holmes, Arthur. Can Impacted Teeth Cause Moral Delinquency? The Psychological Clinic, Vol. IV, No. 1, March, 1910, p. 19.

McHENRY. Medical School Inspection in Cleveland. The Cleveland Medical Journal, Vol. VIII, 1909, p. 888.

Orr. The New Medical Inspection Department in the Cleveland Public School. The Cleveland Sunday Leader, Magazine and Workers Section, March 18, 1910.

Russell Sage Foundation. What American Cities Are Doing for the Health of School Children, 1911.

Sneed, C. M., and Whipple, G. M. An Examination of the Eyes, Ears and Throats of Children in the Public Schools of Jefferson City, Mo. The Psychological Clinic, Vol. II, No. 8, January, 1909, p. 284.

Taussio, A. E. The Prevalence of Visual and Aural Defects Among the Public School Children of St. Louis County, Mo. The Psychological Clinic, Vol. III, No. 6, November, 1909, p. 149.

CHAPTER XVII

EFFICIENCY IN SCHOOL ORGANIZATION AND THE CONSERVATION OF THE MENTAL

HEALTH OF CHILDREN1

The preservation and promotion of the mental, physical, educational, social, moral and vocational efficiency of the individual is not only the most vital problem that confronts each human being, mature or immature, but it is also the problem par excellence of the family, state and school. Owing to the disintegrating, and ofttimes demoralizing, influences exerted upon the institution of the home by the modern urbanization and industrialization, together with the frequently attendant pauperization, of a large part of our population, the obligation for the reclamation, conservation and improvement of child life is being largely transferred to the state. But we are rapidly learning that the state has no agency which is able adequately to cope with the numerous problems involved except the public schools. And so the obligation to care for the welfare of the children is more and more being placed primarily, and very properly, upon the institution of the public schools. This is the only institution established under state control in all communities which can be invested with sufficient police power and which commands in largest measure the confidence of the community.

i Delivered, in part, at the Annual Meeting of the Child Study Department of the Pennsylvania State Educational Association, Pittsburgh, December 31, 1913.

That the public schools have responded to the new demands made upon them by the people during the last decade or two is well known. They have assumed functions not dreamed possible only a few years ago. Witness the growth of the social center or wider-use-of-the-school-plant movement, the establishment of evening continuation and trade school work, the introduction of school feeding, the organization of school medical inspection systems, school medical, dental and psychological clinics and playgrounds and social service departments. Splendid as have been these recent attempts to reformulate, revitalize and modernize the functions of the schools, and wonderful as are the results which have already been attained, it must, nevertheless, be admitted that we are even now but in the beginnings of the new order of things—of a new movement of social and educational reconstruction which is destined to sweep over all the land.

Among the forces tending toward a more efficient organization of school work is the growing recognition of the fact that the basic condition of efficient instruction and of the effective conservation of the mental health and special talents of children is the adjustment of the educative processes to meet the varying needs of varying children, and the adjustment of the individual to his social and vocational environment. Education, indeed, is fundamentally a process of adjustment. But only a few of the best modern school systems (leave alone the average or poor ones) have thus far succeeded in making a measurably complete adjustment of the educational agencies to the varied needs of all the children of the people, and the varied needs of all the communities of all the people. It is the purpose of this paper to emphasize the fact that many, if not most, of the schools of the country fail properly to conserve the educational health of all their pupils because they fail to adjust the processes of the schools to the individual requirements of the pupils. This often renders much of the work of intellectual and moral instruction and training quite unscientific, inefficient or nugatory.

Before attempting to preach a moral, however, we should first be reasonably certain about our facts. Before attempting to advise or prescribe, we should thoroughly scrutinize the evidence and accurately diagnose the case. Only after the existence of defects in the existent social, educational, or industrial order has been proved, is the critic or advocate ready for the public forum, and only then will he receive the critical attention and arouse the determined action of thoughtful people. It was the exposure of the demonstrated existence of repellent conditions in the Chicago slaughter-houses and stock-yards that led to the enactment of meat inspection laws. It was the high degree of refinement and differentiation of medical diagnosis that led to specialization in medicine, to the development of various kinds of medical specialists, and which made imperative the organization of various kinds of hospitals and the differentiation of wards and clinics within hospitals. Just so surely as the refinement of scientific medical diagnosis has led to the development of new specialties in medicine, which has resulted in the improved differential remedial treatment of sick people, so surely will the refinement of scientific educational diagnosis develop new specialties and new methods of treatment in education. One of the peculiar benefits of this advance step, toward which education is surely tending, is that the schools (like the hospitals in respect to medical care) will develop differential or remedial or corrective educational treatment designed to meet the individual needs of all those children who differ from the standard of mental and pedagogical health in the same sense that different kinds of sick persons differ from the standard of bodily health. When our schools have been organized scientifically to diagnose educationally abnormal pupils as hospitals are now organized to scientifically diagnose sick people, then, and then only, will the schools be prepared intelligently maximally to conserve and to improve the mental, educational, moral and physical well-being of all the children, and economically and efficiently to train them for the social, civic and vocational responsibilities for which they are fitted. Then, and then only, will the work of rearing children be made as dignified and as scientific as the work of raising cattle and horses. Then, and then only, will school supervision be made efficient, and school organization minister effectually to the needs of all the children. But I have anticipated my conclusions in the preamble. I must therefore proceed at once to present some facts to justify the above assertions, which may sound to you like the pipe-dreams of a beclouded mind. What you demand are actual concrete facts—facts which are capable of duplication and verification in any large school system anywhere. Nowhere are such facts—abundant, verifiable, incontestable—more easily accessible than in the clinic files of the modern well-organized psycho-educational clinic. The facts now to be presented consist of a dozen clinical pictures selected from the files of the educational clinic in the School of Education of the University of Pittsburgh. These pictures fail to furnish an adequate idea of the great variety of educationally unusual children—some easily diagnosed and others extremely baffling—which have been coming to the clinic for examination from various sections in Western Pennsylvania. However, the cases discussed will not only furnish clinical pictures of the two opposite types of educational deviates—the subnormal and the supernormal—but they will also give a faint idea of the great variety of subtypes of abnormal children which will be found within any given classification, or within the same grade of mental arrest or acceleration, and which must be adequately differentiated unless the public will continue to be satisfied with the type of crude and amateurish educational diagnosis which is now tolerated in most school systems.

I shall begin with the subnormal cases, using the word subnormal in its broadest connotation, as inclusive of all cases on the minus side of the curve of distribution. I shall first present five types of imbeciles, pointing out the moral for the schools and for the community in connection with the discussion of each case. It is well to dwell on these cases for two reasons: first, because it sometimes happens that these cases never get to the schools and therefore receive no educational attention whatsoever; second—and this happens more frequently—because all types and grades of imbeciles actually do get to the schools, and when there they are scarcely ever recognized by the teachers, principals, nurses or school inspectors, unless teachers and inspectors have taken special courses on feeble-minded and backward children. The claim has frequently been made, and presumably still is made, in all sections of the country by teachers, superintendents and medical inspectors that cases so low-grade as imbeciles, particularly the low-grade imbeciles, never get into the schools. We now know that this statement is without foundation. I shall first cite two cases, however, which did not receive any school instruction.

Case 1

My first case is an Irish-American girl, aged eleven years eleven months at the time of the clinic examination in November, 1913.

She is reported to have been a fine, healthy babe, weighed twelve pounds at birth, nursed for one and a half years. Cerebro-spinal meningitis, accompanied by convulsions at the time of teething during the tenth month, left her sickly, fretful and backward. The first teeth did not come through until the age of two and a half and the second set began cutting during the tenth year. The anterior fontanelle did not close until about three. At three she was too weak to walk, stumbling and falling, but walked unsupported at about the age of four; the control of the fundamental reflexes was acquired at about four. Measles at four and a light attack of pertussis, and scarlet fever, at five. Speech has remained undeveloped except for very few words and various inarticulate sounds (nuh=no; uh-huh=yes lah=Jennie, her sister; nah=her usual response).

Eats heartily and sleeps soundly at present. Table manners good but cannot sip soup; drinks it and slobbers on clothes. Usually good-natured, but has spells of stubbornness, displays violent temper when aroused and will chase boys on the street who annoy her.

Home conditions and home treatment fair. Is able to scrub floor, iron dust-cloths, sew fairly well, dress herself, but cannot button her clothes or wash her face clean or go errands. She cannot persist in her work.

The clinic examination disclosed the presence of several dental cavities and strabismus due to muscular paralysis. Dental treatment was advised and has been provided.

In anthropometric development[2] she was quite normal. [2] In all cases the anthropometric measurements are compared with the norms furnished by Smedley (percentile and age tables), Boas, In standing and sitting height, head circumference and weight she was equal to the normal twelve-year-old girl, while in strength of right-hand and left-hand grip she ranked between nine and ten and ten and eleven, respectively. Her weight was correct for her height and the proportion between standing and sitting stature was also right (ponderal index equals 28.1, normal equals 28.8; statural index equals 58.2, normal equals 58.2).

But mentally she tested only to about the age of three, while in motor development she was like a child of four.

She was unable to copy a square, could not show her right hand and left ear except in a vaccillating manner, could not state the number of fingers on the two hands, but was sometimes able to hold up as many fingers as the number of fingers held up by the examiner. When shown a key and asked what it was she picked a key from her mothers handbag. Cannot distinguish between pretty and ugly pictures or execute a triple order, is sensitive to the presence of observers, but makes fair effort to respond and some effort to talk.

Here is afforded a very interesting case of partial aphasia superposed upon a background of imbecility of developmental origin (due to inflammation of the pia mater), with practically normal anthropometric develop-

Hastings, Quandelet and Montessori. The norms from these authorities are sometimes discrepant, whence it has at times been necessary to make approximations. In all cases the intellectual age has been determined by the Binet-Simon scale, 1908 edition, the authors guide (Experimental Studies of Mental Defectives, Baltimore, 1912, pp. 116f.). The motor age has been determined by the Vineland form-board. Data are also given for the two Healy-Femald construction puzzles (Tests for Practical Mental Classification, Baltimore, 1911. It has not yet been proved that these construction puzzles have the value for mental diagnosis claimed for them. I have a number of instances where the child failed utterly to do the tests on one occasion but had no difficulty on another occasion. The outcome, apparently, depends too much on chance).

ment. Although almost twelve years of age, this child has never received any systematic instruction either at home or in school. The educational possibilities of a case like this are, to be sure, quite limited. But corrective speech work, applied several years ago, would not have been entirely futile, and the right kind of sensori-motor training would have developed a degree of motor skill which would now enable this girl to make more profitable use of muscles which are not very far below normal strength. The time almost invariably comes in the lives of these unfortunates when society must support them, and it is only a just demand of society that the schools so train them in their youth that they may be able to contribute more to their own support in institutions than they can do if left to grow up untrained in their homes.

Case 2

The following case, an American girl, age sixteen years eleven months at the time of the examination in December, 1912, grades about the same in intelligence, but represents a different type. She furnishes another illustration of educational neglect.

According to the record, her birth was normal and on time, weighed about eight pounds at birth, bottle fed, appeared bright and intelligent as a babe but did not kick like the normal child; six or eight teeth appeared simultaneously during the sixth month; walked at about the age of two but required braces until three; began to talk more or less at three or four. Mental peculiarity first noticed by parents at six years, particularly the lack of progress in speech development. Pubertal development somewhat retarded (first menstruation at fifteen and one half years).

Chicken-pox, mumps and measles during fourth year; scarlet fever, followed by diphtheria, rendered the child weak for five or six weeks. Always more or less nervously unstable, easily excited, nervous jumps/ but without violent outbreaks.

At home, she is amiable and obedient, understands commands and is willing to do what she can comprehend. Can sweep, scrub, set table, put on shoes and stockings. Does not know the alphabet nor understand the meaning of such words as or and if, and cannot read or count.

Mother very weak and nervous before childs birth; father not always temperate; one cousin of father weak-minded; a child of fathers sister acted peculiarly and could not talk; a child of the daughter of a sister of the father had chorea.

Attended school a few days at the age of six, but was sent home because she was too nervous. No other schooling.

The examination at the clinic revealed an excitable but pleasant type of imbecile, with pronounced neurotic stigmata, gross finger twitches, occasional nervous starts, two slightly enlarged tonsils, two carious teeth, an asymmetrical chest and a very unsymmetrical physical development. In head girth, she graded eight years, in standing and sitting height, over eighteen years (statural index equals 52.7, normal equals 52); in weight, a little over fifteen (ponderal index equals 22.7, normal equals 28.6); in strength of grip, about normal, but in vital capacity notably deficient. She is thus both too tall and too light and her head is exceptionally small. Her speech was very indistinct; she was color blind and possessed very little comprehension of form.

Intellectually, she tested at about three and a half years.

She knows the value of the four smallest United States coins, can point to her nose, eyes and mouth, names a knife and a key, knows her sex and can distinguish the difference in weight between six and fifteen grams. She can repeat only the last of two digits or the last word of six syllables pronounced to her, says she has two fingers on her right hand, makes no reply for the left, and two fingers on both hands.

This girl had been examined repeatedly during the last ten years, but the mother had never yet been told what was fundamentally wrong with her—a low degree of imbecility of the simple and excitable type, probably of combined primary and secondary origin.

Because the girl was able to understand a little and do a few things, the mother had been permitted to continue to indulge the fond, but vain, belief that she would some day grow out of it. She was, however, assured at the clinic that her girl will never advance beyond a child of four or five, that she will need lifelong protection, especially against the exploiters of defenseless girls of her type, and that, as she had already passed the pubertal epoch, she should be given the protection of institutional care, especially if such protection could not be guaranteed at home. As a result of this advice, application was filed about a year ago for her admission into the state institution at Polk, but it has thus far been impossible to get her admitted.

In theory, the public schools should not be required to train any child below the level of high-grade imbecile. In practice, however, they are forced to accept these children, unless society is satisfied to have them idle their time away in the homes or roam the streets, as so many do, and drift into vagabondage, prostitution and criminality. No state in the union has sufficient institutional provisions to accommodate 25 per cent of all its feeble-minded children. Moreover, many parents, owing to the sympathy which they feel for their unfortunate progeny, refuse to institutionalize them (and will not do so in the absence of mandatory laws), and cannot reconcile themselves to allowing them to remain in institutions even after they have been admitted. This may be illustrated by the following case who was admitted, after special pleadings had been made, to the state institution.

Case 3

A boy, aged nine years ten months at the time of the examination in May, 1913.

The record indicated that the child was born normally, the last of eight children from the second husband; age of mother and father at the time of childs birth forty-two and forty-eight, respectively. He was unable to nurse after the eighth week, thenceforth bottle fed; developed catarrh from cold contracted during the third week; nose operation at one and a half years, nasal obstruction removed at two and a half; same operation repeated in the same nostril at three and a half; nose operation again in November, 1911. Has been examined again and again, but mother has never been told that there was anything wrong except nasal obstruction, catarrh and adenoids. Fell on the forehead at one and a half years; mumps at four, typhoid-pneumonia at five, scarlet fever at five and a half; frequently suffered from styes; has been subject to enuresis. The mental peculiarity (slow development) was noticed by the mother between the first and second years.

Restless and active in disposition, always doing something. Enjoys roller-skating. Able to dress and feed himself. Bad temper at times, but obedient if taken in right way.

Started to kindergarten at five and a half; at seven, was placed in the first grade, but was soon returned to kindergarten; at eight, was again advanced to first grade, where he went over the first half years work three or four times with as many different teachers; then was advanced to 1A; he learned to write his name and a few words, although they meant nothing to him; but could not learn to count.

The clinic examination revealed a diminutive, restless type of boy, crying because he was afraid his nose would be operated on, suffering from rhinitis, pharyngitis and running ears; he kad a tongue slightly fissured transversely, stubby fingers, with the little finger somewhat inturned, rather sandy hair, a rounded, diminutive head, with a girth less than for a six-year-old boy. In standing height and weight he had a development of seven and a half years, in sitting height six and a half, in hand grip between eight and nine for the right hand and about nine for the left hand. Thus in physical development he ranges from the child of six to seven and a half, while his manuometry is about normal. Relatively to total stature his trunk is too short, but his weight is about right (statural index equals 58.2, which is about normal for age twelve; ponderal index equals 28.7, normal equals 28.5).

At the age of nearly ten years he had an intelligence of only four and a half years, which is less than the intelligence he should have had when he first entered the first grade. His motor development was even less, namely, four years. His mental development is thus from two to three years inferior to his physical development.

He is unable to repeat three numbers or six syllables; does not know which is his right hand and left ear, says he has three fingers on the right, four on the left and six fingers on both hands; says he is seven years old, cannot distinguish pretty from ugly faces, cannot state whether the time of the day is forenoon or afternoon, or copy a diamond or square, or locate missing parts in pictures. Says a horse is a horse, a dog is a dog, mamma is a mother, a table is table cover, a chair is make one table chair. Calls a quarter five cents, names red and blue correctly, but calls green blue and yellow red; says three two and three one cent stamps are eight stamps and cost ten cents. Is able to read such monosyllables as in, it to.

This child is a mongolian imbecile, although not so easily recognized as such because of the attenuation of the mongoloid characteristics. Mongolian defectives unusually attain a mentality of about five years, rarely falling below four or exceeding seven. They usually come from the later pregnancies of parents of between forty and fifty of good hereditary qualities. Another boy with glaringly obvious mongolian features, six years old, who was more recently examined at the clinic, had a mentality of about two years and was the tenth of a family of fourteen children. He had been examined more than a dozen times and had been treated for all kinds of troubles, but the mother had never been told before that he was an incurable mongolian imbecile. It is very important to recognize this type early for two reasons: first, because these children are naturally affectionate and agreeable when understood and properly treated, but quite mischievous, stubborn and irascible when not understood. Unfortunately they are rarely understood in the home, school or on the playground, where they are teased and bullied. Second, because they require differential educa tional treatment in special classes. It is a waste of time to try to train these children to read, write and cipher, while speech training yields very meager results because of their limited intelligence. They should be trained in simple domestic and industrial tasks which do not entail very much strain on their vascillating attention. The proper place to train them is in state institutions, but unfortunately, as has been said, it is difficult to persuade the parents to part with them while they are young and plastic and to keep them in commitment once they are admitted. Case 3 was admitted to the state institution at Polk in August, 1913, but was removed after only three weeks of residence by his mother. Until we have mandatory commitment laws the public schools will be obliged to train low-grade defectives. But they should under no circumstances be permitted in the regular classes, there to waste their years on work which has utterly no meaning or value for them, there to monopolize the time of the teacher (but some teachers, I have found from first-hand reports, ignore them and let them sit idle), and there to rob the normal and bright pupils of the advantages which by right are theirs. It looks almost like criminal negligence on the part of the school administration to have kept this child two or three years in the first grade. There is a fine irony in calling education an art based on scientific principles so long as this state of affairs is permitted to continue in the public schools. Some types of defectives, it is true, cannot be infallibly diagnosed at four or five years of age because the deficiency accumulates gradually and is not very patent at four or five, but not so with this type of defective.

To what an extent the public schools are wasting the peoples funds–of course not intentionally, but because of the failure to provide the means for scientifically classifying pupils–by trying to train in the regular classes both low-and high-grade defectives will appear from a consideration of the following high-grade imbeciles.

Case 4

An American boy, aged eleven years eleven months at the time of the examination in December, 1913.

From his history we learned that he was the fifth born of nine children, two of whom died in infancy; he was diminutive at birth, bottle fed for one and a half years, unable to sit up until one and a half, unable to walk until three, although he is reported as talking at about two; neglected, poorly nourished and puny as a babe.

The present home conditions are reprehensible from the hygienic, sanitary and moral points of view. A four-room tenement house, lacking a bath and abounding in dirt and vermin, in a densely populated section, is occupied by ten persons. Seven children sleep in a small, unventilated bedroom, three boys in one bed and four girls in another. The food supply is inadequate in quantity and quality. The home life is upset and disturbed and the children are neglected and poorly disciplined. This boy spends much of his time roving around and playing in the streets.

The father, now a bookkeeper and apparently a drug fiend, formerly held an educational position in a higher institution of learning in the state of Pennsylvania, and springs from a stock having several illustrious names to its credit. The mother was subject to scrofula during the first sixteen years of her life, and apparently is of inferior stock.

The boy entered school at six, has been very irregular in attendance and is reported as a total failure, poor in all branches, but best in music. At twelve he can count to ten, but cannot add, multiply, divide or subtract, cannot read or spell, is very poor in writing and spelling, and at the end of fifty-three months of schooling he is still in a regular first-grade class. The school report indicates that he is chatty, sociable, good-natured, kind, cheerful, impulsive, but also restless, nervous, at times excitable with outbreaks of laughing or of destructive tendencies. He inclines to be heedless of reproof, although he takes reproof with good grace, and is likewise heedless of danger. He is careless, slovenly and acts like an old man of seventy.

The examination at the clinic revealed a poorly nourished child with eight dental caries, two enlarged tonsils (for which dental and medical care was recommended, but nothing has thus far been done owing to the indifference of the father), and an anthropometric development ranging from about five to seven years. His standing stature was nearly equal to seven, his bust, weight and vital capacity nearly equal to six and a half, and his head girth less than five. On the other hand, in strength of grip he ranged between eight and nine years, and his weight was about right for his stature (although tke ponderal index was 28.2 instead of 22.8, normal for height), but his bust was too long (index of stature equals 55 instead of 58; brachyscelous type). No one of his two sisters and his two brothers, varying in ages from eight to fourteen years, who were examined in the clinic, had a head girth equal to the normal seven-year-old child, while the average for all the five cases was less (19.5 inches) than for the five-year-old boy or girl.

In the clinic, on superficial examination, he appeared bright, but with a highly distractable attention, his speech was distinct, fluent, but also glib, and he took delight in talking about his interests and in narrating his possible and impossible experiences–among others that on Halloween he had dressed up and pointed a make-believe revolver at a man, securing from him twenty dollars, which he had deposited in his bank at home.

His intellectual age was only about six years, while his motor development was about seven and a half. In this case there is a fair correspondence between the physical and mental retardation.

He said he had ten fingers on the right hand, eight on the left and two hundred on both hands; thirteen pennies were counted as seventeen; nine cents worth of stamps cost fifty-two cents; in was read as it, bed as ed while to was read correctly; he was unable to write from dictation, to count backwards, to state the difference between common concepts, to select in order five weights differing by three grams, or to give descriptive definitions. Monday, October 18, 1918, was said to be Monday, May 84, second year. He named the four smallest coins, recognized the four fundamental colors and repeated the week days correctly.

This boy is a perfectly typical quasi-microcephalic, unstable, high-grade imbecile of congenital origin, whose condition is possibly aggravated by insufficient feeding and bad home conditions; but after five years of schooling in the same grade he was not recognized by the school force as a true imbecile, but only as a case of marked stupidity or backwardness, complicated with a certain degree of waywardness. For over five years he has been permitted to mark time in the regular grades, but has practically nothing to show for his years of toil and trouble, the teachers labors have accomplished merely negligible results, and the schools have wasted for the instruction of this boy alone at least 150 of the taxpayers money in the vain attempt to educate an imbecile as if he were a normal child. It is almost incomprehensible that we should tolerate in this day of scientific efficiency such wasteful expenditures of the public funds in the education of misfit pupils in the regular grades. This boy, at the very beginning of his school career, should have been given an educational examination by a competent educational examiner, supplemented by a medical examination, and then should have been assigned to a special class. The teaching of reading, writing, language and arithmetic by ordinary methods is unavailing for all imbeciles and for most morons. Taught the things they are able to master, imbeciles can be made measurably efficient in the very humble tasks of life.

Incidentally I may say that the school records of the five children from this family examined in the clinic are one series of failures. In the aggregate, these children have spent 24.5 years in school, but have completed only 12 years of work. They have thus repeated at least 12 years. Since the cost of instruction for each grade pupil in the schools of this system amounts to 30 a year, the economic loss to the community amounts to 360. This, of course, does not include the added outlay required to provide equipment and seating for these repeaters, nor does it include the educational and economic loss which the community ultimately must suffer from allowing deficient children to continue in the regular classes where they monopolize the teachers time and impede the progress of the normal pupils. And this family is only one among scores of similar or worse families in the same community. Witness the following record from another school of another group of five children from two related families, all of whom were examined in the clinic. One of the mothers was kidnaped at thirteen by her uncle, with whom she subsequently lived without being married to him, and by whom she was infected with venereal disease. Fortunately only three of her eighteen children survive. The other woman also lived, without being married, with her uncle, a brother of the former man. Both men deserted the mothers of their children. From these unholy alliances have issued two boys with immoral tendencies, and one boy was at one time confined to an institution for the mentally disordered. The five school children (having an average head girth of only 19.9 inches, or about the same as the five children from the other family) have spent 29.5 years in the regular classes, but have completed only ten grades, thus having repeated fully 19 years of work at a cost for wasted instruction alone of 570. If the school efficiency expert wants proof of inadequacy in the organization of public school instruction let him turn to the files of a modern psycho-educational clinic, where he will find evidence galore of wasted educational endeavor and misspent funds. And for this state of affairs the intelligent public is itself to blame. I feel, however, that just so soon as the facts regarding the educational waste due to faulty organization of class instruction are fully realized by the public, every large school system will be forced, on purely economic if not educational or humanitarian grounds, to employ the services of expert educational examiners to properly classify and direct the education of all mentally unusual children. Let me emphasize that the quality of the total output of the schools will always depend very largely on the ascertainment of the individual peculiarities and needs of the pupils. But if the schools are under obligation to provide the type of classes and instruction which will conserve the mental health of special children, the obligation of the state is equally clear. The state must take steps to prevent the formation of families of this type. The schools must do their duty by the children already born; but society must cut off the sources of supply.

Case 5

My next case, a boy of eleven at the time of the examination in January, 1913, represents an extremely variable type of children, 90 per cent of whom stop short very early in their mental development, many of whom make little or no progress in school, tending rather to dement as they advance in years, many of whom manifest more or less frequent fluctuations in working capacity, and very few of whom should ever be permitted in the regular classes, not only because they require a special educational regimen but because their unpredictable paroxysmal outbreaks tend to frighten normal children and upset the order of the entire classroom.

The record indicates that the boy was the fifth child, born normally, at birth weighed from seven to seven and one-half pounds, delicate and very cross as a babe, suffered from indigestion, did not increase properly in weight, dentition delayed until the second year, did not walk or talk until about the third year. Membranous croup and measles between the third and fourth year; the victim of many accidents; was run over by vehicles but never severely hurt; several falls; at about the age of six fell from the barn, cutting his head. At about nine, he developed diurnal and nocturnal grand mal seizures, recurring once every two or three weeks and later more frequently. They were not preceded by any aura, but were attended by loss of consciousness and contortions of the upper and lower limbs, and with post-convulsive tendencies to walk around and talk off. One of his older brothers who died at six was reported to be just like him.

At the age of seven, he was on three occasions sent to the primary room of the schools, staying in the aggregate about four months, but was dismissed because he was constantly playing with the other pupils and disturbing the room. After this, he was given private instruction at home by five different teachers, but only in the literary branches. His worst reported fault was his inability to concentrate.

In the clinic examination, he was found to have the intelligence of a child of 6.2 years, which was less than his chronological age when he entered school four years earlier.

He was unable to state his age, to carry out three commissions, to repeat a sentence of sixteen syllables, to read, to descry the missing parts in pictures, to write from a copy, to draw a diamond, to count thirteen pennies or to count backward from twenty to zero. He said that he had four fingers on his right hand, five on his left and five on both hands, that three two-cent and three one-cent stamps cost six cents, he called yellow green, and counted thirteen pennies as twelve. But he was able to give functional definitions, describe pictures and name the four smallest coins.

Here is a typical case of epilepsy superposed upon a substratum of imbecility. Restoration to mental normality in cases of this sort is out of the question even if the epilepsy were curable (which it is not, except in from 5 to 10 per cent of the cases). All we can hope to do for this type of mental abnormality is to supply discriminating hygienic, dietetic and educational treatment. Whether educated in the home, school or institution, these children should receive the kind of manu-mental training which will specially prepare them for the type of industrial service which they can render in after life. These individuals will require constant surveillance and supervision both because of their seizures and because of their mental deficiency. Proper care can usually only be secured in the state colonies. Hygienic, adaptable occupations in the open air will contribute most to keep them healthy and happy. The obligation of the public schools is to afford epileptics (as well as other types of mental defectives) differentiated treatment in segregated classes between the ages of six and thirteen or fourteen, and then at the beginning of the pubertal period graduate them into the state colonies where they should at once be assigned congenial employment.

I shall now present a few defective types of a still higher grade of mentality. There are thousands upon thousands of these children in the schools of the nation, but they are very seldom recognized as defectives, partly because their physical development and physical exterior are often quite normal, partly because they are able to apprehend the simpler relations of life fairly well, and frequently can talk quite fluently—a child who has attained a mentality of seven years or more usually has a free and fluent use of language—and partly because they frequently possess a degree of superficial brightness which deceives all except the experienced expert on mental deficiency. Some of the children of this type examined in the clinic who were indubitably feeble-minded have been promoted into the fourth or fifth grades, admitted into ungraded coaching-classes and elementary industrial schools, and placed, by so-called vocational counselors, in responsible positions which they were never able to hold, without the slightest suspicion on the part of the teachers or vocational directors that they were genuinely defective. There is no more difficult task in diagnosis than the differentiation of high-grade morons from border-cases and seriously backward children, and to trust anyone to make this differentiation but an experienced psycho-clinical expert is preposterous. Surveys or estimates made by teachers, principals and medical inspectors of the number of feeble-minded children in the schools are demonstrably worthless and misleading. These people do not recognize a high-grade moron or border-line defective when they see one; to have amateurs attempt to diagnose these cases by formal tests is pernicious.

Case 6

The first of these cases, a German-American boy, aged fourteen years seven months at the time of the examination in November, 1912, presents no special diagnostic difficulties to the experienced examiner.

He did not walk, talk or cut his teeth until over two years of age; was at one time badly burned under his right arm so that it was feared that he would perish; pertussis at two and measles at six; holds his mouth open all the time just like his father and grandfather did.

Lives in a poor section but in a clean, well-ventilated and comparatively well-furnished flat. Plenty of food. The mother, apparently of low mentality, is divorced from the childs father, a drinker who would not support his family. Mother says the great-grandmother was peculiar.

He started to school at six and at the end of eight years of schooling had reached only the second grade. He was then permitted to enter an elementary industrial school, where he remained last year without making progress. He did not return to school this year and his present whereabouts are unknown to the clinic. The school record indicates that he has learned to write fairly well, to spell a few words, and to add and subtract simple combinations. He cannot read or measure, but has a fairly good memory, and knows all the slang phrases and uses them constantly.

The boy was brought to me by one of the students in the clinic who is teaching in the aforesaid industrial school and who suspected that all was not right. He was found to suffer from three carious teeth and enlarged tonsils, to secure treatment for which he was referred to dispensaries. In physical exterior, he appeared absolutely like a normal child. Measurements, indeed, showed that he was equal to the boy of somewhat over fifteen in standing height, of seventeen in sitting height, of sixteen in hand grip, of about fourteen and a half in weight but of only thirteen in vital capacity. His weight is too light for his height, and, in spite of his limited lung capacity, he is quite long-busted or brachyscelous (ponderal index equals 22, normal equals 28.1; statural index equals 55.7, normal equals 52).

On the other hand, in intellectual development this boy has grown to only about eight and one-half years, while in motor development he ranks somewhat over ten years, as determined by the form-board test, and eight years and between ten and eleven years for the right and left hand, respectively, as determined by the tapping test.

He fails on both of the Healy-Fernald construction puzzles (A and B) after trying for nearly two and one-half minutes. His memory was limited to less than five digits, he was unable to count backwards, to write six syllables from dictation, to perform the weight test, to give descriptive definitions, to draw the two designs presented for ten seconds or to point out the absurdities in silly statements. He required twenty-one seconds to read ten words with aid in the reading selection, and was able to reproduce three memories. He could name only thirty-six words in three minutes, said that three two-and three one-cent stamps cost ten cents, gave the date of November 22 as December 21, constructed three separate sentences instead of a single sentence with the three designated words, gave the months of the year as August, September, December and February and gave as rhymes of spring the words ring, king and rang.

It is almost inconceivable that this boy, a middle-grade moron of the simple type, should be retained as a backward boy for eight years in the first two grades with the hope of restoring him to normality, then to be transferred to an elementary industrial school for motor-minded boys (what a beautiful phrase to conjure with and behind which to conceal the profoundest ignorance), and finally to come before a bureau for vocational guidance. No matter how apparently impossible and inconceivable, such are the facts. Could there be a more tragic indictment of the unscientific manner in which the majority of public schools and vocational guidance bureaus are now administered? Is it not evident that there can be no talk of vocational guidance so long as not the slightest attempt is made to evaluate scientifically the mental, physical and vocational status of many of the applicants? Vocational guidance without psychological, vocational and physical diagnosis for at least all abnormal cases is not merely dilettantish and absurd, it is impossible. Let us call this sort of work by its true name, vocational placement and not vocational guidance. Most of the modern school vocational guidance bureaus are largely misnomers: they are merely vocational survey and employment bureaus. But the schools of the country are going to provide genuine vocational guidance based upon a bedrock of scientific diagnosis of the individual applicant, just as soon as society conies to realize that the future health and prosperity of the children leaving the schools for work depend fundamentally upon their placement in positions whose exactions are compatible with their general level of mental functioning and not incompatible with their individual physical weaknesses. To place children in positions which they cannot possibly fill is mischievous and reprehensible.

Let me reinforce these conclusions by the two following cases.

Case 7

A boy, aged sixteen at the time of the examination in April, 1912.

His record shows that he was the youngest of four children; he learned to talk at least one and one-half years late; pertussis and measles at three; diphtheria at five, which seemed to impair his power of retentiveness; he showed a tendency to play by himself.

He entered school at six, reaching the fourth grade after eight years; always had difficulty, making no progress in number work, especially in subtraction, and never learned to read. A good boy, but played truant because he did not like school, especially did not like to be in a class of smaller children, and dropped out entirely some time after being examined in the clinic.

In the examination the eyes and tonsils were found defective, and he was referred to a dispensary, where glasses were supplied. Superficially he appeared to be perfectly normal in physical development. As a matter of fact, in standing height and weight, he was only a trifle short, measuring 15.5 in the former and nearly the same in the latter, while in sitting stature he measured less than 15, in head circumference 18, but in vital capacity only 12.5. In strength of grip he was about normal for his age, although relatively stronger with the left than right hand. He was slightly too light for his height and age and his bust was rather too short (ponderal index equals 22.7, normal equals 28.4; statural index equals 50.7, normal equals 51).

But his significant deficiency was mental not physical. In intelligence he measured only nine years and in motor development only seven and one-half.

He succeeded with the simpler of the Healy-Fernald construction puzzles (A) after 181 seconds, but failed on the more difficult one (B) after three and one-half minutes. He was able to add five and six, and seven and eight correctly, but unable to subtract seven from thirty-one, or sixteen from twenty-eight; twenty-five cents minus six cents in the change test gave twenty-four cents. He could not define descriptively, or correctly distinguish the five weights, or give three monosyllabic rhymes, or repeat six digits, or perceive absurdities. He named the months as April, July, May and June, but was able to recognize all the coins.

This boy was recommended to a special class as a case of high-grade defectiveness (of higher caliber than indicated by the Binet tests), complicated with alexia. Think of the years of wasted effort spent in trying to teach a word-blind, feeble-minded boy to read by ordinary methods!

On December 19, 1918, or nearly a year and eight months after the initial examination, the boy came to the clinic for the third time. By the Binet system, he now ranked 10.2 years; that is, he had gained 1.2 years; but this considerable gain is partly due to the fact that he passed the ten-year standard, on which he had failed the first time. He still failed on four of the six nine-year tests. He now did the change test and selected the weights in the order of heaviness but failed to repeat the days in order (Monday, Tuesday, Wednesday, Friday, Saturday). He gave the months as April, May, June, July, September, November. He was able to give the date and year correctly but not the month. He gave only forty words in three minutes but solved the absurdities (eleven), resistance-to-suggestion (twelve) and drawing-of-diamond (thirteen) problems. He did the more difficult of the Healy-Fernald construction puzzles (B) in fifty-eight seconds, which he failed to solve the first time, and opened the Healy-Fernald instruction box without hesitation. He did the Vineland form-board in 8.2 seconds less time than at first, thus measuring a little higher than nine years, or 1.5 years higher than the first time. He did not know all the letters of the alphabet, reading f as k, q as o, g as d, z as i, y as u and j as 1. He read to and the correctly but it as in and in as is. He was able to reproduce ten memories from the experimenters reading of the selection as against five the first time. On the physical side he had gained very considerably: two and one-half years in standing height and lung capacity, making him more than equal to the eighteen-year-old in the former and equal to the fifteen-year-old in the latter; he had gained over a year in sitting height and weight, reaching a sixteen-year development; and in strength of grip he had also advanced somewhat. He has thus become increasingly light for his height and also increasingly short-chested.

It is evident that the boy has grown an appreciable extent both mentally and physically during the lapse of the year and eight months. Shall we say that this mental growth is due to the fact that he has been out of school at work? There is, to me, not the slightest doubt that a boy of this type will improve more mentally if kept busy at out-of-school tasks which he can do, than if confined in the regular classroom and compelled to labor over work for which he has no aptitude and which he can never comprehend. There is no doubt that our unscientific systems of school classification, rigid methods and hyper-uniformity of curricular requirements have immeasurably retarded the mental development of innumerable exceptional children. However, the laboratory study and vocational record of this boy confirmed the earlier diagnosis of high-grade feeble-mindedness. During a period of less than one and one-half years, he has held at least six different jobs, retaining each only from one to three months, and receiving in weekly pay from 5 to 9. One of these positions was given him by his cousin, while his latest position was secured through the friendship of the employer for his grandfather. But his present employer reports that he cannot use him after January 1, 1914, because the boy possesses no independence. He has to be told over and over again how to do a thing and then cannot do it, he has a poor memory and can only do mechanical things. So the boy will soon have to resume his perennial job-hunting. This is indeed the sad but universal story of morons, border-line cases and the very seriously backward children. Is it not worth while for vocational guidance bureaus to make a scientific appraisal of the mental level of vocational applicants? Is it not worth while for the public schools to select these cases early in their school career for special treatment and then transfer them to colonies where they may work contentedly and effectively under supervision?–for without kind and efficient supervision these children nearly always fail. At large in society under modern competitive conditions, they are almost invariably doomed to utter industrial, and frequently moral, shipwreck. Is it not an imperative obligation on the part of society to save the large army of high-grade defectives from unavoidable pauperism, from enforced criminal careers and from the reproduction of their kind, by forcibly placing them in self-sustaining colonies? These are fundamental social questions which the state and the state-supported schools cannot shirk. There are no more important questions in our entire social economy. The public schools are the great clearinghouse, the common Ellis Island, through which all children must pass. The burden of selection and classification thus rests primarily upon the schools.

Case 8

My next case is a so-called defective delinquent who was brought to the clinic by a probation officer of the juvenile court, an Italian boy born in America, aged fourteen years eleven months at the time of the examination in May, 1912.

He was the seventh of eight children, four of whom died during the first year of life; birth and development normal, never ill, bright as an infant. One child died in spasms and the youngest suffered from weak ankles and convulsions. The mother has developed an abdominal tumor.

Learned very little in school/ was never able to read much but was promoted to the fourth grade. He was brought by the mother before the juvenile court in May, 1906, because of persistent incorrigibility and truancy; attended school about two days a week. Released on probation, but was returned after a few months because of truancy and vagabondage. Lived in the streets and rarely came home for meals, but subsisted on cakes and pies from the restaurants. Was committed to a boys industrial home but was again released on probation. On failure to improve, he was placed in the courts detention home in June, 1909, for one week and was then sent home because he seemed so small. A process issued for him in May, 1910, because he had played truant and loafed around the Pennsylvania station, was not served as the school principal reported that he was doing better. In October, 1910, he was committed to a private home away from the city. Here he improved wonderfully physically, worked steadily and his conduct was good, except that he ran away. Was released from the home in March, 1912, on the mothers petition, because she was contributing slightly towards his support and instead wanted the boy to help support her.

In May, 1912, he was brought to my clinic for examination and was found to suffer from bad oral conditions (he was referred to the Dental College of the University where he had ten or twelve fillings made gratuitously). In physical development he was very much stunted, measuring in stature about 10.5 years, in weight between 10.5 and 11, in sitting stature nearly 11.5, in vital capacity nearly 12 and in dynamometry 12.5 with the right and 12 with the left hand. His weight was about normal for his height but he was of the long-busted type of stature (ponderal index equals 28.4, normal equals 28.1; statural index equals 54.4, normal equals 52).

His intellectual development was about on a par with his physical growth, somewhat less than 10.5 years. In motor development, he graded a little better, or 11 years.

He did both of the Healy-Fernald construction puzzles (A in fifteen seconds and B in fifty-three seconds), and opened the combination safe in twenty-five seconds. He gave sixty words in three minutes but failed on the design and suggestion tests in ages ten and twelve. A short time after the clinic examination, he was placed in a private special class.

On December 9, 1918, a social investigator of the clinic found the mother in despair over the boy, who now, at the age of 16.5 years, was constantly changing his jobs, staying out late at night, getting up between twelve and one oclock in the daytime, spending part of his time loafing around the station, where he was the easy tool and cats-paw of hoodlums. He was defiant of his mother, who now had no control over him. She says bad boys make John bad and call him scab when he work. Still I no want him go school. He can earn money, I sick.

On the following day the boy was reexamined in the clinic. He seemed to be very glad to meet the examiner, was very responsive and appeared bright and intelligent. He reported that he had been out of the control of the juvenile court for nine months, that he attended an elementary industrial school for a while but did not like the work because the reading, electrical and wood work were too hard, and because he was punished when he made a mistake. (Here is an unrecognized high-grade defective in an elementary industrial school who is punished because he does not do the required work, when the real fact is that he is feeble-minded and cannot possibly do the work. This reads like a chapter from the medieval inquisition.) He held a job for a couple of months painting vehicles at 6.50 per week, but quit because he cut his finger, he delivered flowers for a while at 4.50 per week, he carried messages at two cents each, yielding from 4.00 to 4.50 per week, for the Western Union three weeks ago for two months (note the discrepancy), but quit because he had to run too much; he now sells peanuts in a theater after noons and evenings, clearing about 2.70 per week. He said the street loafers hit him and called him scab.

The psychological examination showed that the boy did a little better in some things than he did when examined a year and seven months earlier, but that in general intelligence he had gained only about.2 of a year. In motor development, he showed a slightly greater increase but was still far below normal. In physical development, he had improved far more, having grown about 2.5 years in standing and sitting stature and weight, and about 1.5 years in lung capacity and hand squeeze. But even thus, he ranked in bodily development only as a child from thirteen to fifteen.

Here is a so-called defective delinquent who was not recognized as a defective either in the schools or the juvenile court. As a matter of fact, this boy is primarily a defective and only secondarily a delinquent. He has never committed any serious crime, so far as I know. Inherently he is not vicious. But his mental deficiency makes him an easy dupe for evil boys and makes it almost impossible for him to retain a paying position. If left at large he will almost surely drift into pauperism and crime, and society will have to pay the penalty. Would it not be more rational and economical to classify children of this type early in their school careers, supply them with proper manu-mental training, and then graduate them into the state colonies where they should be compelled to live their lives in innocent, happy and useful service?

Case 9.

Somewhat different is the following morally unstable retardate, an embryonic delinquent who comes from a morally and socially defective home, a boy born in Naples, aged twelve years eleven months at the time of the examination in October, 1913.

He was the second of six children, born at full term, weighed eight pounds, nursed for fifteen months, walked and talked at 1.5 years; about this time experienced a stoppage in speech; at five, fell and broke his nose, which since then has been bleeding almost daily so that in the morning his pillow is usually blood-stained. Measles, whooping cough, mumps and scarlet fever at seven, since which time he has acted queer. He is gluttonous, drinks tea, coffee and beer and chews tobacco. Quick-tempered, untruthful, disobedient, cruel to brothers and sisters, lies and steals. When sent to the store to make purchases, he will appropriate the money for his own use and have the goods charged to his parents. He has also appropriated money which he has collected for his church, which he never attends, although he is sent there. When punished at home, he screams and yells terribly, runs away and stays out all night. He has slept in a dog box and on the hillside, and he is never at home except for meals and to sleep; he usually loafs in the woods with a gang of older boys.

The home conditions are fairly good financially, although the mother makes repeated trips to the Associated Charities whenever a child is to be born. She is probably immoral, wishes to get rid of her children, is very lazy, fails to prepare the meals properly and leaves her new house of five rooms in a filthy, unventilated, disordered condition. The house contains nine lodgers, exclusive of two dogs, three cats and a goat. The cats have been seen to walk on the table at meal-time and help themselves from the dishes. The whole family will sleep in the same bed, although other beds have been given to them by the Associated Charities. The home life is tempestuous and degrading. The child is poorly disciplined, whipped, abused and called crazy by the father. The father also abuses his wife. The parents are intemperate, but the family history is negative, except that the mothers father was rheumatic.

The boy has been in school fifty-three months and has reached the fourth grade. He has spent two years each in the first and second grades. His poorest work is in reading (he reads in fourth reader), memorizing and spelling, and his best work is in music, manual training, drawing and abstract work. He cannot do the fundamental arithmetical processes. He has good powers of observation and concentration. Some teachers say that he is one of the best-behaved and others that he is the worst-behaved pupil in the school. He apparently has a dual nature: at times interested, willing, obedient and cheerful; at other times cranky, obstinate, sullen, devilish and resentful of reproof, threatening to kill someone when angry. Also has a dual walk, at times he stamps his feet, at other times he walks normally (but his gait is poor). After his mother had reported his incorrigibility to the school authorities, he changed for the worst and tried to live up to his reputation; but punishment in school resulted in improvement. His teacher says he has been well-behaved for the past nine months.

The clinic examination showed that the child was suffering from a slight degree of astigmatic myopia, two dental caries, enlarged tonsils, enlarged adenoid growth, enlarged left turbinate and deviating septum (he was referred to a dispensary for treatment but nothing has been done because of parental objections). He was retarded in both physical and mental development, in hand grip measuring about 12 years, in vital capacity 11, in weight 10.5, in standing and sitting stature a little over 9.5, and in head girth 6. His ponderal index was a little better than normal (28.8 vs. 28.1), while his statural proportions indicate that he is a little brachyscelous (58.8 vs. 58).

In motor development, he grades between nine and ten and in intelligence ten (although he passed two of the thirteen-year tests).

He passed all of the tests in age nine, two in ten (months and money), one in twelve (three rhymes) and two in thirteen (diamond and reversed triangle tests).

Here is a boy who is just as genuinely deficient as a feeble-minded boy but to a lesser extent. The difference is one of degree. His is a case of pronounced instability of disposition superposed on a background of pronounced backwardness, aided and abetted by a demoralizing home environment. The orthogenic treatment indicated here is not merely surgical attention and corrective pedagogic treatment in a special class, preferably in a parental school, but the reconstruction of the social and moral conditions in the home. Eventually the schools will have their educational laboratories and clinics with a staff of social workers who will study the social influences of the home and street which predestinate many children to deficiency or delinquency. And eventually the state will take steps to forcibly reconstruct the home whenever it tends to debauch childhood, or the children will be removed from the homes and placed in institutions.

I turn now to three types of supernormal children. The need of scientifically classifying supernormal pupils is even more urgent and the value to be derived from their efficient pedagogical training is even greater than the classification and special treatment of subnormal children.

Case 10 An American girl of English-Scotch ancestry, aged eight years four months at the time of the examination in August, 1912.

An only child who developed normally save for delayed dentition (teething began at two). Typhoid-pneumonia at three and one-half, attended by loss of consciousness, and by severe intermittent convulsions for three days. Convulsions recurred once six months later. Measles at four. For five years affected by convulsive tics of the shoulders and arms, which, however, had shown improvement five weeks prior to examination. Sleep restless and disturbed by dreams; loses temper constantly; takes cold easily.

The home conditions are good. Father decidedly restless from childhood; subject to impulsive tics, picks up objects repeatedly, is intense in action. Mothers father is alive at seventy-eight, but subject to convulsions about once a week, said to be brought on by excitement. Mothers mother died at seventy of nervous prostration, fathers father accidentally killed at forty-seven; fathers mother died at fifty-nine of chronic inflammation of the bowels.

This girl had been in school twenty-three months and was seven months advanced in her work (IV B instead of III B); is good in all branches, especially in reading, spelling and telling stories. Worst faults, restlessness and quick temper.

At the time of the clinic examination, she was subject to tics of the arms and nervous starts affecting the whole body. The roots of eight deciduous teeth were in very bad condition (she was referred to the Dental College for expert examination and treatment). In physical development she was about normal, rating about 9 in hand grip for the right hand and 8 for the left hand, 9 in standing stature, 8.5 in sitting stature and vital capacity, and about 8 in weight. But she is too light for her weight and is somewhat short-chested (ponderal index equals 22.4 instead of 28.8; statural index equals 54 instead of 55).

In intelligence she grades twelve years, or 3.5 accelerated, passing all the tests in age ten and all except one each in ages nine (making change), eleven (absurdities) and twelve (problems).

This is a beautiful illustration of distinct youthful precocity resting upon a pathological background. Judging from the standpoint of intellectual maturity, this girl was marking time in the schools. She should have been advanced at least two years instead of seven months. However, this girl cannot be classified purely according to her degree of intelligence. She distinctly belongs to the neuropathic type of supernormals, and requires a most discriminating educational and hygienic regimen. Unless this fact is recognized and appropriate treatment is accorded her in the schools, the schools certainly will be guilty of contributory negligence in furthering the development of possible adult instabilities in this child. Many adult neuropaths and psychopaths have been manufactured by the unscientific and indiscriminating treatment which mentally abnormal children have received in the home and school.

Case 11

My next case is also a nervously, although non-patho-logically, precocious child, an American girl, aged nine years four months at the time of the examination in March, 1913.

She is the oldest of three children, with a record of normal birth and normal development; scarlet fever at four years and three months, pertussis and measles at six; is nervous, sleepless, easily fatigued, suffers from frontal headache, subject to fears, afraid to go to her room in the dark. Operated at six for adenoids and enlarged tonsils. One feeble-minded aunt and an epileptic relative.

She was advanced in her school work, being in the fourth grade after twenty-seven months of schooling. She was good in all branches, but best in reading, drawing and music.

In the clinic she was nervous and fidgety. Her tonsils were found to be considerably enlarged and infected. In physical growth, she was distinctly superior to the average, measuring fully 12 years in strength of grip and sitting height, 11.5 in weight, 11 in standing height and 10 years in vital capacity. She is long-busted, but her weight is about normal for her height (ponderal index equals 28.6, normal equals 28.5; statural index equals 55.9, normal equals 55).

In intelligence, she graded 11.8 years but in motor development only 10 years. In the tapping test she graded a little less, but she solved (in two minutes) the construction puzzle (B) which requires intelligent adaptation. She passed all the tests in ages nine and ten, all except the association test in eleven, two tests in twelve (rhymes and memory for sentences), and the diamond test in thirteen.

Intellectually this girl had the capacity to do work one or two years in advance of her school classification, and there is no reason why she should not be permitted to work at an accelerated pace, provided she is kept in good physical condition and provided the pressure is relaxed somewhat during her periods of accelerated physical growth.

On the advice of the clinic, the father, a school principal, immediately had her tonsils dissected, and during the months of July and August he kept her on a farm in the country where she received plenty of wholesome food, fresh air and out-of-door exercise. As a result, the girl returned at the beginning of the present school year in excellent condition physically and mentally. The nervous symptoms had disappeared and she now ranks first in her class. It is uneconomical of public funds and wasteful of human brain power to keep children eight years in the grades who can finish the course just as well in six years.

Case 12

This conclusion will be further enforced by the consideration of my final case, a healthy type of supernormal child, a girl aged five years seven months at the time of the examination in August, 1912.

She was the second of three children, weighing ten pounds at birth, walked in the fourteenth month, used words in the twelfth and sentences in the sixteenth and had ten teeth in the tenth month. Chicken pox and severe stomach trouble in her third year.

Mothers mother got overheated and died of inflammation of the brain at forty-four (during climacteric), a paternal aunt suffered from tuberculosis, and neurasthenia, developing into a type of insane dementia, from which she died at thirty-six.

Home conditions excellent; she is good in handwork, can clear table, iron plain clothes and do construction work with building blocks.

At the clinic, her muscular coordination was good, her eyes were good in respect to binocular coordination and distance and light accommodation, but her nasopharynx was slightly congested and she was somewhat flat-footed.

In physical growth, she was distinctly superior to the average, equaling 9.5 years in dynamometry, 7 years in standing height and weight and 6.5 in sitting height.

Her physical superiority was paralleled by her mental superiority. In intelligence and motor development, she graded about 7.5 years.

She passed all the tests in age six, five in seven (she could not write from copy, describe pictures or recognize a twenty-five cent piece), three in eight (passing the stamp, color and statement-of-difference tests), one in nine (repetition of week days) and none in ten. She failed on the construction puzzle (B) after seventy-five seconds.

There are hundreds of healthy, gifted children such as this girl in every community of any size who would be able to finish the eight elementary grades in six years or less if they were only afforded the opportunities by the schools, and they would do so with distinction and without in the least imperilling either their physical or mental well-being, provided, of course, due checks were kept on their temporary health deviations and growth accelerations.

The conservation of the mental health of school children demands not only that we shall select, classify and provide specialized training for children of inferior ability, but (even more insistently) that we differentiate children of superior attainments and organize for their benefit systems of flexible grading, special supernormal or special opportunity classes, and differentiated pedagogic treatment. Surely the conservation and promotion of the mental health of gifted children, who are destined to become the leaders of social progress, is even more important than providing special opportunities for defectives. One inventive genius is worth more to society than a hundred drones. It is the mission of the schools to foster and not to suppress genius. The school systems of the past, with their emphasis on uniformity, on the essential likeness of children, on equivalence of pedagogical treatment and on mass results, have tended to develop sameness, subservience and mediocrity. The school systems of the future, with their emphasis on diversity, on the essential difference of children, on differentiated pedagogical treatment and on individual results, will foster individuality, independence and genius. The ideal of the past was: a uniform program of work and a uniform rate of progress for all the pupils. The slogan of the future will be: expert educational diagnosis as a basis for differentiated programs of work to be given at differentiated rates of speed to meet the needs of all kinds and classes of pupils. Education, I repeat, is fundamentally a process of adjustment, and only so far as the schools succeed in adjusting the educative processes to meet the needs of the individual pupil will they conserve the mental health interests of children.

The conclusions at which we have arrived may be summarized as follows: 1. It is impossible scientifically or effectively to organize instruction in any large school system without segregating or grouping together pupils who are measurably similar either in respect to mental normality or mental abnormality. The instruction of palpably abnormal with normal children is an injustice to both the abnormal and normal pupils, and to the teacher, and can only be regarded as a survival of pedagogic barbarism.

2. It is impossible efficiently to group together or to teach children who depart from the standard of mental normality without a prior scientific diagnosis of each case.

3. So far as concerns the differentiation of mentally unusual children, the work of diagnosis requires the services of a technically trained and experienced psycho educational examiner, and not a school nurse, teacher, principal or medical inspector. It is absurd to suppose that an amateur is qualified to perform the extremely difficult work of mental diagnosis.

4. Every large school system should maintain as an essential part of its administrative organization, an educational clinic and laboratory for the study and differentiation of the numerous types of deviating children who must receive instruction in the schools, who will apply for vocational guidance and who prospectively or actually come before the juvenile court. The schools themselves should adequately diagnose children before they are recommended to the employer or before they come before the juvenile court.

In large cities the clinic should be established as an independent department of the schools–or as a division of the department of special education. It should be closely affiliated with the training school for teachers and with the department of medical inspection. The staff should consist of the following: (1) One director of the psycho-educational clinic and the department of special education, in executive charge of the department and directly responsible to the superintendent of schools. (2) One supervisor of special education, directly responsible to the director of the department. (3) One or more social workers. Teachers or school nurses may be used, provided they have received a certain amount of special training for the work. (4) One or more mental testers for some of the routine testing. Adaptable grade teachers may be trained for this work. (5) One medical man, to serve as a clearing house, or general utility man on the medical side. (6) One or more clerks for stenographic, record, tabulation and computation work. Under this scheme of organization the director of the clinic will have authority over the special classes, and will make the influence of the clinical work felt in the training of teachers.

5. The differentiation and specialized training of children who depart from the average standard of mentality will ultimately prove an economic gain to the community and a boon to the individual pupils; the conservation of the nations brain power demands such differentiation early in the school career of the child.

6. The authority of the schools must be so extended as to include control of the childs out-of-school environment when this is demoralizing to the mental, physical or moral health of the child, thereby rendering the work of the schools nugatory; and also so as to include the right by statute to graduate or transfer anti-social types of children into custodial and industrial colonies where they may spend their lives as harmless, productive servants and wards of the state.

7. Finally, a word in regard to the situation in Pennsylvania. The effort to scientifically differentiate and classify exceptional children educationally may be said to have originated in Pennsylvania. Both of the Pennsylvania universities now maintain free clinics for the psycho-educational diagnosis of children. There is probably no state in the union that offers superior university facilities for rendering this type of philanthropic service to the community. But the public schools in Pennsylvania have,

in the large, failed to do their duty in the establishment of special classes and special forms of instruction for educational deviates. I make this statement after a careful canvass of the replies made to a questionnaire which was sent last October to over 1,350 school systems throughout the country (unfortunately even some of the larger systems in Pennsylvania have made no reply). Space does not permit me to give the detailed results of this inquiry. But let me point out two facts.

First, in regard to the character of the work being accomplished in a state which has rapidly assumed a position of leadership in the enactment of constructive educational legislation, namely, New Jersey. State school laws, enacted in 1911 and 1912, now make it compulsory for every local school board in New Jersey to ascertain the number of subnormal (three years or more below the normal), blind and deaf children in the schools, and to establish special classes for the training of these types of children whenever ten children of each type are found in any school district (provided the blind or deaf are not or cannot be cared for in an institution). No class may contain more than fifteen pupils, and for each teacher employed in one of the special classes the state appropriates 500. Under these laws 102 classes for subnormal children, with an enrollment of about 1,400, had been established up to November 24, 1913 (according to information received from G. A. Mirick, Assistant Commissioner of Education), and practically all of the large cities have established psychological clinics or their equivalent, or utilize university clinics. When may we hope to have similar laws enacted in Pennsylvania? With similar laws on the statute books Pennsylvania would now have from 500 to 1,000 special classes for backward and feebleminded children alone. Is it not a legitimate function of this Association to urge upon the legislature the enactment of laws for the compulsory segregation of seriously backward and feeble-minded children in special classes in the public schools?

Second, in regard to the recent marvelous increase of the psychological clinics. According to questionnaire replies which have arrived to date we now have the following number of psychological clinics in the United States, more or less expertly manned: nineteen in public schools; sixteen in university schools of education and departments of psychology; seven in medical schools; three in normal schools; five in public and private institutions for the feeble-minded; six in penal and correctional institutions; two in juvenile courts; and five in hospitals for the mentally disordered; or a total of sixty-three. This does not include scores of public schools, institutions and courts in which a few formal psychological tests (particularly the Binet) are given by teachers or medical inspectors. I may add that fifteen school systems (exclusive of suburban schools located near clinics) are utilizing, to some extent, university of privately supported psychological clinics, so that about thirty-five large school systems now attempt more or less systematically to psychologically and educationally diagnose unusual children.

To conclude: the schools must forever renounce the rigidly inflexible curricula of the past, which have proved veritable ponies asinorum to hundreds of thousands of children who do not conform to the assumed typical or normal child, and provide, instead, remedial, corrective or differential instruction designed to meet the varying needs of all types of talent and of all types of educational abnormality or deviation.

Some one has said: the sum of our failures in education is measured by the number of our failures with individuals. I would add: there cannot be efficient school organization or effective instruction without individual diagnosis.

CHAPTER XVIII
PUBLIC SCHOOL PROVISIONS FOR MENTALLY UNUSUAL CHILDREN

On October 29, 1913, a questionnaire on public school provisions for mentally exceptional children was sent to the superintendents of public schools in all the cities of the United States of America having a population of 4,000 and over. On December 12 copies of the same questionnaire were again sent to a considerable number of superintendents in the larger cities of the country who had not replied to the earlier letter. In some cases as many as three or four inquiries were sent before any response was forthcoming. As a result of these repeated inquiries, replies were received from all the cities of the country with a population of 100,000 and over (50 cities), from 53 per cent of the cities of 25,000 up to 100,000 (96 out of 179 cities), and from 156 with a population of less than 25,000. In all, replies were received from 302 cities, or somewhat less than one-fourth of the number addressed (about 1,350).

Special classes of some kind are supported by all of the cities of 100,000 and over, except Scranton, Pa.; by 65, or somewhat less than 68 per cent, of the 96 cities of 25,000 up to 100,000; and by 57, or somewhat less than 37 per cent, of the 156 cities of less than 25,000. It is probably safe to conclude that the majority of the cities which failed to report do not maintain any of the special classes enumerated in the questionnaire: namely, classes for the feeble-minded and seriously backward, ungraded classes for giving individual attention merely to pupils retarded in various subjects, epileptic, speech-defective, disciplinary or truant, bright, blind, deaf, etc.

i My thanks are due to the superintendents or their subordinates who took pains to answer the questionnaire; without their kindly interest this study would have been impossible.

The value of the replies varied considerably. Some were prepared with singular regard for accuracy and completeness, at great expense of time and labor. Some respondents answered certain questions very completely, but others very incompletely or not at all. Others gave rather incomplete data on all questions, or occasional ambiguous answers, with the result that it was sometimes difficult to determine whether the classes reported should be tabulated as special classes for the feeble-minded or seriously backward, or as ungraded classes for giving individual attention merely to pupils retarded in various subjects, or whether the psycho-educational examinations were made by teachers, principals, physicians or psychologists. A few superintendents merely sent copies of their annual reports. Unfortunately, these seldom gave all the information contemplated by the inquiry. It is a serious handicap that we do not have a central federal Educational Bureau in the United States, legally vested with the power of exacting reports on all phases of education from all the schools of all the states. It never has been possible, and probably never will be, through private inquiry to secure replies from all the public and private schools of the country. However, the replies received to this inquiry are sufficiently numerous to afford a considerable fund of new data, as well as a solid basis for drawing important deductions, particularly as respects the type of classes in which we are here specially interested and to a discussion of which most of this chapter will be devoted, namely the classes for the feeble-minded and seriously backward.

Special Classes for the Feeble-Minded and Seriously Backward

From an inquiry made by the United States Commissioner of Education in March, 1911, it appeared that out of 898 cities reporting, 99 supported classes for the mentally defective (including classes for epileptics), and 220 had classes for backward children (see Bulletin No. 461), or a total of 319. The latter classes include instances in which special teachers are employed to assist slow pupils. My returns indicate that 108 cities maintain special classes for the feeble-minded and seriously backward (although it is probable that some of these classes are not conducted strictly as special classes), and 111 cities have ungraded classes for the retarded, or a total of 219. Since my figures are based on about one-third as many answers as the Bureaus survey, but show 68 per cent as many classes, it is very probable that there has been a material increase in the number of cities supporting special and ungraded classes. However, the data may not be strictly comparable, owing to the difference in the terminology employed in the two inquiries. The Bureau made a survey of (1) classes for defectives and (2) classes for backward children, while I collected data on (1) special classes for the feeble-minded and seriously backward and (2) ungraded classes for giving individual attention merely to pupils retarded in various subjects. It is quite probable that many classes recorded as special in the Bureaus report did not provide a special curriculum of manual work, and would therefore be registered as ungraded classes in this study.

The term defectives is objectionable, because it carries no fixed connotation. Usually when applied to school cases it is restricted to children who are obviously feeble-minded. But there is no scientific warrant for thus restricting its application, because pupils who are seriously backward are just as truly deficient or defective as the border-line or feeble-minded cases, but only less so. Fundamentally, the difference is quantitative rather than qualitative. Again, the practice of referring to special classes for defectives is pernicious because it creates the mistaken idea that these classes are intended only for those who are actually feebleminded; indeed, the first public school special classes (those started in Germany) were organized solely for the feeble-minded. This idea has become almost universally and ineradicably intrenched in the habit of thought of the average schoolman. The special class for defectives or deficients always means to him the class for the feebleminded. But the special classes in the public schools should receive not only the imbeciles and morons, but also the border-line and seriously backward cases. The seriously backward children should be given the same kind of manumental and industrial program (with modifications, to be sure, to meet the needs of each case) that is provided for the morons. Negatively, they should not be consigned to the ungraded classes, as is now the custom, where they are only given individual attention and coaching in the usual academic subject-matter. What the seriously backward child needs is a different kind of subject-matter and not increased drill on the same contents.

The study of my returns has emphasized again and again the great necessity of clearly distinguishing between the functions of various kinds of special classes for imbeciles, morons, border-cases, seriously backward, backward and retarded children. It is particularly important sharply to distinguish between the so-called special and ungraded classes. The following recommendations are therefore offered in the interest of consistency:

First. Special classes in which imbeciles, morons, borderline and seriously backward cases are taught should be designated special classes/ or, better still, orthogenic or orthophrenic classes, because the word special is generic and applies to eight or ten different kinds of special classes; but only provided such classes furnish a special curriculum of manumental and industrial work.

Second. The term ungraded classes should be applied to classes in which children who are retarded in one or more branches are given individual attention, singly or in small groups or in separate classes in the branches in which they are deficient. These are essentially coaching classes, giving intensive attention to the contents of the regular curriculum. No child should be assigned to these classes who is considerably deficient in all-round intellectual capacity.

Third. Elementary industrial classes should be provided for young adolescents (say, from twelve or thirteen to about sixteen years of age) who are appreciably backward or who are over age because of inability to cope with the regular curriculum, and who withal are industrially inclined. In these classes the minimum of academic work provided should be closely correlated with the manual and industrial work. Those pupils in the special classes who meet the requirements should be graduated into these classes on reaching the age of twelve or thirteen.

No school system of any size can adequately care for the different types of children on the minus side of the curve of mental and pedagogical distribution without organizing the above three types of classes.

That the public schools of the country have merely made a good start in the organization of work in this important field of special education may be inferred from the following percentages of cities which thus far do not support a single special class for feeble-minded and seriously backward children: 16 per cent (or 8) of the cities above 100,000 in population (Kansas City, Mo., St. Paul, Atlanta, Syracuse, Memphis, Scranton, Omaha, Lowell); 60 per cent (or 57) of the 96 cities reporting with a population ranging from 25,000 to (but not including) 100,000; and 83 per cent (or 130) of the 156 cities of less than 25,000. Certainly every city with a school population of 2,000 should have at least one special class. Not only so; in the cities in which special classes have been organized the provisions are wholly inadequate. Thus Baltimore, New Orleans, Pittsburgh and San Francisco support only one special class each; Los Angeles, Spokane and Denver only two; Cambridge, Richmond and New Haven only three; Milwaukee and Minneapolis only four. Even New Yorks 180 classes care for only.38 per cent of the elementary school population, or only about one-third of the pupils in that city who should be trained in special classes. Rochesters twenty-nine classes are said to furnish accommodations for only about 15 per cent of the subnormal children of that city. Some of these cases, however, probably belong rather to ungraded and elementary industrial classes. No city anywhere in the country makes anything like adequate provisions for the segregation of feeble-minded and seriously backward children. Relatively to size, Montclair, N. J., with eight classes, makes the best provision of any city in the country, but in New Jersey every school district having ten pupils retarded three years or more must, under the state law, segregate them in special classes (see p. 381).

The first city to organize special classes was Providence (1896), followed by Springfield, Mass. (1897), Chicago (1898), Boston (1899), New York (1900), Philadelphia (1901), Los Angeles (1902), Detroit and Elgin (1903), Trenton (1905) and Washington, Bridgeport, Newton and Rochester (1906). The New York class, which was started about 1874, and the Cleveland class, started in 1879, were for disciplinary or truant pupils. Although these classes undoubtedly contained seriously backward or feeble-minded children, it is not apparent that the program of studies consisted of special class work.

The enrollment is limited to 15 pupils per class in forty-two cities, 20 in nine, 12 in six, 10 in three, 15 or less in sixty-seven and 20 or less in ninety-two cities. In only five cities is the enrollment permitted to exceed 20. In some cities the permissible register is very elastic, varying from 7 to 20, 5 to 12, 8 to 15, 20 to 30 and 18 to 24 (see Table II). The general tendency thus appears to be to limit the class register to about 15–the limit fixed by state law in New Jersey.

In order to meet the demands of instructional efficiency, no special class should ever contain more than fifteen imbeciles or morons, or twenty seriously backward cases. The chief objection urged to thus limiting the enrollment is the considerable expense required to provide equipment and expert instruction at advanced salaries for children who, as a class, can achieve only mediocre or indifferent success. It is argued that our chief obligation is to the normal, precocious or merely slightly retarded children, who may be trained to responsible socio-industrial service, constructive achievement and leadership. While this objection is well founded, it should not be forgotten that one of the potent reasons for segregating the subnormals is to free the regular grades of driftwood and dead weights. When we provide special opportunities in segregated classes to the subnormals we at the same time improve the working conditions for the normals. However, it is better to permit a register of twenty or twenty-five than to dispense entirely with the special classes and permit the neer-do-wells to encumber or demoralize the regular grades. In the regular grades these children are almost always irritated, disheartened, depressed or embittered by the progress and not infrequently jibes, jeers and ridicule of the normal pupils. Here they soon lapse into indifference or become chronic rebels. They tend to rebel against the tension of the normal pace, against the attempts to force them to apply themselves to subject-matter which to them is a meaningless jargon and against the seeming neglect or harshness of teachers who frequently fail to understand them and who, at best, are precluded in the regular grades from giving them the attention which they require. Because of their indolence, eccentricities, abnormalities and not infrequent vicious, depraved or immoral practices, they often exert an injurious influence upon the normal children. Even when good-natured, virtuous and kindly disposed, they frequently become the innocent dupes and cats-paws of their wiser but designing fellows. Hence they should be removed from the regular grades, not only for their own welfare, but for the sake of the normal pupils.

In Germany, the general, although not the invariable, practice is to establish in congested centers special schools (Hilfsschule) instead of special classes. In London, the practice is to establish centers (special school centers) with two or three rooms in small buildings located in a corner of the school yard and separated from the regular building by a high fence. In America, the prevailing tendency is to organize separate classes in the regular grade buildings rather than separate schools. From Table II it is not possible to infer the exact type of organization in effect in each city. Apparently Dayton, Washington, St. Louis and Salt Lake City maintain schools, although the schools are probably not all housed in separate buildings. The objections to segregating the children in detached buildings are: the grouping of many abnormal children throws their idiosyncrasies and abnormalities into conspicuous relief; it makes the children feel that they are a group set aside from normal children and that they are essentially different or inferior; parents object to placing the children apart because they feel that it stigmatizes them; the pupils have no occasion to mingle with the normal children on the playground, or to partake in the general exercises, hence they are robbed of the opportunities to learn imitatively by association with their normal fellows; and many children must travel long distances or be transported to the school at considerable expense. The advantages of organizing schools rather than single classes are: it allows of a closer grading of the pupils, and of grouping them according to their level of intelligence; this obviates the necessity of having all grades of defectives associate together; it makes possible group instruction, and this makes for economy, as each teacher will be able to instruct a larger number of pupils; the central school permits of the introduction of departmental work, enabling the teachers to restrict their instruction to their specialties, which makes for increased instructional efficiency; the organization of schools will probably insure a better equipment of didactic materials, as the industrial, manual training, kindergarten and other rooms can be used in rotation by the different classes.

The best plan probably is to establish centers of three or four rooms in the regular buildings in congested sections and separate rooms in the regular grade buildings in the less populous districts. Moreover, the larger cities may very well consider the advisability of establishing a farm residential institution near the city limits for the industrial training of educable feeble-minded indigent children. The majority of these children after finishing their course of training should be transferred at the age of, say, fifteen or sixteen years to state colonies, where they should be obliged to utilize in self-supporting occupations the skill which they have developed. The city residential institution should prepare them for efficient service in colony life.

The Examination of Feeble-Minded and Backward Children

The practice of requiring some kind of special examination before a child may be assigned to a special class is becoming well-nigh universal. The 103 cities in Table III so reported except Elgin, Washington, Pa., Columbus and New Orleans; the latter two, however, give the examination after admission. The following cities failed to answer this question: Pittsburgh, Bridgeport, Fall River, Portland, Worcester, Aurora, Ft. Wayne and Stonington, Conn. It is, of course, impossible to state how thorough or valuable these admission examinations are.

Eighty-one of the cities provide a medical examination, two do not, while twenty-one failed to answer the question (see Table III).

Fifty-nine (or 57 per cent) of the schools give educa-tional tests, while the other forty-four leave this question unanswered. It is impossible from the data to determine the character of the educational examination, but it is improbable that any standardized pedagogical efficiency tests have been used to any extent. The tests given are probably only the ordinary examination questions of the schools, or the school record of the child.

That the psychological study of candidates for special classes is rapidly becoming universal is apparent from an examination of Table III. Eighty-four (or 81 per cent) of the 103 cities report that psychological tests are given either by employees of the school boards or by outside agencies. This includes all of the 19 cities of 250,000 population and over, all the cities except 5 (or 76 per cent) of the 21 with a population of 100,000 to 250,000 (including Indianapolis), all except 12 (or 68 per cent) of the 38 cities between 25,000 and 100,000 (Aurora, however, brings some children to Chicago for examination), and all except 2 (or 92 per cent) of the 25 cities of less than 25,000. Psychological testing is thus relatively more prevalent in the groups of cities having the largest and smallest populations. The names of the cities which do or do not conduct psychological testing may be obtained from the table.

While this is an extremely creditable showing, particularly in view of what it portends for the future, it is necessary to emphasize that the psychological testing in most of the cities is exceedingly meager and crude, being conducted by teachers, principals, educators, psychologists and physicians who are not specialists on the physiology, psychology and pedagogy of feeble-minded, backward or other types of mentally abnormal children. This fact is revealed by an examination of the columns in the table giving the extent of the psychological examination, and the extent of the technical preparation and professional affiliation of the psychological examiners. (The answers supplied to these questions were in many cases extremely i ambiguous, evasive or unsatisfactory.) Fifty-two cities report that the testing is confined entirely, or almost entirely, to the Binet tests. Twenty-four respondents failed to answer the question. It is entirely probable, I believe, that at least seventy-five (or 72 per cent) of the 103 cities do not go beyond the Binet and form-board tests. In some cities, less than this is attempted. In only twenty-one cities is it safe to infer that the psychological testing exceeds this minimum. Of the seven cities of less than 100,000 which report giving additional tests, it is probable that only two or three attempt anything approaching an exhaustive examination.

But more important than the extent of the formal testing is the adequacy of the preparation and the experience of the psychological examiners. Immeasurably more important than the tests is the man behind the gun. An analysis of the table with respect to the professional affiliations and attainments of the examiners, including those employed both by the schools and by outside agencies–a total of 115 examiners– shows that 52 are special class teachers, 11 supervisors of special classes or principals, 4 superintendents of schools, 5 alienists or neurologists, 22 medical inspectors or physicians, 8 psychologists and 13 clinical psychologists (restricting the application of the latter term to those only who are trained experts on the psychology and pedagogy of mentally unusual children). It should be said that when the examinations were reported to be made by the medical inspector, special teacher and principal, each was separately counted in the above summary, although it is possible that in many of these reported instances only the special teacher made the psychological examination.

These data point to various interesting conclusions: 1. In the vast majority of cases the psychological testing (and possibly also the diagnoses) of mentally exceptional children in the schools is made by Binet testers–in other words, by amateurs. This includes all the special teachers and the majority of the supervisors, superintendents and medical inspectors. After a careful scrutiny of the qualifications of the examiners, I am forced to the conclusion that not more than thirty psychologists, physicians, alienists and educators occupy a status other than that of the Binet tester. Accordingly 74 per cent of the testing is done by Binet testers.

2. The extent of preparation of the great majority of the Binet testers (cf. data given in the column in the table entitled extent of preparation of psychological examiners) consists in having taken normal school, college or university courses in the usual branches of education and psychology, and a summer course on mental tests and on feeble-minded children; or in having taken a regular medical course and then reading literature on feeble-minded and backward children, learning to give the Binet system, or paying a visit to a psychological clinic. Even if we concede that it is possible thus to prepare psycho-educational testers, the conclusion remains true: that such testers are not expert psycho-educational diagnosticians, and that to prepare expert psycho-educational diagnosticians requires three or four years of technical training and clinical experience.

3. The vast majority of psychological examiners are educators. By including among the educators the clinical psychologists, psychologists, teachers, supervisors, principals and superintendents (a total of eighty-eight), and among the physicians the medical inspectors, alienists or neurologists (a total of twenty-seven), it appears that 77 per cent of the examiners are educators and only 23 per cent are physicians. This represents, I believe, a true appreciation of what the problem of mental exceptionality involves. The psychological diagnosis of school children cannot be divorced from their educational diagnosis. It is essentially pyscho-educational in its nature. Its aim is essentially educational, the correct pedagogical classification and differential pedagogical training of the child. Therefore the directing authority in the diagnosis and training of educationally exceptional children must be the educationist rather than the sociologist, physician, experimental psychologist, biologist or heredity worker. This is no more exclusively a medical problem (except in certain cases) than it is exclusively a social, heredity or psychological problem. But by educationist I do not mean the ordinary teacher, principal, superintendent, or child, experimental or educational psychologist; I refer to the technically trained psycho-educational examiner who possesses the qualifications described on pp. 114 f., 132 f., 157 f., 210 f., and 216 f.

Moreover, that the psychological examination of school children is already regarded as a function of the schools is indicated by the fact that in the overwhelming majority of cities the examinations are now conducted in the educational divisions rather than in the departments of medical inspection or in the boards of health. Sixty-four cities conduct the examinations in the educational divisions of the schools and only twenty-two in the divisions of medical inspection. The two divisions conduct the examinations jointly in some cities. Moreover, at least seven (possibly fourteen) of the departments of medical inspection are under the control of the boards of education, so that 82 per cent of the work is supported by educational boards (exclusive of the cooperative work by outside agencies). These figures indicate a growing conviction that this work should be placed directly under the executive control of the superintendent of instruction.

The best indication that the schools will not long be content with crude or amateurish psycho-educational diagnoses is the remarkable growth of the psychological or psycho-educational clinics in the schools. Laboratory clinics have been established in the following schools: Chicago, 1898; Rochester, 1907; New York, 1908; Providence, Oakland, Hibbing and Cincinnati, 1911; Grand Rapids, Seattle, Philadelphia, Springfield, Mass, (supports a psychologist on part time), New Orleans and Milwaukee (temporarily discontinued), 1912; Buffalo, Washington, Albany, Los Angeles and Trenton, 1913, and Detroit, 1914 (supports a consulting psychologist on part time)–a total of nineteen public school clinics.2 2 The first twelve psychological clinics established in any kind of institution (including the institutional psychological laboratories) are, in the order of organization: University of Pennsylvania, 1896; Chicago Public Schools and Minnesota School for the Feeble-Minded and Colony for Epileptics, 1899 (discontinued but reestablished in 1910); Mclean Hospital, Waverley, Mass., 1904; The Training School at Vineland, N. J., 1906; Rochester Public Schools and Government Hospital for the Insane, Washington, D. C., 1907; Colorado State Teachers College, Greeley, 1908; University of Washington, University of Minnesota, Lincoln State School and Colony of Illinois, and

Several other cities already have good rudimentary clinics, and others are ready to organize clinics.8 It is safe to prophesy that within the next five or ten years every city with a population of 100,000 and over will have its school psycho-educational clinic, and smaller cities will make some provision for the more adequate psychological examination of their mentally exceptional school children.

All of the existing clinics are under the control of the superintendent of instruction except four, two of these being administered by the board of health (Buffalo and Providence), one by the department of medical inspection (Philadelphia) and one by a municipal university (Cincinnati). Six of the directors of these clinics are clinical psychologists. However, by adding two medical directors who have considerable psychological training and extensive experience with the feeble-minded, and three psychologists, the number may be increased to eleven. Only two or three clinics are in charge of medical inspectors, one is in charge of an alienist, and three are in charge of Binet testers.

Juvenile Psychopathic Institute, Chicago, 1909. Psychological testing was begun on a small scale in the Los Angeles public schools in 1895, but a psychological clinic was not established as an independent division until July, 1913.

On April 14, 1914, the Board of Education of the city of St Louis authorized the establishment of a psycho-educational clinic, as an independent division in the department of education, and appointed the writer as the first director. The clinic will be located on the grounds of the Harris Teachers College, with which it will be closely affiliated. The director of the clinic will have administrative supervision of the clinical and educational work with mentally unusual children. The actual work of class supervision will be in charge of a special supervisor, working under the directions of the clinic. The director will offer courses at the Harris Teachers College on mentally. exceptional children. The form of organization adopted by St. Louis corresponds, in the main, to the plan suggested on p. 375.

Number of Psychological Clinics in All Kinds of Institutions.

In public schools, as above 19 In universities (see p. 57), including the Psychopathic Laboratory in the School of Education,

University of Chicago 17 In medical schools (see p. 58) 7 In normal schools (seep. 58) 3 In Girard College 1 In institutions for the feeble-minded and epileptic (including Lapeer, which has a consulting psychologist, see p. 70f.) 6 In hospitals for the insane (these clinics perhaps are psychological laboratories rather than psychological clinics, see p. 70) 6 In penal and correctional institutions (see p. 78). 6

New York Probation and Protective Association. 1 In juvenile courts (see p. 74) 2 In municipal criminal courts (Boston and Chicago) 2 In immigrant stations (Ellis Island). 1

Total 70 (According to recent press reports, psychological examinations are also given in clinics established in connection with the criminal branch of the municipal court in the city of Cleveland and in connection with the juvenile court in Philadelphia. The Ohio Board of Control for state institutions is erecting a central observation cottage, which will serve as a clearing-house for children who are to be sent to institutions. Here defectives and delinquents of doubtful mentality will be given a mental and physical examination before being placed in an institution. The Board is given the power to examine and transfer cases. No special legislative appropriation has yet been made for this clearing-house which, evidently, will contain a psychological clinic.)

Seventy-five cities, or 75 per cent of the cities tabulated in Table IV, pay increased salaries to teachers of backward and feeble-minded children, 8 per cent give no increase, 3 per cent of the answers are ambiguous, and 18 per cent failed to reply to the question. One city gives an initial increase of 300; two cities an increase of 250; one, 240; eight, 200; one, 160; three, 150; thirty-one, 100; one, 75; one, 60, and thirteen, 50. New York pays a minimum of 860 and a maximum of 1,820, with a 100 annual increase. The advance most frequently given is thus 100 a year, followed by 50 and 200.

The justification for raising the salaries of special-class teachers is twofold. First, the arduous nature of the work. I am not certain, however, that this point is well taken, for, while subnormal children require far more drill, individual attention and patient care than normal children, the special teacher is relieved of the drudgery, monotony and formalism incident to mass instruction and the discipline of large numbers of children. Many teachers who desire to escape from the lock-step of class work will regard the opportunities of doing individual work with small numbers as sufficient compensation in itself.

Second, the specialized preparation required by the work. The teacher of the special class must be an expert; she must be able to psychologize each pupil and individualize instruction; she must be able to grasp the essentials of the diagnosis submitted with cases on admission, so that she can adapt treatment to individual needs; she must be able to observe scientifically, so that she can modify and adapt her methods to the developmental needs of each pupil; she must be thoroughly grounded in cor rective pedagogics; in a word, she must be an expert in orthophrenics. But no teacher can be considered an expert in this field who has not pursued extended technical courses. A professional course pursued during a summer term suffices merely to lay a good foundation.

That school administrators are gradually becoming convinced that no one should be appointed to teach a special class who has not made a special study of the problems, is apparent from an examination of Table V. Seventy-two, or 70 per cent of the 102 cities tabulated, answered in the negative (or gave data which seemed to justify a negative answer) the question, Do you appoint teachers of special classes for the feeble-minded and seriously backward who have not received special preparation? However, this figure is probably slightly too high, because it includes cities which propose in future to require special training as the eligibility condition for appointment, and cities which expect teachers to take a training course after instead of before appointment (this may be good for the teacher, but it is bad pedagogy and hard on the pupils). Moreover, gratifying as these results are, it should be stated that the standards of what constitutes special preparation for this work are still quite vague and fluid. Shall we regard as specially trained teachers who have taken a kindergarten course, or who have merely taught young children, or who have taken or taught a little industrial work, or who have merely observed the work of a special class for a few weeks? Hardly. The training which teachers need for this work is just as specific, precise, detailed and extended (in fact, more extended) as the training needed to become an expert kindergartner, or manual or domestic arts teacher. New York City is, I believe, the only city in the country which gives a special eligibility examination to all candidates for appointment to a special class for feeble-minded and seriously backward children.

Ungraded Classes

About 102, or 33 per cent of the 302 cities reporting, maintain ungraded classes. This is exclusive of one city in which the principals give a little attention to slow pupils, and of a few cities in which the classes are divided into slow, medium and fast divisions, and in which the slow pupils are given industrial work. But it includes cities in which teachers give individual instruction before, during and after school hours, during the regular terms or the summer term only, to pupils separately, or in ungraded classes, or in the regular grades, in small groups or in unlimited numbers, by substitute, assisting, unassigned, ungraded or regular teachers. It includes cities in which the instruction is available to the slow pupils in all grades, or is limited to those in the first three or four grades or to those in the seventh and eighth grades. It is evident from the returns that the types of ungraded class organization which obtain throughout the country have little in common except the element of coaching or individual attention. It is also evident from many of the replies that the function of these classes is frequently confused with the function, on the one hand, of the elementary industrial classes and with the function, on the other hand, of the special (orthogenie) classes. It is quite clear to my mind that the ungraded class has become the dumping-ground for the misfits of the schools, just as the special class once was (and still is in many places) the dumping-ground for the flotsam and jetsam of the schools. Here one finds all types and all grades of deviating children, from the imbeciles and morons to the motor minded or industrially inclined. It has been my fortune to examine a considerable number of pupils who have been consigned by the educational authorities to the ungraded classes because they were merely temporarily retarded on account of absence, sickness or transfer and therefore needed only individual attention from the ungraded teacher. I have frequently marveled over the blundering diagnoses which have consigned morons and seriously backward children to the coaching classes, as well as children who should be given academic work almost entirely in correlation with elementary industrial training. There is no justification for the supposition that psycho-educational diagnosis is necessary only for the extreme abnormal types, and not for the children who grade nearer the normal. The correct diagnosis of some of the latter is no mean task. There is urgent need for a thoroughgoing study of all aspects of ungraded class organization. What is the most efficient type of organization? Should the class merely be divided into slow, normal and fast divisions, and each division be instructed by the regular teachers, or should the slow pupils be grouped together in a separate ungraded class, or should they be taken out occasionally, singly or in small groups, and be given special attention by ungraded teachers? What should be the enrollment of the ungraded class? The practice varies considerably. In twelve of the cities tabulated the register is 20; in eleven, 25; in nine, 15; in four each, 20 to 25, and 15 to 20; in three, 24; in two each, 20 to 24, 15 to 18, 12, and 80. In others it varies from 15 to 70, 20 to 30, 5 to 20, 5 to 12, 4 to 9, 3 to 8 and 1 to 4 (the latter figures probably refer to the size of groups instead of classes). In thirty-eight cities the register is between 20 and 30 (inclusive), in thirty between 15 and 20 (inclusive), and in eight less than 14. What is the true function of the ungraded class? What are the practical results of ungraded work? What types of pupils are really benefited by individual coaching in the regular academic branches? What are the qualifications required by the ungraded teacher? What special preparation does she require? It is obvious that a teacher who is unable to study each child, to unearth the causes of his peculiar pedagogical handicaps, to psychologize the child and individualize the instruction, has little place in the ungraded room. All these questions deserve careful study.

From the following tabulation it appears that the feeble-minded and backward classes are relatively more numerous in the larger cities (above 25,000), while ungraded classes are relatively more numerous in the smaller cities (below 25,000):

Percentages of the 302 cities maintaining

Special Classes Population Ungraded Classes

Per cent Per cent 84 over 100,000 74 43 25,000 to 100,000 35 17 under 25,000 20

This is probably not due to the fact that there are relatively more feeble-minded and seriously backward pupils in the larger cities, but is due to the fact that the smaller cities have not yet become thoroughly alive to the administrative educational problems affecting these children. The alleged explanation that there are not enough seriously deficient children in smaller cities (say, conservatively, in cities of 10,000 and over) to make up a class, is without foundation.

For data bearing on the other types of special classes the reader is referred to Tables VII to XV.

Classes for the Feeble-Minded and Seriously Backward

Cities of 500,000 and over

City Year Started No. of Pupils per Class No. of Classes Types of Pupils, or Character of Class

Baltimore, Md 7 to 20 1 Mental defectives

Boston, Mass 1899 15 30 provable type

1898 20 50

Cleveland, O 1879 10 to 20 17

New York, N Y 1900 15 180

Philadelphia, Pa 1901 16ave 90

Pittsburgh, Pa 1912 15 I process of organ ization

St Louis, Mo. 1907-08 15 34 for the backward and defi-cient

Cities of 250,000 and less than 500,000

Buffalo, N Y 1909 15 7

Cincinnati, O 1909 15 10 F.-M

Detroit, Mich 1903 15

Jersey City, N. J 1911 15 g mal

1902 12 2 Defectives

Milwaukee, Wis 1908 12 4

Minneapolis, Minn Newark, N. J. 1912 1910 15 15 4 15 P.-M.

New Orleans, La 1910 14-15 1 Defectives (F-M)

San Francisco, Cal 1 of exceptional children

Washington, D. C 1906 12-16 14 ives. Hope to organize a school F.-M. and seriously back-ward; 4 colored; 10 white

Cities of 100,000 and less than 250,000

Albany, N. Y 1913 12-20 backward

10 1 F.-M.

1906 20 1 Defective

1913 15 3 Deficient children

Columbus. O Dayton, O 1909 1911 15-20 10 Slow and mentally defective

1911 10 2

Fall River, Mass 1913 15 4 vation classes F.-M.

Grand Rapids, Mich 1910 1907 12-15 16-18 4

Louisville, Ky 1913 12-14 1 Defectives

Nashville, Tenn 1912 (?)40 school for F.-M. Retarded?); 4 teachers in 1 bid.

New Haven, Conn Oakland, Cal 1913 1911 15 14 3 Subnormal

City Year Started No. of Pupils per Class No. of Classes Types of Pupils, or Character of Class

Paterson, X J 1912 15 4 Mentally deficient

8-12

Providence, R. I. 18 18 8 F.-M.

1910-11 15 3 Mentally deficient

Rochester, N. Y 1906 15 29
Seattle, Wash 1910 12 10 F-M.
1911 15 2
1913 Backward
Toledo, O 1910 15 I5 F.-M. and seriously backward
18-24 16 C lasses for defective and back-
ward
Cities of 25,000 and less than 100,000
    Allen town. Pa 1910 15 1
1914 8-15 1
Auburn, N. Y 1911 10-12 1
1912 15-18 1
Bayonne, N. J 1911 15 5
20-30 1
Cam den, N. J 1912 15 5
Chester, Pa 1912 17 1
Decatur, 111 4
Elffin, in. 1903 15 1
Elizabeth, N. J. 1909 15 2
Erie, Pa 1910 20
Ft. Wayne. Ind 1910 20 2
1908 14
? 8-12 6
1912 10-12 8
Little Rock Ark. 1912 11 1
1909 16 1
1909 15 1
Mt. Vernon, N. Y 1913 17 1
New Britain, Conn New Rochelle, N Y. 1907 12 1
10-20
1906 40
Niagara Falls, N. Y. Passaic, N. J 1912 1907 15-20 15 1 3
Perth Amboy, N. J Reading, Pa 1912 1908 15 1 1
20
Saginaw, Mich 1907 10-15 1
Salt Lake City, U
Schenectady, N. Y 1912 1910 20 15 3 2
Springfield, Mass 1897 1911 15 5-12 2 1
Tacoma. Wash 1910 10 1
Waltham, Mass 1905 10-15 8
W Hoboken, N J. 1912 15 1
F.-M.
    Expect to start a class for mental defectives in 1914
    F.-M.
    F.-M. and speech defectives

F.-M.
Defectives Institutional children and mentally weak
F.-M. and backward
Classes for F.-M., slow, deaf, disciplinary and speech defective
F.-M. and retarded
Mentally inferior
One school for F.-M.
State School takes care of defectives
F.-M. and seriously backward
F.-M., seriously backward, speech defective
F.-M. and seriously backward
Mentally defective
F.-M.
F.-M.
F.-M.
Defectives
Mental defectives
Classes for P.-M. and seriously backward
Seriously backward; 4 teachers
Subnormal
Mentally defective
F.-M.
Seriously backward, including deaf, blind, epfleptic
Mentally defective
One hundred in one atypical school
F.-M.
F.-M.
Mentally defective
Mentally defective
Mentally defective
Mentally subnormal
Utilize Waltham State School for F.-M.
F.-M.
City Year Started No. of Pupils per Class No. of Classes Types of Pupils, or Character of Class
Ashcviue, N. C. Plan to start classes
Bloom field, N J 15-21 2 below class
Bnglewood, N J. 1910 15 1 below normal
Everett, Wash 1911 15 1
Goldsboro, N C 1913 20 1
1911-12 15 3
Hempstead. N Y 1913 20 ly backward F.-M.
Hibbing, Minn 1913 15 1
1909 12 1 Subnormal
1913 12 1 pedagogically

1911 15 for exceptional children
1912 15-20 1
Long Branch, N. J 1912 15 2 Subnormal
Mason City, la. 1911 10-15 1 F.-M.
Montclair, N J 1910 I5 8
1913 15 1
I5 Classes for F.-M
New Brunswick, N. J. N Bergen, N Y 1911 1913 15 15 2 1 Mentally defective F.-M.
1913 13-15 1 Subnormal
Pawtucket. R. I. 20 1
Plainfield, N J 15 3 below grade Mentally deficient
1913 15 2
Raleigh, N. C. 1913 28 1 ward
Somerville, N. J 1913 15 1
1912 24 2 class Mentally defective
Summit, N J. 15 2
Washington, Pa 1913 18 1 age and truants
Cities of 500,000 and over
City Special Examination Befoee Admission Character of Examination Official Conducting Examination
Med. Psy. Ed. Ed. Psy.
Baltimore Yes Yes Yes Yes Yes Yes Yes Yes Director of Phipps Clinic
Med. Insp. for Spec. CL
Chicago Yes Yes Yes Yes Yes Yes Yes Yes Yes Clin. psys. ch. study dept. Binet tester, spec. tch. M. D. s. psy., grtd students, insp. of Un. Cl.
Cleveland Yes Yes
New York Yes Psy. City College, Insp. of Un. Cl.
Philadelphia Yes Yes Yes Yes Chief of med. insp. 5 M. D. assts., 10 dist. supts.
Pittsburgh Yes Yes Yes Yes
St. Louis Yes Yes Supt. of Spec. Cl. Clin. psy., Sept., 1914 Clin. psy., beginning Sept., 1914
Cities of 250,000 and less than 500,000 Cities of 500,000 and over
Yes Yes Yes Yes Med Insp, Biandet
Yes Yes Yes Yes Supv. of Spec. Cl. testers Psy. of U. of Onn.,
Detroit Yes Yes Yes Supv. of Spec. Ct
spec. tch. Spec. Med Insp. and M. D. s
Jersey City Yes Yes Yes Yes Supt. of Spec. Cl. Snpt. of Spec. Cl.,
Yes Yes Yes Clin psy Med. Insp. Clin. psy
Milwaukee Yes Yes Yes Yes Tch. Psy.
Yes Yes Yes Yes Spec. tch. Spec. tch.
Newark Yes Yes Yes Yes Spec. tch.
No Yes Yes Yes Director of Dept. of
Yes Yes Yes Ed. Research Spec. tch.
Yes Yes Yes Binet tester, din
psy.

Agencies Conducting Psy. Examinations Extent of Preparation of Sch. Psy. Examiners Extent of Ply. Examinations Child Study Laboratory or Psychological Clinic Med. Ed. Dlv. Outside Agency Year In what dept. Approx-imate cost Dlv. started

Phipps Clinic, Johns Hopkins Phipps Director, a leading psychiatric authority Binet and other lab. tests None None

Yes State Psycho-pathic Hospital, Harvard U. 2 clin. psys., Ph. D. s and 1 asst. Courses on mental tests and subn. ch. Adequate Various psy. and anth. tests Binet tests 1898 None 1908 Ed. 15,000

Yet Yes Yes City College Not confined to one set of tests, test de-pends upon the type of child Binet and other psy. tests Ed. Ed. 900 Nominal

For 12 years co-operation from the psy. clin., U. of Penn. Psy. clinic, Sch. of Ed. U. of Pittsburgh Med. Director, has specialized on subn. ch. 1912

Clin. psy. De Sanctls, Binet, Healy, Wallin, anth. and other tests De Sanctis. Binet. Healy, Wallin, anth., ed., social, heredi-tary, etc.

Yea Clin. psy., Ph. D. 1914, Sept. Ed. 450 Initial

Cities of 250.000 and less than 500,000 Cities of 25,000 and less than 100,000 Cities of 25,000 and less than 100,000

Ye Yes M. D. Observational clinics Director Ph. D. In psy., 2 asata. tr(. in mental testa and subn. ch. One clin. psy., M. D., and spec, tch., cours-es in subn. ch. Binet tests 1913 1911 B. of H. 1438

In B. of H. Yes Dept. of psy., U. of Clnn. Binet, anth., and other testa U. of Cinn. 250 Yes Pay., Dept. of Ed., U. of Mich., appointed con-sulting pay., Feb., 1914 Binet, form board, educational tests 1914

Yes Yes Normal and coll. grad. univ. trg. Psy., M. A., exten-sive experience Binet test principal-ly Binet, others None 1913 1912 None None 1912 Ed. 750

Yea Med. Insp.

Yes Yes Dept. of pay., U. of Minn. Spec. trg. Binet tests

Yes Ph. D. in psy. Binet, anth., heredi-ty Healy, Binet, form board, anth. Ed. J3.5004 Yes Trg. In acha. for pre-paring tchs. for de-fectives Spec. trg. on defect-ives in summer scha. and unlvs.

Yec U. S. Hospitalfor Insane Binet, form board, audiometer, spirom-eter and other lab. tests 1913 Ed. 200

City Special Examination Befoee Admission Character of Examination Official Con-ducting Examination

Med. Psy. Ed. Ed. Psy.

Yes Yes Yes Yes Yes Yes Yes Director of Medico-Psy. Lab.

Med. Insp., a Binet

Bridgeport Yes Yes Yes Yes Prin., Snpt. of pri-mary sens. tester Tch., Med. Insp., Prin.

No Yes Spec. tch., students from State U.

Yes Yes Yes Yes Yes Yes Yes Prln. Prin., tch. Spec. tch. Spec. tch.

Fall River Yes Spec. tch. since 1913

Grand Rapids Yes Yes Supv. of backward

Yes Yes Yes Yes Yes Yea Yes Yes Yes Yes No Yes and i.; u

Louisville Yes Yes Yes Spec. tch.
Nashville Yes Yes Yes Teh. Spec. tch.
Oakland Yes Yes Yes Yes Yes Yes Yes Yes Prin., spec. tch. Tch. Grade tch. Estimates by tch. Clln. Psy. Director of Ch. Study Dept.
Providence Yes Yes Alienist Spec. tch.
Richmond Yes Yes
Rochester Yes Director and Asst, Ch. Study Dept.
Seattle Yes Yes Yes Yes Yes Prin., tch. Tchs. Head spec. tch.
Spokane Yes Yes Yes Yes Yes Spec. tch. Supt. of Spec. Sen.
Toledo Yes
Yes Yes Yes Yes Spec. tch
Agencies Conducting Pay. Examinations Extent of Preparation of Sch. Psy. Examiners Extent of Psy. Examinations Child Study Laboratory or Psychological Clinic lied. Div. Ed. Div. Outside Year started In what dept. Approx-imate cost
Yes Agency M. D., M. A., tch., sch. administrator, work in f.-m. institu-tions 3e Sanctis. Whipple, Fernald, etc. 1913 Ed. 190
Yes Chiefly Binet
Psychopathic Hospital, Dept. of Psy., Harvard Dept. of Psy., State U. Psys. and psychi-atrists of Harvard Binet and other tests
Yes One tch. with spec. trg. on defectives, others from books Courses on mental tests and subn. Binet (incidentally),. esults of book and ndv. trg. Binet tests
Yes Yes Clin. psy., State Teh. College since 1911 Planningtowork under State Inst. F.-M., Waverley Binet tests 1,000
Yes Ind. U. during 1910-11 Spec. courses in mental tests and subn. ch. Binet and other tests 1912 Ed. ff
Yes Summer courses on subn. ch. Binet and other indv., and phy. tests 0
Yes Clin. psy. at Yale Summer courses on subn. ch. B. A., grod. work in Binet and other tests Binet andothertests 1911 Ch. study dept. 417"
psy.
B. of H. Alienist, Butler Hospital M. D., alienist 1911 B. of H.
Yes Yes Summer courses on subn. ch. Summer courses on subn. ch. and tests Binet, assoc. tests and form board Binet, De Sanctls, Healy and other tests. 1907 1912 Ed. 500 50"
Yes Director of Ch Welfare Founda tion, U. of Wash Clin. psy. and tch. with spec. trg. Ed.
Yes Yes Wash. Summer courses on subn. ch. Binet andothertests Binet tests
Yes Yea Binet tests
snbn. ch.
City Special Examination Before Admission Character of Examination Official Con-duct ins- Examination
Med. Psy. Ed. Ed. Psy.
Altoona Ye. Yes Yes Yes Yes Med. Insp. Spec. tch.
Yes Yes
Brockton Yes Ye Yes Yes Yes Yes Yes M. D., sen. nurse
Decatur Yea Yea Yea No Yes Yes Yes Yes Primary Snpv. Binet teter

Elizabeth Yes Yes Yes Yes Yes Yes Yes Yes Yes Yes Yes Prin., tch. Spec. tch. M. D. since 1910 Med. Insp.

Brie

Ft. Wayne Yes Yes Yes Yes Yes Ye Yes Yes Yes Yes Yes Yes Yes Yes Yes Yes Yes Med. Insp. and spec-tch. Spec. tch.

Yes Prln., spec. tch. Med. Insp., spec. tch. Prin. M. D. M. D. since 1907 Spec. tch.

Little Rock Yes Yes Yes Yes Yes Yes Yes Yes Yes Yes

Maiden Prin.

Mt Vernon Yes Yes Yes Yes

New Britain Yes Supt. Prin., frade tch. Spec. tch. since 1910

Niagara Palls Yes Yes Yes Yes Yes Spec. tch.

Passaic Yes Spec. tch.

Pawtncket Yes Yes Yes Yes Yes Yes Prin. Spec. tch. since 1912

Agencies Conducting Psy. Examinations Extent of Preparation of Sch. Psy. Examiners Child Study Laboratory or Psychological Clinic

Extent of Psy. Examinations

Med. Ed. Div. Outside Agency Year started In what dept. Approx-imate cost Div.

Ym Yes Ed. dept., Cor-nell U., during 1911 Summer courses on subn. ch. Binet tests Binet tests

Yes Chicago Spec. tch. from Newark Summer courses on subn. ch. Binet tests

Yes Psych, clin., U. of Penn. 7 years supv. Binet and other tests Binet tests

Ye Yes Spec. trgr. on subn. ch. and tests Binet tests

Ye Yes Yes Yes Summer courses on subn. ch. Summer courses on subn. ch. Summer courses on subn. ch. Summer courses on subn. ch. M. D. Binet tests Binet tests

Yee

Yes Yes Yes Simple ed. tests Binet tests

B. of H. Yes Yes Bluet tester from Vineland. 1913 Summer courses on subn. ch. Summer courses on subn. ch. Very limited Binet tests Binet tests Binet tests No spec, tests Binet tests

Yes Con. tru summer courses on subn. ch., 10 yrs. experience with subn. Binet tests

Yes Summer courses on snbn. ch. 3inet tests

City Special Examination Before Admission Character of Examination Official Conducting Examination

Med. Psy. Ed. Ed. Psy.

Reading Yes Yes Ym Spec. tch.

Salt Lake City Yes Yes Yes Yes Yes Yes Yes Yes Yes Yes Yes Yes Grade tch. Prin. of atypical sch. Spec. tch. since lr Prin. of atypical sci M. D. spec. tch.

Yes Yes Yes Yes Yes Yes Yes Yes Yes Prln. and tch. Spec. tch. since 1W Director of Py. Lib

Yes Yes Yes Yes Yes Yes Yes Yes Ye Prin. and tch. Prin., tch. Tch. Supv. of Spec. Ed. Spec. tch. since 1912

W Hoboken Yes

Cities of less than 95,000 Cities of less than 25,000 Annual budget, 8,000.

Yes Yes Yes Spec tch since 1913
Yes Yes Spec, tch
Everett Yes Yes Yes
Yes Yes Yes M. D, spec tch
Yes Yes Yes Yes Spec, tch
Yes Yes
Hibbing Yes Yes Yes Yes M D, 1911 spec tct
Yes Yes Yes
Yes Yes Med Insp
Yes Yes Yes Prin., Supt. 1911 Supt
Yes Yes
Yes Yes Yes Yes Prin. Spec, tch
Mason City Yes Yes Spec, tch
Montclalr Yes Yes
Yes Yes Yes Spec tch
Agencies Conducting Pay. Examinations Extent of Preparation of Scn. Psy. Examiners Extent of Psy. Examinations Child Study Laboratory or Psychological Clinic
Med. Div. Ed. Div. Outside Agency Year started In what dept. Approx-imate cost
Yes Psy. clln., U. of Penn. for last 5 years Six yrs. contact with subn. ch. Blnet tests
Binet tests
Yes Yes Yes Yes M. A., summer cours-es on subn. ch. M. D. with spec. trg. in psy. spec. tch. trg. in Binet Summer courses on subn. ch. Clin. psy. Ph. D. Binet andothertests
Yes Binet tests
Yes Anth., Healy, Binet and other tests 1912 Ed. 300
Yes Yes Yes Clin. pay., U. of Wash. U. of Wash., clin. psy. Clin. psy., Ph. D. Binet, anth., social and other tests Binet testa 1913 Ed. 200
Summer courses on subn. ch.
Yes Yes Yes Spec, summer cours-es on subn. ch. Spec. tch. Binet tests Binet tests Blnet and other tests Binet tests Blnet tests
Clin. psy., U. of Wash. Psy. in U. of Wash., spec. trg. Special course in summer schs. Summer courses on subn. ch.
Yes
Yes
Yes Yes
Yes Spec. trg. Spec. trg. in testing Binet and reaction tests Binet tests 1911" Med. and Ed. 500
Yes Binet tests Binet, Whipple
Yes Yes Yes Yes Yea Yes Spec, courses in ed. psy. and tests Binet tests Binet tests Binet tests Binet tests
Spec, summer course on subn. ch. Summer courses on subn. ch. Spec, trg., state cer-tificate
City Special Examination Befoee Admission Character of Examination Official Conducting Examination
Med. Piy. Ed. Ed. Pay.

Yes Yes Yes Yes Yes Yes Yes Yes Yes Yes Yes Yes Tch. Med. B., Snpv. spec. Spec. tch., 1911 Supt., ipec. tch. Supt., Prtn., tch. M. D., spec. tch. M D, spec tch
N. Bergren Yes
Ottumwa Yes Yes Supt., Prin., tch. Prin.
Plalnficld Yes Yes Yes Yes
Raleitfh Yes Yes Yes No Yes Yes Yes Yes Yes Yes Spec. tch. Spec. tch. M. D., spec. tch.
Not an organized department.

Examinations are made after assignment.
Total amount of budget for Department of Research.
The nucleus of a laboratory has been formed.
Examination is given after admission.
Equipment contributed by friends.
Except that one or two special teachers voluntarily examine some pupils.
May start a clinic in 1914-15.
Classroom equipment. 911.
Also have use of the equipment of the University of Washington.
In modified form.
Agencies Conducting Psy.   Examinations Extent of Preparation of Sen.   Psy. Examiners Chdd Study Laboratory or Psychological Clinic
Extent of Psy. Examinations
Mod. Ed. Div. Ontside Agency Year started In what dept. Approx-imate cost Div.
Yes Yes Summer courses on ni. ii. ch. Summer courses on subn. ch. Both have special courses on subn. ch. Binet, anth., and
Yes other tests Binet tests
Yes Blnet tests
Yes
Yes Both, summer courses on subn. ch. Teh. spec. trg. in Psy. Binet tests Ed. and Binet tests
Yes Yes Dept. of Pay. Princeton Univ., 1913
Yes Summer courses on subn. ch. Summer courses on subn. ch. Both, spec. trg. on subn. ch. Binet tests Binet tests Binet tests
Yes
Abbreviations:
Anth.=anthropometric. Assoc.=association. Asst.=Assistant.
Back.=backward. B. of. H.–Board of Health.
Clin. Psy.=cllnical psychologist. Cl.=class or classes. Ch.=children.
Dept.–department.
Ed.=educational. F.-M.=feeble-minded. Grad.=graduate.
Indv.=indlvidual. Lab.=laboratory. Med. Insp.=medical inspector.
Psy.=psychologist or psychological. li in.-principal.
Spec. trg.=special training. Supv.=supervisor. Spec.=special. Sch.=school.
Subn.=subnormal. Spec. tch.=special teacher.
Un.=ungraded.

Annual Salary Increase For Teachers Of Special Classes For The Feeble-minded And Backward

Citiet giving an increase of 240 or more:

Muskegon (start at 300 above regular scale); Buffalo, Harris-burg (850); Los Angeles (840). Citiet giving an increase of 300 to 150:

Bayonne, Detroit, Elizabeth, Lakewood, Louisville, Montclair, New Haven, Richmond (200); North Bergen (160); New Brunswick, Paterson, Superior (150). Citiet giving an increase of 100:

Boston, Bloomfleld, Bridgeport, Cambridge, Columbus, Cincinnati, Everett, Grand Rapids, Hackensack, Hempstead, Houston, Lynn (expect to give 100 increase), Milwaukee, Minneapolis, Morristown, Mt. Vernon, Newark, New Britain, New York, Philadelphia, Plain-fleld, Portland, Providence, Raleigh, Reading, Saginaw, Schenectady, Somerville, Spokane, St. Louis, Trenton. Cities giving an increase of 75 to 50:

Somerville, Mass. (75); Jersey City (60); Auburn, Baltimore, Brockton, Chester, Chicago, Dayton, Denver, Fall River, Little Rock, Memphis, Passaic, Rochester, Worcester (50). Citiet giving an increase of 50 to SO per cent over regular scale:

Allentown (50 per cent increase); Lancaster (some get 50 per cent increase); Goldsboro (33.3 per cent increase); Newton (head teacher gets 33.3 per cent increase over highest paid teacher). Citiet stating the amount of salary given or giving an indefinite increase:

Birmingham (100 per month); Elgin (not settled); Englewood (slight increase); Hibbing (about 500); Pawtucket (same as grammar maximum); Princeton (1,000 per year); Summit (900 to 1,000 per year); Niagara Falls (75 per month); Indianapolis (slight increase over maximum grade salary); Mason City (10 more than regular scale); New Orleans (tendency to increase); Springfield (amount varies); Washington, D. C. (one grade higher than regular teacher). Cities granting no salary increase:

Albany, Cleveland, Maiden, Oakland, Ottumwa, Perth Amboy, Seattle, Tacoma. Cities giving no reply:

Aurora, Camden, Decatur, Hoquiam, Kalamazoo, Leominster, Nashville, New Rochelle, Salt Lake City, San Francisco, Stonington, Waltham, Washington, Pa.

Qualifications Of Teachers Of Backward And Feeble Minded Classes

Cities not appointing teachert without tpecial preparation:

Albany (plan to send teachers for special training–one teacher has had training), Allentown, Altoona (will place a trained teacher when class is started), Auburn, Baltimore, Boston, Bloomfield, Birmingham, Bridgeport, Buffalo, Cambridge, Chester, Cincinnati, Dayton, Denver, Detroit (expect teachers to take training after appointment), Elgin, Elizabeth, Englewood, Everett, Fall River, Goldsboro, Grand Rapids, Hackensack, Harrisburg, Hempstead (try to get especially trained teacher), Hibbing, Hoquiam, Houston, Indianapolis (both teachers have special training), Jersey City, Kalamazoo, Lakewood, Long Branch, I. us Angeles, Louisville, Lynn, Mason City, Minneapolis, Montclair, Morristown (special teacher has had training and two years of experience), Newark, New Brunswick, New Haven, New York, North Bergen, Niagara Falls, Oakland, Passaic, Paterson, Perth Amboy, Plainfield, Portland, Princeton, Providence, Raleigh, Rochester (teachers who are adapted and show special ability to take training), Saginaw (appointed with the understanding that they are to get training), Schenectady, Seattle, Somerville, Mass, (teachers are to take special training after appointment), Somerville, N. J., Spokane, Springfield, Summit, Superior, Tacoma, Toledo, Trenton, Washington, D. C., Washington, Pa., West Hoboken.

Citiet appointing teachers without special preparation:

Bayonne, Brockton, Chicago, Erie, Maiden, Milwaukee, New Britain, New Orleans, Newton, Oakland, Ottumwa, Philadelphia, Reading, Rochester, Stonington, Worcester.

Citiet appointing teacher for other reasons:

Columbus (select teachers who are optimistic and skilled in industrial work), Lancaster (have thus far selected teachers because of apparent adaptability), Solvay (teachers appointed who are especially qualified for this work), St. Louis (appoint teachers with inclination and adaptability).

Citiet giving no reply:

Aurora, Decatur, Leominster, Mt Vernon, Muskegon, Nashville, New Rochelle, Pawtucket, San Francisco, Waltham.

Ungraded Classes

Cities of 500,000 and over

Year Started T aa K I f. Increase of Salary per Year

City I OJS Character of Class

z. B ISO 50

80

Chicago, III ed pupils 50

Cleveland, O.-10-20 10

New York, N. Y. 18,746 pupils in E classes for

Philadelphia, Pa backward pupils capable of rapid restoration

60

small groups 100

cannot best be cared for in regular grade schools

Cities of 250,000 and less than 500,000

Buffalo, N Y pupils without mental de-fect, but retarded

Cincinnati, O 1910 25 8 50

Los Angeles. Cal–Milwaukee, Wis 1902 1912 20-24 15 75 30 Ungraded Over age, but not mentally defective Retarded 240 100

Newark, N J 1913 25-30 7 100

1910 half-time kindergartners in afternoons Ungraded. Class not now in

Washington, D. C. 1905-6 16 1 operation

Cities of 100,000 and less than 350,000 Cities of 95,000 and less than 100,000 Cities less than 23,000

Albany, NY. 1913 46 salary

25 7

Bridgeport, Conn. 1912 20-25 1 Backward 50

Dayton, O 1911-12 retarded 50

Denver, Col 1911 20 m mer classes, continuation classes 50

Fall River, Mass. Grand Rapids, Mich. 1913 15-18 2 S 21 10 Retarded and ungraded

50
1910 1909 5-20 20-25 Ungraded Backward so
Kansas City, Mo. 1908 1 For pupils failing to do regular
1913 15-18 work, also 8 industrial class-es, since 1910 Retarded
1912 15 to 20 substitute teachers
1911 5 work with the backward 50
bright
City Year Started u! Character of Class Increase of Salary per Year
If 2
Oakland, Cal 1912 25 i ago. abandoned, opened again in 1912
Omaha, Neb 1907 20 i
Paterson, N. J 1912 25 t
Portland, Ore 8-12
Providence. R. I. 1896 1913 25 20-24 3 Ungraded Retarded 50
4 100-200
Rochester, N. Y St Paul, Minn 1910 1906 23 No 2 Ungraded, each school gives special
help to backward ch. 50
Seattle Wash 1912 limit 40 ward
Spokane. Wash. 1907 25 1
Toledo, O. 15-20 and backward
24 f, 2 or more years (SO
Camden, N J 20 2 mentality Ungraded
Charleston, S. C. 1913 30 1
12-18
Elgin, IU 1913 14 1 in various subjects 50
Elizabeth, N J. 1
Fitchburg, Mass
Holyoke, Mass Huntington, W. Va. 1910-13 15 3 Ungraded Increase expected
1911 20 4 ing coaches the retarded
20-25 4
1912 25 8 count of crowding. Back-ward and precocious
Manchester, N H 1911 25 2 backward pupils J100
New Britain, Conn. 1913 30 1
Newport, R I 2
New Rochelle, N. Y. 10-20 indiv. attention
1906 15-20 ?-
Pasadena. Cal 1907-8 15-20 classes
Poughkeepsie, N Y. 1910 20
Roanoke, Va 20 4 slow
San Diego. Cal 1908 15 fi rooms for backward chil-dren
Salt Lake City, U. 15-70 and slow Ungraded
Schenectady, N. Y. 1912 1912 20 8 None
4-9 attention in 5 schools
City Year Started "0:3.2 du O en Character of Class Increase of Salary per Year
zs ll

1910 25 i
22 150
15-20 i
1894 25 9 speaking. Also 2 practical arts classes, since 1913 Special aid
1911 5-12 4 60
Varies Ungraded
1905 2 Dull
1913 4 possible in ungraded rooms for retarded
1912-13 1
24 1
1911 15 1 ungraded classes 100
Bismarck, N. D. 1911 because of lack of room
20-30 small classes Retarded grouped in various
Claremont, N H 15 1 classes
Denison, Tex 1900 12 4 Industrial instruction to re-
Eveleth, Minn 1909 20 1 tarded 100
Everett, Wash. 1911 1 groups of from 1 to 6 pupils
Goldsboro, N. C 1913 20 1
Great Palls, Mont after school
1 1 i M."iv. Minn. 1913 Slight
Hillsboro, Tex. 1913-14 15 1 hand-minded increase
Ironwood. Mich 1912 1911-12 20 15 1 more subjects Backward and truant 50 50
4
Lead, S. D 1913 20 1
Long Branch, N. J. 1912 25 4 Ungraded
Ludington, Mich tional children
Mason City, la 1913 10-15 2
Munhall, Pa 1912 20 2
Paris City, 111 3-8 ward 90-100
Parkersburg. W. Va. 15 give special attention to re-tarded
Rockland, Me es in each building
Rockland, Mass 1912 16 6 grades
Southington. Conn. 20-25 1
Stonington, Conn. 1912 24 7 Special classes for 1st three
Summit, N. J 15 1 grades Retarded
I" n i. ml own Pa. 4th grades
City Year Started lh No. of Classes Character of Class Increase of Salary per Year
Winchester, Ky 1901 1-4 Modification of Batavia plan
in every grade
Winchester, Mass. 1913 12 1
work
1912 1
Winsted, Conn 1911 16 I
TABLE VII
Classes for Epileptics

City Year Character of Class
Started
Baltimore, Md. 1912
Chicago III 1914
Cleveland, O
Reading, Pa 1908
TABLE VIII
Classes for Disciplinary and Truant
Cities of 500,000 and over sal 8
City Year Started i Character of Class
= 0
Zfl.5 20
Chicago, 111 1908 25 12
Cleveland, O 1902 2 250 pupils in one parental sch. for truants
New York. N. Y Pittsburgh, Pa About 1874 1913 33 I5 Disciplinary or truant
1 ent and delinquent
Cities of 250,000 and less than 500,000 Cities of 100,000 and less than 850,000
Buffalo, N Y 25
Los Angeles, Cal–1904 1899 15 8 Incorrigible
-ssl No. of 1 Classes
City Year Started i! Character of Class
Newark, N. J 1898 20 ciplinary and truant 100 colored and 100 white pupils in Chil-
Washington, D. C. 1906 16-25 drens Harbor and Reform Sch. One sch. for disci-
plinary and truant
Dayton, O. 1910 1
1911 20 1
Grand Rapids, Mich. 1910 20 2 4 One truant sch.
1910 30 2 attendance
2
Oakland, Cal 1910 20 7
1913
Paterson, N J 1912 1
Portland, Ore
Providence, R. I Rochester, N. Y St Paul, Minn 1896 1899 1911-12 15 16 5 Disci-
plinary Truant. 2 teachers
Seattle, Wash 1906 1
Spokane, Wash 1909 1913 25 1 One parental sch. Cl. for incorrigibles
Cities of 25,000 and less than 100,000 1909 1
Camden, N J 1912 1
Decatur, HI 1912
Elizabeth, N J. 1912 1
action Incorrigible and truant Classes
Harrisburg, Pa 1902 30 2
Pueblo, Col. 1911 25 1
1908 I5 1

Trenton, N. J 1905 15 8
Waltham, Mass
Cities of less than 25,000
    Bloomfield, N J 1912 1
Montclair, N. J 1910 1
1913 1
Plainfield, N J. 1909 1
1913 1
Washington, Pa 1913 f
Classes for Foreigners
    City Year Character of Class
Started
1912
Cleveland, O 1910
1911
Fall River, Mass 1913
15 years of age
Hackensack, N J 1912
1913
1908
1910
New York, N. Y 1.474 pupils In C classes
Philadelphia, Pa 1913
Pittsburgh, Pa 1912
Rochester, NY 1899
Solvay, N Y speak English
1910
1894
Syracuse, N. Y classes
Trenton, N. J 1905
Washington, D. C Day (1) and night (12) classes
Winsted, Conn
TABLE X
    Classes for the Deaf
    City Year Started Character of Class
Appleton, Wis. 1913
Atlanta, Ga 1912
1895
Dayton, O 1911
Decatur, 111 1912
Detroit, Mich
Grand Rapids, Mich 1910
Jersey City, N. J 1911 1 class
Kenosha, Wis 1913
1913 1 school

1900
Milwaukee, Wis 1876
Newark, N J 1910
New York, N. Y 1909
Oakland, Cal 1901
Portland, Ore
Reading, Pa, 1908
City Year Character of Class
Started
Rock Island, 111 1903 1 class, limited to 10 pupils
San Diego, Cal 1912 1 class
1907 1 class
Seattle Wash. 1911
St. Louis, Mo Deaf placed in Gallaudet School
St Paul, Minn 1913
Tacoma, Wash 1909 1 class
Toledo, O 1 class
TABLE XI
    Classes for the Blind
    City Year Started Character of Class
Chicago, 111 1899
Cleveland, O
Detroit, Mich Classes
Classes
Milwaukee, Wis 1908
Newark, N J 1910
New York, N. Y 1907
New York, N Y 1912
pupils Blind placed in defective class
Reading, Pa 1908
TABLE XII Classes for Speech Defects
    City Year Character of Class
Started
Appleton. WIs 1896
1912
Chicago, 111 Visiting teachers cover) of city twic
each week
Dccatur, 111 1912
Detroit, Mich Classes
1908
Jersey City, N J. 1911
1913
Milwaukee, Wis 1912
1912
City Year Started Character of Class

New York, NY. 1911
Pittsburgh, Pa 1912 tions of city Mentally deficient through speech de-
Princeton, N. J 1913 fect 1 class
Rochester, N. Y. 1913
Rock Island, 111. 1 class
St. Paul, Minn 1913 School for speech and hearing defects
TABLE XIII Classes for Bright Children
    City Year Started Character of Class
Baltimore, Md 1913
Hempstead, N, Y 1902
1912
1912
1910
Methuen, Mass Montclair, N. J 19i6 Special class
Parkersburjf, W Va 1907-8
Salt Lake City, U 1912
Solvay, N Y 1913
Washington, D. C 1913
TABLE XIV
Orthopedic Classes
    City Year Started Character of Class
Baltimore, Md 1912
Detroit, Mich
Newark, N. J. 1913
New York, N. Y 1906
Philadelphia, Pa 1913
Open Air Schools
    City Year Started Character of Class
Buffalo, N. Y. 1910 2 open air schools, 1 in prospect
Chicago, 111. 1910
1911 For anemic children
1911
1911 3 tubercular classes, 1 open air
New York, N Y 1910 class Anemic, 41 classes, 21 pupils to each class Pre-tubercular
Pawtuclcet, R. I.
Philadelphia, Pa. 1911
Pittsburgh, Pa 1912 1912 1 tubercular One class for tubercular children (-started
St Louis, Mo. by Tuberculosis League of Civic Club of Allegheny County in 1907).
One class for anemic children (started by Tuber-culosis League in 1911)
Syracuse. N. Y
I am indebted to Miss Eva Webb for assistance in tabulating these returns, and to my
wife for considerable stenographic work in connection with the book.
    CHAPTER XIX
    A SCHEMA FOR THE CLINICAL STUDY OF
    MENTALLY AND EDUCATIONALLY

UNUSUAL CHILDREN

The scientific study of the educationally exceptional child should follow a definite plan of procedure and should be sufficiently comprehensive to include an investigation of all the important intrinsic and extrinsic factors which may mar his development. A complete investigation should include the study of the childs developmental, family, hereditary and school histories, an investigation of his past and present social and physical environment, and an examination of his present physical condition and anthropometric, educational and psychological status. A completely satisfying investigation thus requires the cooperation of the social and hereditary worker, the teacher, the medical expert and the psycho-educational clinician.

The following schema is offered as a guide to the scientific examination of mentally abnormal children. It may be used in either of two ways. First, the various forms may be reprinted on separate blanks with appropriate vacant spaces, to be filled in by the investigator. The chief objection to this plan is probably financial: blanks are expensive, and in few cases will it be possible to fill out all the spaces, while in many cases it will not be necessary to do so. Second, the investigator may thoroughly familiarize himself with the contents of the various forms, and follow them as a systematic and comprehensive guide to his investigation; but instead of entering the data on printed blanks he may write up a running history, giving the essential facts of the case, on blank sheets. Whether the one plan or the other is followed, it is desirable that every investigator should append a brief summary of his findings and recommendations.

It cannot be too forcibly impressed upon social, field and laboratory investigators of children that parents and relatives—or any from whom bio-social data are sought— must be approached with much tact and judgment. Gathering hereditary, personal and social data is, at best, a very delicate undertaking, subject to many errors, and many investigators fail utterly to secure, or otherwise they pervert, the significant factors, either because they do not know how to approach parents so as to win their confidence and put them in a communicative attitude, or because they suggest answers by their indiscreet use of leading questions. While, therefore, a guide will prove of the greatest value to child investigators, they must know above all else how to use the guide with tact, common sense and discriminating intelligence.

Social and hereditary investigators must also be cautioned against drawing premature or unjustifiable conclusions from hearsay evidence. They must accustom themselves to weigh reports very carefully, and to verify them in every way possible. There is a large amount of work done today in heredo-biology, heredo-psychology and social investigation which is careless, unscientific and worthless. Do not conclude that someone was feebleminded or insane simply because someone reported him to be slow, stupid, feebly-gifted or as acting queerly. Do not conclude that a child is feeble-minded simply because he appears stupid or feeble-minded to you, or because he happens to test three years, or even four or five years, retarded. Science cannot be founded on guesswork. Gather all possible facts bearing on your case, and avoid hasty generalizations. It is rather for the trained specialist to supply the diagnoses.

It need scarcely be said that when the same person gathers the developmental, hereditary and school data, it is not necessary to re-record on each blank the identical facts called for in the different blanks unless there is a discrepancy in the statements.

FORM I

DEVELOPMENTAL HISTORY

No. Diagnosis Source of data Date

Full name Age: date of birth yrs. mos. Address (with phone) Fathers name Mothers name Guardians name By whom referred for investigation (Underscore appropriate words, and fill in other data)

Conciptive Conditions: diseases, syphilis, gonorrhea, tuberculosis, scrofula, alcohol, drugs, health, overwork, starvation, fright, accidents, anxiety, excitement, aversion, etc., before or at time of conception in mother in father

Pregnancy Conditions: above data for mother during pregnancy. Also pelvic diseases, attempts at abortion, "maternal impressions, legitimacy of child

Birth Conditions: premature (how much) full term, weight labor normal, prolonged (how long) or difficult; delivery with instruments or anesthesia; difficult animation, breathing or crying, cyanosis; injury or deformity (especially of head) or paralysis; inability to suckle

Growth Conditions: nursed (by whom, how long) Bottle fed (how long, what) What fed when weaned Sickly as baby or child First teeth, when (any fever or illness) Second teeth, when Fontanel, closed when First crawled, when Stood alone, when

Walked (unsupported steps), when Walked well, when Ran well, when Supported head, when Talked–single words correctly applied, when Short phrases, when Complete sentences, when Specific speech defects, what, since when, circumstances Able to hold or grasp well, when Control of fundamental reflexes (acquisition of tidy habits), when Beginning of puberty

Of menstruation (difficult)

Diseases And Accidents (age, attributed cause, severity, subsequent effects, recovery): measles, smallpox, whooping cough, scarlatina, scarlet fever, mumps, diphtheria, cerebro-spinal meningitis, infantile paralysis, rickets, malnutrition, inanition, scrofula, swollen glands, adenoids, enlarged tonsils, nose, eyes, ears, nervousness, muscular twitches, where chorea, periodical headaches, fainting spells, convulsions (infantile or epileptic, with data) enuresis (nocturnal or diurnal), falls, injuries, orthopedic deformities, pubertal or menstrual troubles Vaccinated, when, effects Hospital or surgical record

M. D. s by whom examined or treated

Diagnoses by different M. D. s

Habits: sleep (past and present): hours of retiring and arising sound, restless, insomnia (cause). Drinking: tea, coffee, wine, beer, whisky; drugs (how much, how frequently) Appetite: hearty, poor, capricious, gluttonous, food preferences, usual menu Chews or smokes: cigarettes, cigars, pipe. Excessive indulgence in sweets Masturbates, sexually immoral or perverse.

Mental And Physical Peculiarities In Infancy And Chiij hood (age first observed, parents explanation): queer or bizarre ideas, action, behavior, speech, disposition

Fits of crying or laughing, with or without cause Outbreaks, tantrums, continuous or periodic Night terrors, sleep-walking

Morbid fears Criminal, intemperate, immoral or destructive tendencies Running away Solitude or company preferred Shut-in, solitary disposition

Playing or seeking younger or older persons or opposite sex Dull, stupid, lazy, indifferent, bright, talented, precocious (with facts)

Record Of Delinquencies (with ascribed causes, institutional, court and probation records):

Agencies which have previously been interested in this child:

Additional Remarks:

Recommendations (by whom):

Results Of Following Recommendations (as reported later):

Sionatuhe:

FORM II

FAMILY AND HEREDITARY HISTORY

No. Diagnosis Source of data Date

Full name Bom, where Age: date of birth yrs. mos. Lives with at (street, with phone) Name, with birthplace, nationality and religion of father of mother

Language spoken at home Order of childs birth no. of sisters, alive dead of brothers, alive dead Age of father at childs birth of mother

Blood relationship between parents Parents living apart, together, divorced. Occupation and weekly earnings of father of mother of other children of child

Health, morals, habits, diseases, sexual habits, etc., prior to birth of child, of father of mother (see Form I)

i

i

1 1 ! x

X I

a S-3

IgeASK gs

OS

a

j ! l

Incouru, , S

ill

i

I JH

X

Bh

i il

Criminal Tenden-cies

a ;1 JO

i C !!

il

u v l

Health
8 ill J ill 1 ill 1 1
,
and -" Z 6 fe 6 6 6
323 x55e
S! H js a a a coo 55 COC U and. and. and. and. SSXO
"S g
  be 4 ts.
  S 3 -3
  III!
  Elll isi Ill -all
  If?
  FORM III
HOME AND NEIGHBORHOOD ENVIRONMENT
  No. Diagnosis Source of data Date
  Full name Age: date of birth yrs. mos. Address (with phone) Laves with Parents address, if different
  Fathers name Mothers name
  Parents alive Parents living together If separated, divorced or deserted. Guardians name and address
  Childs birthplace Language spoken in home Referred for investigation by
  Successive places of residence (with sanitary, hygienic and moral conditions of each)
  Present Home Influences
(Underscore appropriate words, and fill in other relevant data)
  Financial: rich, moderate, poor, impoverished, proverty-stricken, charity case. Weekly earnings of father mother children Breadwinners, who Influence of financial conditions on childs care
  Food: quantity quality Drinks: what how often how much No. of meals (typical menus)
  Clothing: ample, insufficient, shabby, soiled, tasteless, immodest (effect on child)
  Bathing: frequency
  Housing: flat, tenement, house; no. of rooms of bedrooms bathroom no. of lodgers in family of boarders
  Clean, bright, sunshiny, artistic, attractive, dark, dingy, damp, filthy, disordered, well or poorly ventilated. Garbage Sewerage
  Childs bedroom: quiet, good ventilation, light, sleeping companions, no. in room Hours of retiring and arising
  Home Life: excellent, tranquil, religious, moral, refined, upset, disturbed, boisterous, raw, quarrelsome, brutal, fighting, vulgar, degrading irreligious, immoral, bad.
  Home Treatment: excellent, good, kindly, good care, indifferent, neglectful, poor care, parents away, petted, coddled, well or poorly disciplined, ridiculed, rebuffed, irritated, maltreated, whipped, frightened, abused, by father, mother, stepmother, siblings, guardians, etc. Overworked

Childs Deportment At Home: excellent, good, average, poor, bad; obedient, disobedient; mischievous, quarrelsome, fights, cruel to animals or siblings or playmates, incorrigible, destructive; cheats, steals, squanders money, pawns, gambles, plays craps, deceives, lies, untrustworthy; neat, careless, indolent, immodest, immoral; runs away. Attitude toward parents, siblings, playmates, strangers Toward reprimands and punishment How punished

Deportment of siblings at home

Amusements At Home: what, cards, games, plays, singing, music, reading, proper, improper. How does child spend leisure time?

Chief interests at home Vacations, when where spent

Work: complete record of jobs, with dates, how long held, hours, pay, success, reasons for changes or discharge Age on taking first job I 1.1 u-mu- Disposition: religious, irreligious or indifferent. Attends church, where, how often, willingly or reluctantly Attends Sunday school, where, how often, willingly

Neighborhood Influences

Physical Surroundings: sanitary, insanitary, dark, smoky, filthy, shimmy, densely populated, foreign population, saloons, dance halls, gambling joints, picture shows, immoral resorts.

Social Environment: character of chums or associates (boys, girls, adults), good, bad, vulgar, gamblers, crap players, immoral, corrupt, criminal, thieves. Belongs to clubs or gangs, as leader or follower, what kind (social, amusement, literary, predatory, criminal, etc.), effects of on child Tendencies toward loafing, vagrancy, migration.

Recreation facilities of neighborhood: playgrounds, public, private, supervised, unsupervised, streets, home yard, athletic field, gymnasium, social settlement house. Seeks what kinds of amusements (games, plays, loafing, running around, ball, gambling, crap playing, immoral practices, selling papers, theaters, picture shows, etc.). Plays with boys or girls, older or younger. Attends picture shows or theaters, how often What kind of shows preferred

Effects of on child

Recommendations :

Results Of Recommendations (from later investigations):

Signature :

FORM IV

SCHOOL HISTORY

Teacrebs Reports On Fedagogical, Psychological, Social And
Moral Traits

No. Diagnosis Reported by (with position)

Date Full name Sex

Age: yrs. mos. Birthday Address (with phone) Parents or guardians name (and address, if different from childs)

and religion of father

Language spoken in childs home

Nationality, language mother By whom referred (Underscore appropriate words: once for moderate, twice for marked, and thrice for extreme degree. Also fill in data in blank spaces.)

Attendance Record: Age on entering first school (kindergarten included)

Names of schools attended, in correct time order Location of School Time, from to No. of months in attendance Grades completed Grades repeated

(1)

(2)

(S)

CO

Repetition: number of months spent in each grade child has repeated

Total time (years or months) spent repeating work Bttardation: grade in which child should be according to age Present grade

Amount of pedagogical retardation (yrs. and mos.) Attendance, regular or irregular, during past or present time (ascribed causes of irregularity)

Past Record: character of work, conduct, disposition, traits, etc., as reported from previous teachers or specialists

Present Pedagogical Status: School efficiency in general: excellent, good, fair, poor, very poor, total failure. Prospects of promotion: excellent, good, fair, poor, none. Poorest work in which branches Best work in which branches

Special aptitudes, what Greatest interests, or likes, in school work Greatest dislikes

Pedagogical traits in which strongest In which most deficient Learning capacity: is child good or poor in ability to observe to concentrate to memorize (mechanically, logically, understandingly) to retain to express orally or in writing to form habits to adapt self to new or changing situations, conditions or emergencies to think, judge, reason, under stand to do independent work to lead to direct to originate, invent to keep a level head (easily confused) Learns best by repetition, rote, memorizing, reasoning, imitation, reading, being told, doing or experimenting for self (hit or miss). Accomplishments: in reading: knows alphabet (letters not known) reads in what reader how well reads at sight, syllables, short words, long words, spells out words In arithmetic: counts, how far Ability in addition, subtrac tion multiplication division problems How far advanced Best in concrete or abstract work In spelling; sample words child can spell Words child cannot spell In writing In drawing In grammar In language work In speaking, dramatizing In music In kindergarten In manual train ing In shop work In domestic science In school gardening In gymnastics, games In history In geography Ability of brothers of sisters

Reported defects or capacities of mother of father

Attitude Toward School Work: interested, willing, tries, industrious, energetic, cheerful, trustworthy, lazy, slovenly, careless, shirking, despairing, diffident, non-persevering, easily wearied or fatigued, grows sleepy, dopey, disinterested, bored, inattentive, complaining.

Attitude Toward Correction, Reproof oa Punishment: heedless, resentful, head-strong, obstinate, talks back, abusive, sensitive, cries, indifferent. Very responsive, tries to improve, takes it with good grace.

Attitude Toward Plats And Games: seeks or avoids games. Plays much or little. On playground Plays with boys or girls with younger or older children

Fond of what games or plays Plays make-believe plays ability to plan or lead games Gets confused in games Loses self-control

Behavior in games

Mental, Moral And Social Traits: Circumspect, deliberate, thoughtful, thoughtless, impulsive, careless, slothful, slovenly, lazy, inert, slow, dull, stupid, apathetic, unresponsive, taciturn, reticent, diffident, retiring, bashful, quiet

Bright, talented, precocious, quick, responsive, talkative, loquacious, communicative, entertaining, boring

Cheerful, good-natured, gay, humorous, kind, affectionate, sympathetic, helpful, generous, frank, obedient

Moody, sensitive, despairing, fretful, cranky, resentful, malignant, defiant, angry, meddlesome, complaining, quarrelsome, trouble maker, brutal, fights, kicks, scolds, nags, spiteful, jealous, sullen, selfish, self-centered, proud, domineering, bossy, changeable moods, capricious disposition or character

Graceful, artistic, neat, awkward, clumsy, poor gait, poor motor control, stumbles, falls, injures self

Bold, reckless, heedless of danger, venturesome, blustering, noisy, fearsome, cowardly

Restless, fidgety, nervous, scowls, twitching movements (of what) excessive movements, emotional, excitable, impulsive, passionate, violent

Strange or peculiar actions, habits, speech (what) Sudden or capricious outbreaks of passion, anger, fear, destructive tendencies, love, gaiety, laughing, crying, tantrums, fits, fainting spells. Automatic actions (when excited or otherwise) Suspicious, solitary, seclusive, shut-in, avoids company, dreamy, observant

Honest, truthful, pure, modest; dishonest, untruthful, steals, lies, profane, swears, obscene, lewd, masturbates, immoral Any sense of shame, of difference between right and wrong, of guilt, remorse, sorrow, reverence, religion

Speech: stutters, stammers, lisps, lalls, indistinct, inarticulate, sluggish, mumbling, thick, incoherent, halting, jerky, rambling, pointless, labored; clear, fluent, logical, sensible, braggadocious, egotistical, gossipy; declaims, recites, sings

Headaches, eyestrain, holds eyes near work, mouth open, poor hearing, takes cold easily, running nose, gets sick, tired Smokes, chews. Data from school medical record:

What special measures have been taken to overcome the child pedagogical deficiencies? To overcome his physical defects His moral or social shortcomings

Results Of These Measures:

Recommendations:

Results Of Following Recommendations (from later inquiries):

Signature :

FORM V PHYSICAL AND ANTHROPOMETRIC EXAMINATION

No. Diagnosis Examiner Date

Full name Sex Birthday

Age: yrs. mos. Address Parents or guardians name (and address, if different, with phone)

Brought by Referred by (Underscore appropriate words: once for moderate, twice for marked. and thrice for extreme degree. Supply all relevant data in blank spaces.)

Defects, Diseases, Disorders And Stigmata
(Anatomical, physiological, neurological)

General Appearance: Expression nutrition

Fat, corpulent, lean, emaciated, fair, normal.

Skin: complexion; pallid, sallow, ashen, oily, moist, dry, leathery, wrinkled, baggy, florid, scars, birthmarks.

Teeth: carious (number, degree) roots, tartar, impacted, irregular, malocclusion, rachitic, serrated, pointed, Hutch-insons Gums

Tongue: thick, pointed, large, small, furrowed, enlarged papillae.

Throat: tonsils, enlarged, atrophied, submerged, pitted, soft, removed. Pharyngitis. Laryngitis. Mouth breather. Lymph glands. Thyroid, enlarged, atrophied. Adenoids.

Palate: cleft, V-shaped, arched, narrow.

Lips: normal, hare-lip, thick, thin, everted, fissured.

Nose: deflected septum, enlarged turbinates, polipi, rhinitis, broad base, sunken bones, squat, mongoloid, cretinoid.

Eyes: acuity, R L Astigmatism Small palpebral fissure, exophthalmos, choked disc, scotoma, hemiopsia, irregular or eccentric pupils, ptosis, oblique mongolian, epicanthus. Nystagmus, strabismus, diplopia, accommodation to light to distance Argyll-Robertson Iris, color, R L Wearing proper or improper glasses

Ears: acuity, R L Kinm-Otitis media,

R L Impacted cerumen, perforated drum, otorrhea.

Large, small, Darwinian tubercle, lobule absent, fossae absent or irregular, pinna (size, shape) asymmetries

Face: immobile, mobile; forehead, Bombe, receding, low or narrow; prognathous jaws, asymmetries

Head: hydrocephalic, macrocephalic, microcephalic, rachitic, syphilitic, cretinoid, asymmetries. Hair: color coarse, dry, oily, scant, brittle. Pediculosis.

Shoulders: round, square, stooped, asymmetrical. Scaphoid scapula

Spine: scoliosis C D L lordosis, C D L kyphosis

Chest: flat, rachitic, pigeon, funnel, barrel-shaped, asymmetrical. Lungs Respiration, rate character

Upper Limrs:

Lower Limrs: Flat foot

Circulation: good, poor. Heart: dilation, murmurs, displacements. Pulse: volume rate rhythm pressure Veins

Arteries Blood examination: red corpuscles white corpuscles hemoglobin color index

Widal Wasserman

Alimentation: appetite digestion abdomen stomach intestines

Gestito-urinahy System:

Neuro-muscot. ar : tone, relaxed, flabby, tense. Corrugation, over-action of frentals. Tremors, coarse, fine, unilateral, spastic, jerky, intermittent, rhythmical, of what parts Hand balance: relaxed, tense, drooping, asymmetrical, finger twitches Station: relaxed, unsteady. Head balance Gait: normal, lively, clumsy, shuffling, spastic, ataxic, waddling. Paralyses Contractures Fainting spells Tics

Habit spasm Convulsions Chorea

Epilepsy Hysteria Headache, migraine

Anesthesias

Reflexes: patellar, R L Clonus Babinski

Other reflexes Defective speech

Other Defects Or Stigmata:

Active Disease Processes: record the diseases, and indicate whether slight or serious, of the integumentary, skeletal, muscular, nervous, nutritive, respiratory, circulatory, lymphatic, excretory and reproductive systems.

History Of Diseases, Deformities And Accidents, With Previoub Medical Diagnoses:

Name Of Examiner:

Physicians Recommendations:

Results Of Recommendations (as later ascertained): Physician or hospital recommended:

Anthropometric Measurements

Weight: Ibs. kg. Stature, net standing (mm.)

Sitting Ponderal index Statural index

Statural type Spread of arms

Spirometry: 123 Chest girth (below level of axille): maximal inhalation exhalation normal Vital index

Dynamometry: Rl 3 3 LI 2 3 Head measurements: circumference height length (antero- posterior diameter) breadth cephalic index

Other measurements

FORM VI

PSYCHOLOGICAL EXAMINATION It has been deemed wise to omit a schema for conducting psychological examinations for the following reasons. First, a considerable number of graded scales for testing intelligence (particularly versions of the Binet-Simon scale) are now easily accessible in English. Second, hundreds of different psychological tests and experiments are equally accessible in the standard books dealing with psychological tests (e. g., the manuals by Whipple, Franz, Titchener, Sanford, Starch, Scripture). It would be futile to attempt to print a selected list of such tests here, because the expert experimental psychologist is qualified to make his own selection, while the inexperienced psychologist (physician, nurse, teacher) would scarcely be able either properly to conduct the experiments without technical training, or elaborate explanations, or correctly to interpret the findings. Third, there is little profit in outlining a comprehensive series of tests until reliable clinical nornu are available. Unfortunately such norms are not yet available. The fact that this is so makes it all the more necessary that the clinical psycho-educational examiner should possess very extensive first-hand experience with many types of mentally unusual children, so that he will be able to diagnose cases fairly accurately with the aid of a minimal number of tests.

FORM VII

PEDAGOGICAL EXAMINATION

Until we have available a series of clinical pedagogical age-norms, in various school studies, established by objective tests given under standard and controlled conditions, possibly to individuals rather than to groups–such as the Courtis scores in the fundamental mathematical processes, though these are group norms–it would be of little avail to outline a schema for the pedagogical testing of the child. We have, to be sure, the pedagogical scales by Vaney and Holmes, but the former is very limited in range and not entirely appropriate to pupils trained by American school methods, while the latter has not been experimentally derived by objectively testing individual children of various ages (the method of derivation is not revealed). It is merely an abbreviated course of study for grades two to five which, it is assumed, represents the pedagogical accomplishments of normal children. Until we possess satisfactory pedagogical age scales of development, it will be necessary to use (but with discriminating judgment) the school record of the child (Form IV).

FORM VIII

SUMMARY OF IMPORTANT FINDINGS It is very desirable that social or field workers epitomize for the busy examiner the chief findings. This blank should be comprehensive, yet very brief: it should contain only the data which seem to have an important bearing on the case, which are important for diagnosis and prognosis. It may also include the chief results of the physical, anthropometric and psychological examinations, the final (or at least the provisional) diagnosis, the recommendations, a record of treatment, the results of treatment, and the final disposition of the case.

The question naturally arises whether it is necessary or indeed desirable to make such an exhaustive investigation of each case as that contemplated by the above schema. The answer is that it is usually desirable, but not always necessary or possible to do so. Unless the clinicist has at his command the necessary staff of assistants he must content himself with a far less thorough investigation. He should, however, at all times attempt to secure a certain minimum of data which bear significantly upon psycho-educational cases. Such a minimum is represented, I believe, by the following abbreviated record blank. It is reproduced from the routine blanks which have been in constant use in my clinic for several years.

FORM IX

ABRIDGED RECORD BLANK

Childs name (with street and city address and phone)

Parents names (with address and phone, if different)

Referred by Brought by Date

Data secured from Recorded by

Exact age: date of birth Age in yrs. and mos.

Place of birth Nationality of father of mother

Language spoken at home I. Pedagogical Record

School now in All schools attended, in correct time order, with dates

Age on entering first school (including kindergarten)

Number of years (or months) in school Present grade In what grade should child be according to age Years retarded Number of years (or months) in each grade (including kindergarten)

Grades repeated (indicate whether one, two or three years)

Will child be promoted this year Attendance

Greatest capacities, abilities or talents shown in school work (best subjects) Greatest interests

Greatest deficiencies, worst faults, poorest school subjects

Physical, mental and moral characteristics, disposition, deportment

Other comments by teachers

School medical inspection record

School record of brothers and sisters II. HOME AND F, vvuins Mcntm CONDITIONS

Parents alive Living together Breadwinner (who) Financial conditions Home sanitary, well ventilated, clean In house, tenement, shack, apart ment In good or bad (slummy or immoral) neighbor hood Social or moral conditions in home

Home treatment (child neglected, cruelly or kindly treated, well cared for) What does child usually eat

What does child drink Hours of retiring and arising Does child keep bad company

III. Childs Developmental History

Birth conditions: on time premature (how much)

Labor, how long With instruments Birth injuries How nursed (length)

Health as babe Infant and child diseases (state age, severity, after effects): Croup Whooping cough

Chicken-pox Measles Diphtheria Scarlet fever Typhoid Pneumonia C.-s. menin gitis Infant paralysis Spasms (describe)

Enuresis Accidents By whom previously examined and diagnoses given

First teeth, when (any illness) Fontanel closed

First stood alone First sat up First steps unsup ported First walked unsupported First used single words Short phrases or sentences

Mental and physical peculiarities in infancy and childhood (age first observed): queer or unusual behavior, talk or ideas; emotional fits or outbreaks, fears, night terrors, destructive, disobedient, vagrancy, truancy, veracity, delinquencies, bad sex habits, social traits, play tendencies, stupid, sluggish, quick, bright IV. Hereditary Factors

Health, habits, diseases, drink, etc., of father and mother before and during conception

Pregnancy conditions (overwork, poor health, infection, drink, abuse, starvation, etc.)

Age of mother at childs birth of father Parents related -as S3 Jjg Order of childs birth

3 Oi i2 il

Number of Sisters

Number of Brothers

Give facts in regard to the following defects, conditions or diseases found in the childs brothers, sisters, mother, father, maternal and paternal great-grandparents, grandparents, aunts, uncles, first and second cousins, etc.: o 03 Mentally Epileptic Alcoholic Ceiminal Sexually immoeal. Diseases (what) Noemal

32 queee Insane a v

-2a2 a lls

22s. Kit ft h Qu:

Coptm of tht prtctding Schtma art available in ttparatt rtprmtt, and can bt Hcortdfrom the publithtrt.

Note To Chapter IV

Some unwarranted assumptions and criticisms relating to the original of this chapter by one of my reviewers call for a brief refutation (E. A. Doll, The Training School Bulletin, March, 1914, 10).

Possibly Dr. Wallin has again confused cause and effect. My critic assumes (he gives no facts in support of the indictment) that my diagnoses are purely diagnoses by symptoms, and that I confuse the facts of etiology with the facts of symptomatology. A perusal of the article will show that it was explicitly affirmed that my final diagnosis was based on all the available facts, facts of etiology and pathology no less than facts of symptomatology. The symptomatological classification was not based purely on symptoms, as the word would indicate unless proper regard were given to the statement made in the text.

Dr. Wallin believes that the percentage (of the feebleminded) is below rather than above 1 per cent, and yet he states that "over 10 per cent of all the elementary pupils in the Pittsburgh public schools are retarded three years or more." This looks very much like a contradiction, since feeble-mindedness is defined psychologically as intellectual retardation of two years at an age below nine or three years at and above nine, which definition the author admits in his Experimental Studies. My reply is threefold.

First, I do not admit this definition. The statement I made in the Experimental Studies (pp. 16, 98, 103) was that children retarded less than three years should probably not be rated as feeble-minded. Since only nine epileptic children were retarded less than three years, while the average retardation for the epileptics who were classified as children was over seven years, I had little need of attempting to apply automatically any rigid two-or three-year standard of feeble-mindedness. In the Practical Guide (p. 116f.) I was careful to avoid laying down any arbitrary standard whatever. My experience with epileptic and insane patients had aroused my suspicion of the propriety of so doing. My later experience with the great variety of cases which come to a university clinic has convinced me that it is futile to attempt a differential diagnosis–even to the extent of differentiating between morons and backward persons–on a confessedly artificial and arbitrary quantitative standard of intellectual retardation. In the 1911 scale Binet himself wisely avoids this pitfall. He merely states that no child, no matter how little he knows, should be regarded as defective unless his intelligence is retarded more than two years. Elsewhere he cites the French policy, apparently with approval, of not placing a child in a special class for defectives for mental retardation alone, unless the retardation amounts to three years or more, or to at least two years if the child is less than nine.

Second, the retardation statistics I gave for the Pittsburgh schools refer to peda-gogical retardation based merely on an age-grade census. As everybody knows these surveys include children who are not even genuinely backward in inherent all-round mental capacity. I merely ventured the opinion that one-half of the 10 per cent retarded three years or more should be placed in special classes, but assuredly not because they were all feebleminded. The special classes in the public schools are designed not only for the feeble-minded but also for the seriously backward. Under ideal conditions 4 or 5 per cent of the elementary pupils should be placed in these classes, about one-fourth of these being feeble-minded, about one-fourth border-line cases and about one-half seriously backward.

Third, no one who defines feeble-mindedness as intellectual retardation of two years at an age below nine, or three years at and above nine has had the courage to follow this definition to its inevitable conclusion. It is indeed amusing that the advocates of this arbitrary standard tell us that only 2 per cent of the elementary school population is feeble-minded. (Possibly they have merely accepted an old English conjecture. As long ago as 1906 Dr. James Kerr, chief medical officer for the London County Council Schools, made the same estimate for a committee of inquiry, but he included in his estimate other types of mental defectives than those actually feebleminded.) Why do they not announce that 8.4 per cent of the grade pupils are feeble-minded, for Goddard found that this percentage of all the pupils in the first six grades in a given township were retarded from three to seven years by the Binet scale? Not only so, if we assume that one-fifth of those retarded two years were at an age below nine, the number of feeble-minded would be 10.4 per cent, instead of 8.4 per cent—or 2 per cent! Are those who defend the amazing accuracy of the automaton method of diagnosticating feeble-mindedness prepared to follow their method to its inescapable conclusion? Are they prepared to stand by their experimental facts instead of preconceived notions as to possibility or impossibility? Are they ready to present incontestable facts to show that the standard which they adopt is not itself nothing but a preconceived notion? If there is a magic infallibility about this standard, why do they not formulate the standard in precisely the same terms? Doll has one standard; Goddard has another, to wit: If a child is more than two years backward while he is still under nine years of age,. he is probably feeble-minded. For a child above nine how about the nine-year old? we allow him to be more than three years backward before we call him defective (italics mine). Does more than three years backward mean three years and one point or four years? We seek in vain for an answer. Contrast this standard with Dolls dictum given above and note the difference. As I have frequently stated elsewhere in this book, my attempt to apply arbitrary quantitative standards of intellectual retardation in the diagnosis of the varied cases coming to a university clinic in a populous district has, in the main, proved quite futile. I have had numerous mentally abnormal cases retarded from five to sixteen years by the Binet tests whom I should hesitate to call feebleminded.

INDEX

Lightning Source UK Ltd.
Milton Keynes UK
03 November 2010

162319UK00001B/63/P

9 780217 803519